Artificial Intelligence in Value Creation

Andrzej Wodecki

Artificial Intelligence in Value Creation

Improving Competitive Advantage

palgrave
macmillan

Andrzej Wodecki
Warsaw University of Technology
Warsaw, Poland

ISBN 978-3-030-06259-0 ISBN 978-3-319-91596-8 (eBook)
https://doi.org/10.1007/978-3-319-91596-8

Printed on acid-free paper

This Palgrave Macmillan imprint is published by the registered company Springer Nature Switzerland AG
The registered company address is: Gewerbestrasse 11, 6330 Cham, Switzerland

Contents

List of Figures

List of Tables

1

Value Creation and Competitive Advantage Models

1.1 Introduction

We have entered the twenty-first century full of fears, with many unresolved global problems such as armed conflicts or unstable financial systems, yet at the same time with the expectation of not only solving the problems but also creating systems that offer unimaginable possibilities. As at the beginning of 2018, we are seeing more and more possibilities in widely understood systems of machine learning and Artificial Intelligence (AI). Increasingly available and more efficient computing power combined with the growing interest from industry contribute to the intensive development of AI methods and technologies, which turn out to be good and efficient and can be used to design and commercialize new, smart, connected products (see e.g. Porter and Heppelmann 2014). This positive relation between the sectors of education, science and industry (see e.g. Shoham et al. 2017) currently causes an exponential increase in the capabilities of systems, resulting in new concepts for products, services or business models.

The AI industry is at a very interesting stage of development. On the one hand, it is in a sense "mature" as, according to various estimates in

A. Wodecki, *Artificial Intelligence in Value Creation*,
https://doi.org/10.1007/978-3-319-91596-8_1

this area, around 2000 (see e.g. Index.co website statistics) to 4000 (see e.g. Tracxn.com) companies operate. On the other hand, the very high dynamics of changes in technology and methods combined with a high rate of development of the entire information and communications technology (ICT) sector (from specialized processors to blockchain or Ethereum technologies) cause a continuous and rapid evolution of products, services or business models. In a natural way, this changes the rules of creating value and competing by generating the need to develop new competencies and being a source of new risks and challenges.

No wonder that many researchers, managers and investors are aware of the potential of systems using AI. Yet they do not quite understand them well enough and thus they have problems with implementing such solutions in practice and recovering business value from them (Bughin et al. 2017; Ransbotham et al. 2017). On the other hand, companies successfully implementing AI invest in these solutions much more than organizations not yet experienced in this area, which deepens the distance between "pioneer" and "passive" implementers. It turns out that the key to adoption of AI competencies is the intuition of AI activity among managers, the ability to formulate good business cases and the ability to manage such projects (see e.g. Bughin et al. 2017; Ransbotham et al. 2017).

This book analyzes various models of value generation by companies using artificial intelligence in their products, services and business models. At the beginning, "classical" models of value generation and competition are presented and the basic concepts, methods and technologies of artificial intelligence are described. Furthermore, on the basis of the analysis of 323 case studies, it is shown how AI systems influence the generation of values (in the primary and support areas of the organization's activity) and the rules of competition, competitive advantages and markets. Based on the above analyses, a proposal for a universal model of recovering values from AI systems and the concept of the so-called cognitive networks is presented.

The basis of the research is an in-depth analysis of 323 organizations and projects using AI in their activities, offering intelligent services or supporting their design and implementation, which for the needs of this study are classified according to 85 criteria. An additional source of information are industry reports and scientific studies from this area.

Using the results of these tests the possible influence of AI systems on the activity in the value chain is shown (including design, production and logistics, marketing and sales, service, after-sales service, human resource management and information and knowledge management). For each of these areas of activity, competencies, the most important risks and challenges significant for the generation of value are also indicated. The next step shows the impact of smart systems on competitiveness and markets, in particular, the roles and strength of producers, customers, suppliers and new players. It also presents the possible impact of AI systems on the competencies and the role of humans in the organization.

The analysis of the impact of smart technologies on the operation and rules of company competitiveness is the basis for the proposal for a value generation model using AI solutions. In the first step, three alternative classifications of AI systems are proposed: (1) according to the influence on the functional area and the applied technologies, (2) according to the place in the knowledge value chain, and (3) according to cognitive functions (cognitive classification). Then, by applying the Case-Based Reasoning method, the value generation model is proposed taking into account AI technology, its impact on a given area and the resulting effects and business values.

The final result of the research is a proposition of the so-called cognitive networks: new value generation structures in markets that use artificial intelligence intensively. For this purpose, in the first step it is shown how the impact of AI systems on the generation of values and rules of competition can be described in the context of "classical" models: chains, constellations, value grids and networks, and within the service-oriented logics. This made it possible to formulate the concept of cognitive networks, and in particular to propose an architecture for these structures (actors, combining their relations and the impact of AI technology on these relations and the control points), control, coordination and optimization mechanisms, services in such networks and key competencies of suppliers, customers and network coordinators.

This chapter, in a synthetic way, presents the most important logics of value creation and methods of achieving competitive advantages (chains, constellations, shops, networks, grids and structures dominated by services), models of data information and knowledge impact on the generation of value and the impact of information technologies on value configurations and competition rules. The whole is complemented by a presentation of the value network model in the telecommunication and IT industries as well as a list of competencies that help achieve a sustainable competitive advantage. The concepts described here will allow for the formulation of the so-called cognitive networks describing the processes of generating value on the markets using the artificial intelligence to a large extent (see Chap. 4).

In Chap. 2, the basic concepts and methods of artificial intelligence are presented. In the introduction, various aspects of Big Data are described and it is shown how crucial they are for the implementation of AI solutions. Next, various definitions, methods, learning mechanisms and technologies used to create intelligent systems are discussed. Finally, the cognitive computing IT solutions that exert an increasing influence on the development of the whole field of AI are presented.

Chapter 3 demonstrates the impact of intelligent systems on the organization's activity and competitiveness. First of all, it presents the results of research on the adoption of AI solutions in companies. It shows the characteristics of the organizations that implement them successfully, and describes key success factors and the most important barriers. Later, on the basis of many case studies, it describes the way AI systems change activities in the value chain (including design, production, logistics, marketing and sales, service, human resource and knowledge management). Finally, it shows how smart solutions can change markets and competitiveness and influence the role of humans in the organization.

In Chap. 4, a proposition of the model, which might describe new value creation logics as a consequence of intelligent systems dissemination, is presented. First of all, a classification of AI technologies from the perspective of value creation models is proposed. As a starting point, classical models of knowledge value chains and models of data transformation processes in information systems are used. They are usually implemented to organize AI systems according to (1) a place in the knowledge value chain (in this approach, AI enables data transformation into information and knowledge), and (2) cognitive functions (for the purpose of the cognitive networks concept introduced later). The above classifications are further used to develop a value generation model at the organization level and the level of network structures. The first of them can be used, for example, by managers or investors interested in assessing the business potential of ventures. The second concerning the concept of cognitive networks constitutes a proposal of a new model of relations and methods for generating value in the network structures, in which key services rely on the enrichment of information by the use of AI systems.

Chapter 5 presents the most important, according to the author, research challenges in the area of the impact of artificial intelligence systems on the generation of values and competitive advantages of AI.

The study is supplemented with appendices. In the first one, the assumptions and the results of in-depth analyses of 323 projects using AI or enabling their design are presented. The most important methods, questions and research hypotheses and a short descriptive analysis of quantitative research results are demonstrated. The reader will also find here (Appendix 3 of Chap. 5) an ordered list of analyzed AI projects in alphabetical order (company/project name and its web address). The following appendices summarize the desired competencies (Appendix 1 of Chap. 5) and challenges (Appendix 2 of Chap. 5) related to the design and implementation of solutions using AI. The list of these elements situated in one place might be helpful for people interested in assessing the potential of such solutions or implementing them in their own organization.

1.2 The Value Creation and Competitive Advantage Models

The concept of value, methods of its generation and sources of competitive advantages have been the subject of research for decades, as a part of management as well as economic sciences. The models, such as chains, shops, networks or value grids in connection with the analyses of the technology impact on value generation and ways of competing, are extremely up-to-date and can be successfully applied while describing phenomena on the markets that use AI methods and technologies intensively.

The purpose of this chapter is to provide a synthetic presentation of the most important logics of value creation and methods of achieving competitive advantages (chains, constellations, shops, networks, grids and structures dominated by services), models of data information and knowledge impact on the generation of value and the impact of information technologies on value configurations and competition rules. The whole is complemented by a presentation of the value network model in the telecommunications and IT industries as well as a list of competencies that help to achieve a sustainable competitive advantage.

The concepts described here will allow for the formulation of the so-called cognitive network model, which describes the processes of generating value on the markets using artificial intelligence to a large extent (see Chap. 4).

1.2.1 Introduction

The sources of competitive advantages have been the subject of research for several decades, both in management and economic sciences. One of the dimensions that allows classifying theories of competitive advantages is the location of the sources of these advantages in relation to the organization. From this perspective, three approaches can be distinguished (Bednarz 2011):

1. **Classical theories** positioning the sources of competitive advantage outside an organization, e.g. in its economic background;
2. **Resource theories** looking for sources of advantage in the resources and processes of an organization;
3. **Mixed theories** connecting external and internal sources.

In classical theories, the source of competitive advantage has been seen mainly in the company's environment. For example, Porter (2008) identifies leadership on the basis of costs and differentiation. He recommends that competitive fight should be based on the market power and introduces the concept of five forces defining the situation in a given market. In resource theories, the starting point is an enterprise that builds its competitive advantage through the use of internal predispositions and resources (Bednarz 2011; Prahalad and Hamel 1990). The authors of the concept appreciate the importance of external factors: to achieve market success, it is necessary to be able to recognize and exploit opportunities with simultaneous, widely understood, efficient management.

In the final decade of the last century, some researchers began to identify intangible assets. Particularly, intellectual capital was seen as a source of competitive advantages. These assets were divided into three types of capital: human, structural and relational (Edvinsson and Malone 1997). The studies were also extended to countries, regions and cities (Bounfour and Edvinsson 2012; Godlewska-Majkowska et al. 2010; Rószkiewicz et al. 2007).

Further part of the dissertation presents various models of creating value and achieving a competitive advantage, relevant in the research on the impact of the systems using artificial intelligence (AI) on organizations and markets. These models will not only constitute a frame for research, but also they will help to formulate research questions and hypotheses. This will allow placing the developed conclusions in a broader context and indicate interesting directions for further research.

1.2.2 The Influence of Technology on the Logics of Value Creation

For years, many researchers have pointed to the strong impact of broadly understood technologies on management and value creation models. Before conducting detailed analyses, it is worth presenting briefly a few fundamental concepts describing the impact of technology on companies.

1.2.2.1 The First Theories of the Impact of Technology on Management

One of the first researchers who studied the influence of technology on management was James David Thompson (1967). He divided technologies into:

1. **Long-linked**, in which tasks are ordered (depend on each other) in a sequential manner and require advanced coordination. They are most often used by large production companies.
2. **Intensive**, used by companies offering their clients various solutions tailored to their needs. Business processes in such organizations have many tasks depending on each other, often carried out in spiral cycles (e.g. analysis, hypothesis, solution, implementation, evaluation), which requires high managerial and expert competencies as well as flat rather than vertical structures.
3. **Mediating**, enabling the provision of services that support the connection between customers. The examples are telecommunications networks, banks, stock exchanges, and especially nowadays, social networks.

In further studies, Thompson linked technologies classified in this way with the interdependence of tasks, organizational units and companies in the structures of values. In particular, he showed that the level and type of mutual dependencies between technologies depend on the type and range of resources shared by the activities they support (Stabell and Fjeldstad 1998).

This has become the basis for broadening the concept of the value chain, which will be presented in more detail later in this study.

The creator of the next theory, important in the context of our research, was Joan Woodward. In the 1960s, she showed how organizational structures adapt to the applied technologies (Woodward 1970). She identified the relationship between the scale of production (unitary, mass or process) and the complexity of processes and organizational structures (measured particularly by the number of managerial staff and the subordinate levels). In the transition from unitary production to mass production, the number of managerial staff and the scope of managing increased, while with the change from mass production to process production, they decreased again. Woodward related these changes to the development of technology enforced by changes in the scale of an organization's operations.

In the 1970s, Charles D. Perrow, when examining the complexity of the organization and its resistance to various types of threats, identified two key dimensions for the technology analysis: task variability and their "analyzability". He proposed that the task variability should be measured with the number of exceptions that an employee encountered while working. He understood 'analyzability' as the degree to which the performance of a given task could be described by procedures: the analytical problems could be solved on the basis of procedures and technical knowledge, while the non-analytical ones required experience and intuition. As part of this concept, Perrow proposed four categories of technology ("ProvenModels – technology typology"): routine (no exceptions, high standardization), craft (no exceptions, but frequent necessity to look for individual solutions), engineering (many exceptions, high standardization) and non-routine (many exceptions, the need to search for unique solutions). The effects of his further research on organizations and organizational units can be summarized in the following points:

1. The diversity of business units can be described by the types of technologies that they use to perform their tasks.
2. Organizational structures and business processes depend on technology.
3. Managers should design their organizational units in such a way that they meet the requirements of the technologies used.

The concepts outlined above have paved the way for further research concerning the impact of technology on management. In the next part of the study, their usefulness for the analysis of the business potential of AI class solutions will be described.

1.2.3 Value Chains

The value chain is a fundamental management concept and it is the starting point for many analyses in the field of value management of an organization and the sources of competitiveness. Below, there is an outline of this theory, with the emphasis put on the logics of value creation and, resulting from them, sources of competitive advantages and strategic options.

1.2.3.1 The Concept of the Value Chain

The value chain concept was proposed by Michael Porter. In his model (Porter and Millar 1985), the value created by a company is measured by the price that customers are willing to pay for its products or services, and the company is profitable when the value it creates is higher than the costs of value creation. The value chain of a company is understood to be a set of related value-providing activities, where actions are combined when one of them affects the cost or efficiency of the other. Connections between activities force their coordination. Precise management of activities is often a source of competitive advantage. Companies should be able to see such connections and skillfully coordinate them. These connections can enforce trade-offs in optimization processes. For example, an increase in design cost (e.g. higher number of hours) or production (e.g. by using better quality materials) can result in a cost reduction in after-sales service (lower repair costs).

In order to achieve a competitive advantage, a company must properly coordinate activities in the value chain and settle the above-mentioned compromises.

1.2.3.2 The Value Creation Logic

The company value chain is an element in a system of interlinked chains. As part of this concept, the process of identifying and understanding competitive advantages comes down to the analysis of processes generating the value for discreet activities that affect the cost advantage and distinguish the company's offers (Stabell and Fjeldstad 1998). The analysis of the activity should be complete, so that it takes into account all the activities of the organization. To make such an analysis feasible, Porter suggests focusing on activities that have

1. Various "economies,"
2. A high impact on the difference between offer and competition,
3. Significant (or increasing) share of costs.

Porter divides the value-creating activities into primary and supporting.

Primary activities are directly related to the creation and delivery of the value to the customer; most often they concern final material products. Due to the fact that the value chain model is used to analyze the value creation logic and not to analyze business processes (e.g. to reengineer them), primary activities do not necessarily coincide with organizational functions: a given primary activity can be implemented by many different business units and the chosen organizational function can contribute to the implementation of many different primary activities.

Porter divides primary activities into:

1. **Inbound logistics**: activities related to the receipt, storage and transfer of materials for production.
2. **Operations**: transformations of input materials into end products.
3. **Outbound logistics**: collecting, storing and physical distribution of products to buyers.
4. **Marketing and sales**: actions ensuring product availability on the market, related to providing ways of purchasing products by customers and motivating them to do so.
5. **Services**: actions focused on maintaining and strengthening the value offered by the product, having a critical impact on its value for the customer.

Supporting activities increase the effectiveness of primary activities: they have an impact on the value offered to a customer only as much as they influence the efficiency of primary activities.

Porter distinguishes the following categories of supporting activities:

1. **Procurement**: purchases of materials and services used in the value chain;
2. **Technological development**: activities aimed at improving products and processes.
3. **HR management**: recruitment, employment, training, development and rewarding employees.
4. **Infrastructure**: general management, planning, finance, accounting, legal services, relations with the public sector and quality management.

The chain of values understood in this way is presented in Fig. 1.1.

Stabell and Fjeldstad (1998) summarize the value creation logic in value chains in the following way:

1. **The value for the customer** is determined either by the level of cost reduction or by the increase in efficiency that comes with the product use.
2. **The goal of technology development** is either the reduction of cost for the customer or raising prices through better adaptation to the customer's purchase criteria.

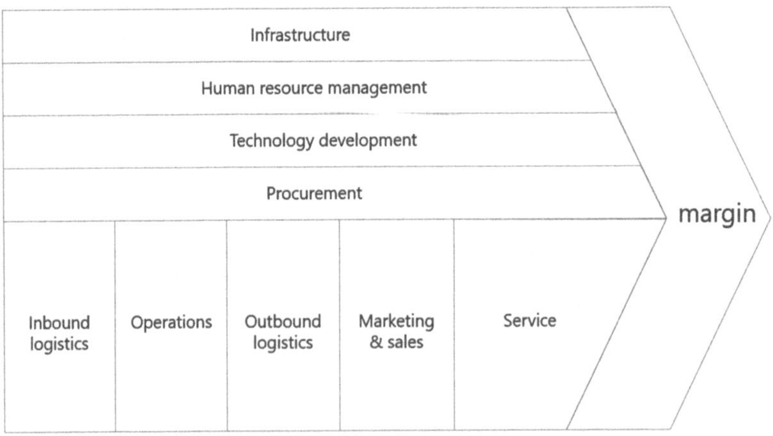

Fig. 1.1 Porter's value chain. (Source: Own elaboration based on Porter 2008)

3. **The product is a medium enabling the transfer of values from the company to the customer.** Raw materials and semi-finished products are transported to the factory, where they are transformed to final products and transported to customers.
4. **Marketing supports two complementary processes:**
   (a) Development and improvement of the chain by providing product specifications and demand forecasting.
   (b) The stimulation of demand for chain products in order to ensure stability of cooperation and optimal management of production capacities.
5. **After-sales service** ensures the correct use of products by a customer and, as a result, prevents failures or extends the life of the product.
6. **The value chain models the activities of chain technologies in the Thompson's typology** (1967), due to which the value is created by transforming the input materials into the final product.

1.2.3.3 Competitive Advantage

Value Systems

The value chain of a company in a specific industry is immersed in the stream of other companies' activities, which Porter defines as the value system (Porter and Millar 1985). It includes the value chains of suppliers, companies, further distribution channels and customers. Activities that create company value are combined with the activities of other organizations; the skillful management of these connections can be a source of competitive advantage.

The Scope and Strategies of Competition

Porter offers four dimensions of the scope of competition (Porter and Millar 1985): segment, vertical integration level, geography and industry. He distinguishes competitiveness:

1. **In a wide range**, involving the exploration of relations between the value chains of companies from many different market segments, industries or geographic regions. For example, an international, coordinated sales strategy based on experience from different markets can be a source of competitive advantage over local competitors, and vertical integration increases independence from external suppliers and can improve, thanks to the coordination of activities, the efficiency of processes.
2. **In a narrow range**, based on precise adjusting of the value chain to the value chains of specific customer groups, and being as a result a source of competitive advantage (cost or differentiation advantage).

To achieve a competitive advantage the organization must perform these activities at lower costs or in a way that leads to differentiation (justifies the premium price by providing a higher value).

Factors Determining the Competitive Advantage

Stabell and Fjeldstad suggest the following stages of analysis of competitive advantages in the value chain (Stabell and Fjeldstad 1998):

1. Organizing activities into groups in accordance with the value chain model.
2. Assigning costs and resources to action groups creating value.
3. The analysis of factors determining the costs of activities and an offered value.

The aim of the analysis of costs and resources is to identify the activities, which have the greatest impact on product costs, assess competitive advantages and improve potentials by comparing with competitors. The benefits that companies derive from such analysis are:

1. **A chance to ask questions that are important to the company**: What is the company's competitive position? What should be improved? And so on.
2. **The knowledge acquired during the analysis process** can be as valuable as detailed information about costs and values.

3. **The assessment of the difficulty of the analysis.** The difficulty in a good understanding of factors affecting costs and value can constitute a measure of the entry barrier and imitation for competitors.

In-depth understanding and management of factors that shape the costs of activities can be one of the main sources of competitive advantage. Porter (2008) distinguishes 10 key factors: scale, the use of opportunities, connections, relations with the environment, degree of vertical integration, location, punctuality, learning, strategic decisions and regulations.

1.2.3.4 Strategic Options

The purpose of the value configuration analysis is to diagnose and improve the competitive advantage. Stabell and Fjeldstad (1998) identify three dimensions of competitiveness:

1. Product.
2. Market segment.
3. Activities that generate value within the value system of interconnected companies, sometimes called the degree of vertical integration.

In order to achieve a competitive advantage, strategic positioning comes down to choosing a place in the product, market segment and business value dimensions. The choice of position in these dimensions depends on factors that generate costs and value. For companies based on chain technologies (sequential), the optimal position is determined by the relation between the scale of operation, the degree of utilization of production potential, market scope, uncertainty in the areas of demand and supply, and the place in the product life cycle (Stabell and Fjeldstad 1998).

1.2.4 Motivation for Extending the Concept of Value Chains

Changes taking place in the world today have inspired researchers to expand the concept of the value chain. Just in 1993, Normann and Ramirez (1993) stated that global competition, rapidly changing markets and new technologies generated completely new ways of creating value. As a result, strategy cannot boil down to a skillfully added value in a chain, but to discovering new methods for creating it. The subject of strategic analysis should not be companies or industries alone, but systems of value creation, under which different actors (suppliers, business partners, customers) produce value collectively. Strategic activities should be oriented on the reconfiguration of roles and relations between partners in order to create new forms of value.

In 1998, Stabell and Fjeldstad in an interesting way showed that the typology of primary activities in the Porter model works well with traditional manufacturing companies, but has many limitations in the analysis of companies from service industries (Stabell and Fjeldstad 1998). As an example, the authors mentioned the insurance company and the bank, for which it was difficult to determine what was provided "at the entrance" of the chain, what was produced, and what was delivered to the end customer. Other qualitative problems were identified in the in-depth analysis of support activities, e.g. technological development. Illustrating this by an example of exploration of deposits in the mining industry, they claimed that in the case of development activities with a large uncertainty factor, the value generated by them rarely correlated with the costs.

Stabell and Fjeldstad proposed three basic logics of value creation using the typology of Thompson's technology (1967):

1. **Value chain** modeling the activities of chain technologies
2. **Value shops** as a model for intensive technologies
3. **Value networks** modeling the operation of mediation technologies

As can be seen, the critical factors that distinguish these three logics of value creation are technologies, at the same time constituting the fundamentals of the theory and methods of analyzing the competitive advantages of a company.

The authors also proposed replacing the value chain analysis with the value configuration analysis. The value chain analysis is a method of decomposing the company into activities with a strategic dimension and understanding their impact on costs and generated value. They defined analysis of value configuration as a method of analyzing competitive advantages based on the theory of the three technologies and value creation logics. As can be seen, the approach changes the goal as well as the method of analysis.

In 2006, Pil and Holweg proposed extending the value chain model to the concept of the so-called value grids (Pil and Holweg 2006). In their opinion, the creation of values is more often more multidirectional than linear, which is why there is a need to modify the traditional, linear value chain. Constant tensions between opportunities and threats force companies to look for opportunities to manage risk, gain influence on demand and generate new ways of creating value. The basis of their research was the analysis of value chain management strategies for many companies, mainly from the automotive industry (car manufacturers, their suppliers and shipping companies), known for their high operational efficiency and a linear approach to the value chain, very fast-changing telecommunications industry (manufacturers of equipment, software and telecommunications companies) and the health sector. The network approach proposed by them offers many new ways to increase efficiency and is an interesting extension of the Porter concept.

1.2.5 Value Constellations

In 1993 Normann and Ramirez (1993) described a value constellation model. They integrated the concepts of products and services into a single term of an offer, from which customers can generate value for themselves. Later on, they stated that the complexity of the offer increases along with the complexity of the network necessary to deliver it. In effect, the strategic goal of the organization is constant reconfiguration and integration of its own competencies and customers.

The new value creation logic proposed by Norman and Ramirez has three key strategic implications:

1. In a world where value is generated in complex constellations (and not linear chains) the purpose of companies should not so much be creating value for customers, but rather mobilizing their independent creation of values for themselves by using the capabilities ("density") offered by the network.

2. As the complexity of offers increases, the complexity of relations between partners necessary to deliver them increases. The best offers involve customers, suppliers and various business partners in various configurations. In effect, the strategic goal of the company is a skillful reconfiguration of these relations in order to increase the value for the customer.
3. Due to the fact that the key to creating a unique value is the mobilization of customers to cooperate, the main source of competitive advantage is the ability to coordinate the entire value creation system.

These implications will acquire a special meaning in structures dominated by AI systems, which will be presented later in this study.

At this point, the outcomes of some research papers are worth mentioning, as they significantly support the development of concepts that expand the theory of the value chain. In 2000, Bowman and Ambrosini proposed differentiation of value creation (understood as a contribution to the usability of the product/service for the end user) from value capture (understood as the difference between the income and the cost obtained from the product/service) (Bowman and Ambrosini 2000). On the other hand, in Lippman and Rumelt (2003) and MacDonald and Ryall (2004), the authors describe the conditions determining the capability of particular actors to value capture, while Adner et al. focus on the factors conditioning the creation of value (Adner and Zemsky 2004).

1.2.6 Value Shops

1.2.6.1 The Concept of Value Shops

In 1998, Stabell and Fjeldstad proposed the concept of value shops (Stabell and Fjeldstad 1998). In their opinion, the companies for whom the concept of value shop is an appropriate model use the so-called intensive technologies (according to Thompson's classification) to solve their customers' problems (Thompson 1967). In contrast to organizations whose activities can be modeled with a value chain, the type and sequence of primary activities, in this case, depend significantly on the specificity of the customer's problem. In other words, the factor determining primary activities and the relations between them is the problem itself.

The value shops can also correctly model selected areas of company activities, whose creation of values for the customer is well described by the value chain. An example of this would be the mining companies whose primary values are represented by the chain, while the areas of technological development supporting them (e.g. exploration of deposits) are much better described with the use of the concept of value shops.

As it has already been mentioned, the primary activity of value shops is solving customer problems. The problem can be defined as the difference between the current state and the desired one (Simon 1977). Therefore, problem solving, which is the basis for generating value in "shops", includes changing states from current to desired with the use of intensive technologies. Examples of this type of activity are consultancy and medical services.

1.2.6.2 The Value Creation Logic

Stabell and Fjeldstad (1998) distinguish the following unique features of generating values in structures using intensive technologies:

1. **Strong information asymmetry** between the company and its customer, which is often the reason why a customer uses company's services.
2. **Value creation process adapted to solve non-standard problems.**
3. **Cyclical, iterative and uninterrupted activities.** The activity flow is not linear but often iterative (between activities) and cyclical (within activity groups).
4. **Important sequential and feedback relationships between activities.** The iterative nature of the problem-solving process results in a high degree of dependence, sequential as well as returnable, between various activities. As a result, it is necessary to efficiently coordinate activities and exchange information between teams of domain experts.

5. Many disciplines and specializations in spiral activity cycles. At the entrance to the next cycle, there is the solution to the problem generated by the previous cycle or the problem that results from it.
6. **Problem-independent operations focused on acquiring information.** Standard problem-independent methods of obtaining data and information.
7. **Relying on the expert knowledge.** Domain specialists constitute crucial and often the most numerous staff.
8. **Efficiency increase through cooperation of support and primary activities.** The management of highly qualified specialists is critically important. Marketing, procurement and technological development are often interconnected, carried out by experts in cooperation with the customer to solve their problems.
9. **A value system based on reputation and relations:**

   (a) References, when the main (general) contractor redirects the customer to another specialist.
   (b) Subcontracting, when the main contractor commissions some of the work to a third party taking responsibility for the work they perform.

The above characteristics of activities determine the structure of primary activities. Stabell and Fjeldstad divide them into five categories:

1. **Problem finding**, which consists of registering, reviewing and formulating a problem that needs to be resolved. This category is similar to marketing activities in value chains.
2. **Problem solving:** generating and evaluating possible solutions.
3. **Choosing the best solution.** This category is characterized by a relatively low cost and effort but is critically important from the perspective of the offered value.
4. **Execution** of solution, including communication, organization and implementation of the chosen solution.
5. **Control and evaluation**, measuring and assessing to what degree the solution solved the problem.

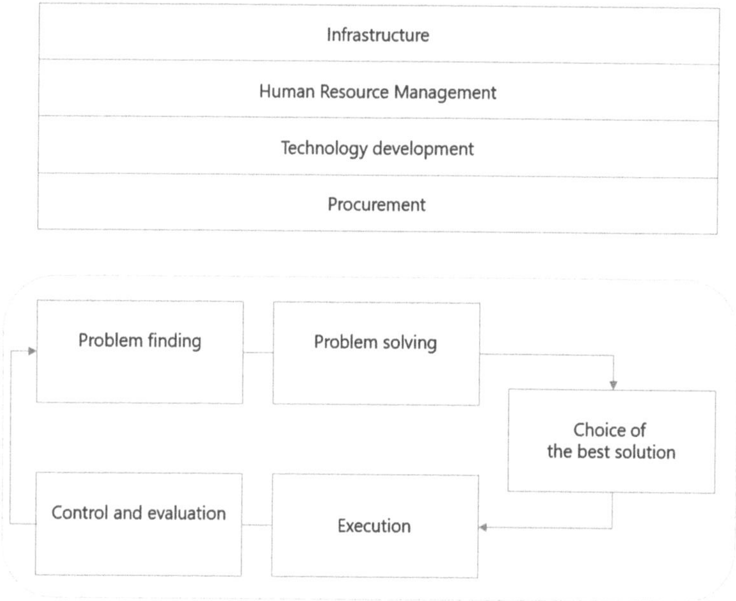

Fig. 1.2 Value configuration in value shops chart. (Source: Own elaboration based on Stabell and Fjeldstad 1998)

As can be seen, the categories of primary activities in value shops are very similar to the cycle seen in consulting projects. The relations between references and subtasks appearing in the problem-solving cycles define, in turn, the vertical range in the value system.

In the area of support activities, the authors use Porter's classical approach from the value chain model. The value configuration diagram can be depicted in the following scheme (Fig. 1.2):

In the scheme, the cyclical nature of primary activities is clearly visible:

1. The evaluation of the solution effectiveness can be an input for activities that define the problem.
2. **The wheels-with-wheels** character of the actions is manifested when the execution phase has the internal structure of the cycle problem→solution→choice→execution→evaluation.

3. **The spiral nature of activities** occurs when the decision cycle refers (or passes control) to a more specialized "shop" that can be implemented by the organization's business unit or another company from the value system.

1.2.6.3 Competitive Advantage

In the case of value shops, the evaluation of an offered value is more difficult than the cost analysis. The relative costs of activities and the values generated by them do not have to correlate (Porter 2008). It may turn out that relatively low-cost activities have a very large impact on the generated value. The reason for that may be, for example, the spiral nature of the actions due to which early actions have a potentially large impact on the effects of subsequent activities. As a result, the challenge is to formulate clear criteria to assess the impact of activities on future values for customers. The value of activity is determined by its effect on the subsequent activity in the cycle.

In the case of value shops, the value-determining factors are more important than cost factors. This is because customers are looking for relatively solid solutions to their problems, not the lowest-priced service as the main attribute. Stabell and Fjeldstad (1998) indicate two key factors determining the competitive advantage: learning and scale effects.

The success manifested in good reputation and relations is a key factor determining the value of companies using intensive technologies. Reputation is a signal of great value and gives access to increasingly demanding customers. The opportunity to implement difficult projects becomes, in turn, an opportunity to learn and, as a result, acquire new competencies. Therefore, learning "across" projects constitutes a very important link between different value shops.

On the other hand, scale effects are related to the scale of the customer's problems and their geographic dispersion. The authors point out that a large number of relatively small value shops lead to its weakening.

1.2.6.4 Strategic Options

The product ranges as well as the business value system are derived from the level of specialized problems and solutions that enable them to be solved (Stabell and Fjeldstad 1998). A high level of vertical integration in the value system implies the wide availability of specialists and the existence of general contractors who can use their competencies. The more different specializations in the industry and the faster the variability of technology are, the smaller the vertical integration of companies operating in the industry is.

The equivalent of vertical integration in the value chain and the scale effect in the value network for shops is the range of engagement in the problem. It is the degree to which the company is able to solve the problem of a given class on its own (without the support of external experts). Management of this scope is not only one of the methods of managing uncertainty, but also a method of improving communication between experts and improving the efficiency of evaluation processes for implementing solutions. As a result, it is a factor determining the reduction of costs as well as the generation of value.

1.2.7 Value Networks

1.2.7.1 The Concept of Value Networks

The value network is another concept proposed by Stabell and Fjeldstad (1998). It is based on mediation technologies—according to Thompson's typology (Thompson 1967)—connecting clients and customers[1] who are interested in creating mutual relations and interdependence. Mediating technologies support relations between actors scattered over time and space. They are used for this purpose, for example, by telecommunications companies, retail banking, insurance companies or postal services.

On the other hand, Pagani (2013) defines the value network as a cluster, in which actors cooperate to provide value to the end user, taking responsibility for the success or failure of these activities. The strategic goal of the actors is to reconfigure their roles and mutual relations in order to create values in new forms and by new players. A key competence of the members of the network should be the ability to manage partnerships (see Dyer and Singh 1998).

1.2.7.2 The Value Creation Logic

A critical determinant of values in networks for each of the actors is the set (network) of entities operating in them. The value creation logic in value networks proposed by Stabell and Fjeldstad (1998) is presented below.

In networks the value is generated by organizing and supporting exchanges between the network actors. Network members may be connected directly—so called Peer-to-Peer (P2P) connections—via intermediaries or shared resources. Network operators act as club managers. They initiate, monitor and interrupt direct or indirect relations. For the operators, all network participants are customers, regardless of the role they play in the network.

The values of services constitute the function of positive external factors on the part of the network demand (network effect). The network value increases with the number of participants. The value is recovered from the access to services and their capacity. Network operators usually charge for access to the network (the ability to use its capabilities) and its actual use (the scope of functionality and the intensity of their use).

Mediating activities are carried out simultaneously on many different levels. Satisfying the random communication needs of a large number of network actors requires a lot of parallel activities that are organized in layers. As a result, the primary activities must have strong reverse connections, not just sequential like in the case of value chains, and errors in synchronization of activities may result in serious network communication failures. For this reason, standardization is a key factor affecting the quality of coordination and feedback in the network, which directly translates into its value to users.

Standardization supports partners' matching and monitoring of their relations. It enables network operators to connect users (compatible with standards) and effectively manage and monitor their interaction.

The life cycles of implementations and operational activities are different. Due to the different needs of network users, the start-up and network sharing phases are separated in time. First, the service is available and widely promoted (implementation phase). Over time, the interested users are gradually starting to use it (operational phase). At some point, a snowball effect occurs: the network effect begins to attract more and more users.

Business relations with partners in value networks come down to cooperation in parallel sub-networks and not, as in the case of value chains, to the supplier–recipient relation. As a result, structures consisting of many cooperating structures are created. For example: telecommunications network operators provide infrastructure for companies offering telecommunications services that provide infrastructure to payment service providers.

Value networks differ in a natural way in the subject of mediation, but they have many common features. Stabell and Fjeldstad (1998) distinguish in them the following common primary activities:

1. **Network promotion and contract management**
   (a) Encouraging potential customers to enter the network; customer selection; initialization, management and interruption of contracts for the provision of services.
   (b) Types and costs of contract service strongly depend on the type and complexity of the network service.
2. **Delivery of services**
   (a) Initiation, maintenance and interruption of connections between network participants; payment support for network services.
   (b) The scope and level of complexity of these activities depend on the nature of the mediation subject.
3. **Network infrastructure management**
   (a) Maintaining the technical and information infrastructure of the network.
   (b) Dependent on the type of infrastructure used.

Among the support activities, the authors point out two interrelated aspects of technology development as particularly interesting:

1. **Development of network infrastructure**, including activities such as design, development and implementation of the network infrastructure.
2. **Development of network services**, especially the development of contracts and the creation of new services.

On the other hand, deliveries and human resource management strongly depend on the type of infrastructure and the specificity of network services.

The diagram of value configuration for the network is presented below (Fig. 1.3).

As can be seen, primary activities overlap due to the concurrent nature of the relations between them. The lack of arrows displaying sequences

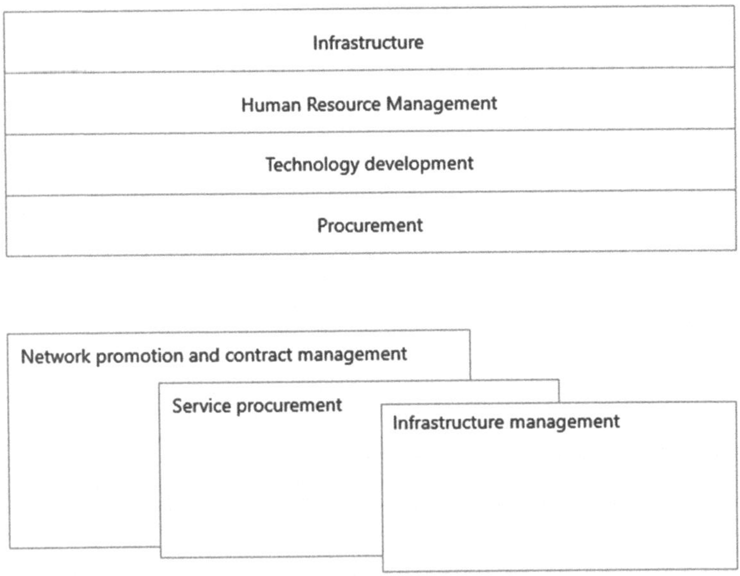

Fig. 1.3 Network value configuration chart. (Source: Own elaboration based on Stabell and Fjeldstad 1998)

indicates that the value is generated by stimulating the interaction between network users.

1.2.7.3 Competitive Advantage

Network structures play a crucial role in cognitive computing systems, which is why it is worth analyzing the theoretical models of factors determining the competitive advantage in networks. Below, the concepts of Stabell and Fjeldstad (1998), and a very interesting model of value creation in service networks by Lusch et al. (2009) are presented.

Factors Determining Cost and Value in Networks

According to Stabell and Fjeldstad (1998) network operators provide value to its users through network access options and the possibility of using services offered within this network. For this reason, the following factors determining the cost and value of the network depend on these two aspects:

1. **Scale and structure**
   (a) Mutual dependence and relations between users are the main value offered by the network: **other users are a key component of the value offered**. Above all, network services provide the opportunity to use these relations. As a result, services in value networks are characterized by a scale effect that is derived from the network effect (the value of the service increases with the number of network users).
   (b) **The scale is also important when it affects the availability of the service**. The large size of the network providing an easy access to its services affects the cost of its use by customers.
   (c) **Common industry standards** are also crucial for the development of network structures and enable connections between networks.

2. **Exploiting the capabilities.** The degree of utilization of network capabilities is closely related to the scale of operation. High level of potential utilization on the one hand reduces costs; on the other hand, it may also reduce the quality of provided services (e.g. network overload).
3. **Connections.** The need to synchronize many parallel activities generates many feedback relations between primary activities.
4. **Learning.** The activities related to customer selection and service monitoring give the highest number of opportunities for learning.

Impact of the Reconfiguration of Forms, Time, Place and Possession on the Offered Value

According to Lusch et al. (2009) the purpose of the network is to provide better value propositions to end customers. It is possible due to raising the level of "density" by reconfiguring forms, time, place and possession of business processes. The maximum density is when "the best combination of resources is mobilized in a particular situation, independent of location to create the optimum value/cost result for a customer" (see Normann 2001). The increase of density may be the effect of changes in the reconfiguration of the network structure. The structure of the value network can be conceptualized in terms of the form of resources, time and place of their availability and possession and methods of their use. Lusch et al. (2009) describe in detail the impact of the reconfiguration of these forms on the final value for the customer—these observations are very valuable for investigating the mechanisms of generating value in structures using AI class systems.

Reconfiguration of Forms

The resources in value networks can exist in material and non-material forms. The examples of material forms are vehicles, warehouses, packaging and other infrastructure. Non-material forms are, for example, legal agreements, licenses, procedures or business processes.

The processes of reconfiguration of forms boil down to the analysis of functions of individual resources in the network of values and the possibilities of optimization by changing their forms. For example, changing the form of a computer from a huge mainframe to a desktop computer has changed its functions in organizations (from computational support for office work), while progressing miniaturization and digitization of devices has made them the basis for platforms that analyze user behavior (Porter and Heppelmann 2014).

The change of form can have a wide impact on interactions in value networks. An example of this is the analysis of the impact of the Walmart package sizes on the environment (it turned out that it was a key factor in energy losses) and the subsequent change in size, which in turn met with strong opposition from Walmart suppliers (Lusch et al. 2009).

Standardization, especially in the form of the use of modular architectures, can also have a very strong impact on the dynamics of relations in the value network.

Reconfiguration of Time

The moment in which the activities are carried out is, according to Lusch et al. (2009) another option of reconfiguration in the value network. It usually results in shortening the time of processes and reducing their costs.

The parallel engineering enables significant reduction of the time needed to enter the market in design as well as in production of physical goods and software (Zirger and Hartley 1996).

The application of start parts and smart parts in Product Lifecycle Management (PLM) significantly shortens the production time while maintaining a high level of meeting the individual needs of users.

The current capabilities of big data analysis allow the inclusion of predictive models as product components in their specifications under PLM (Yunpeng Li et al. 2015); see the description of the implementation of the predictive model as a component in the PLM support system by Aras Innovator (http://www.aras.com/). On the other hand, reusable IT components enable fast creation of new services, for example in the case of Service Oriented Architectures (SOA) (Gebhart et al. 2016).

Reconfiguration of time may also apply to the place of the customer/end user in the value creation process. Some time ago, the product was designed, manufactured and tested internally. Today, due to the possibilities of the Internet as well as smart, connected things, the end user can be directly involved in the design process, the testing takes place wherever a product is used, and the product itself dynamically adjusts its parameters to the user's needs (Porter and Heppelmann 2014).

Reconfiguration of the Place

Modern information technologies (teleconferencing solutions), augmented and virtual reality or systems of smart, connected products enable reconfiguration of the designing place (remote work, conscious involvement of the community, unconscious involvement of customers), manufacturing, production, testing and service (see e.g. Porter and Heppelmann 2015).

Reconfiguration of Ownership

According to service-oriented logic, the value delivered to the customer does not have to be associated with owning the service/product. In other words, it is the access to values that is crucial, not the means to provide them.

As a result, companies may lease (or provide in some other way) but not transfer, ownership to products and services.

This approach is becoming common in today's computing services, for example, cloud computing, where infrastructure, software, development environments and many side services are made available (Stanoevska-Slabeva and Talamanca 2007).

In the systems using artificial intelligence, described later on in the study, this trend can already be observed. IBM provides its cognitive services in this model: (https://www.ibm.com/watson/), while the Algorithmia platform (Algorithmia.com) is becoming a more and more popular platform connecting algorithm providers with customers who use them.

The Role of Intangible Assets in Achieving Competitive Advantage

In the research on supply chain, there is a shift of focus from the supplying and transferring of tangible assets, to creating partnerships, relations, networks of connections, and (co-)creating value (Bovet and Martha 2000; Hoyt and Huq 2000; Lusch et al. 2009; Min et al. 2007). A similar trend can also be seen in marketing (Vargo and Lusch 2004) and in the approaches indicating the key role of intangible assets in the competitive advantage of an organization (Edvinsson and Malone 1997). The detailed analysis of the role of intangible assets in creating value is beyond the scope of this book, but this aspect is worth remembering in further research on the impact of systems using AI on the rules of competition and sources of competitive advantage.

The Role of Competencies, Relations and Information in Value Networks

According to Lusch et al. (2009) the factors connecting the network of values are the competencies, relations and information exchanged between the members of the network. It is no wonder that these categories of resources are perceived as the most valuable for the organization (Evans and Wurster 1997; Vargo and Lusch 2004) while network actors become integrators of these resources (Vargo and Lusch 2008).

The Influence of Intermediaries and Network Complexity on Generating Value

For years, intermediaries (distribution, marketing) have supported the processes of exchanging goods between buyers and sellers. They achieved this by eliminating the gaps: spatial (between places of production and consumption), time (between the moment of production and consumption) and information (between sellers and buyers) (Lusch et al. 2009).

The liquifaction of information in value networks created a space for information brokers, integrators, processors, distributors and sellers of information (detached from their physical component). As a result, the key competence of partners in value networks should be the ability to

1. **identify information intermediaries** that can increase the value of the network,
2. create proper **architecture integrating** those intermediaries with partners in the value network,
3. fully **use the potential of intermediaries to reconfigure forms, time, place and possession** in order to strengthen the value proposition for the customer.

(Lusch et al. 2009)

Additionally, Stanoevska-Slabeva and Talamanca (2007) indicate the need to develop competencies in the field of complexity management, which results from the growing complexity of the relations network. The research on the complexity of systems has been focused on modularity in design, competence specialization, decomposition of tasks and technologies and simplification of interfaces (Lusch et al. 2009). According to Lusch et al. the concept of managing the product complexity that is optimal for service-oriented logic is the product life cycle management model, which divides the stages of material product control into conceptual, development, production and use stages. The authors propose using this model to develop the concept of service life cycle management.

1.2.7.4 Strategic Options

In multilayer network structures, the activities of some network operators are based on activities of other operators, according to Stabell and Fjeldstad (1998). Therefore, the authors suggest two strategic positioning options: one in vertical dimension, the second in horizontal dimension.

Vertical dimension in the mediating industries determines the extent to which the network operator is able to control all levels of activities necessary to ensure communication. In this dimension, the strategic option boils down to determining the scope of control of activity levels in the network.

In horizontal dimension the network operator can expand the market segment by expanding its customer base or through exchange agreements with operators of other networks. The strategic choice comes down to the choice of markets and strategic partnerships in other segments.

1.2.8 Value Grids

An interesting concept complementing the models of value chain, shops and networks is the value grid model, proposed in 2006 by Pil and Holweg (2006).

Constant tensions between opportunities and threats force companies to look for opportunities to manage risk, gain influence on demand and generate new ways of creating value. In Pil and Hogweg's opinion, the creation of values is often more multidirectional than linear, which is why there is a need to modify the traditional, linear value chain.

The basis of the research was the analysis of value chain management strategies for many companies, mainly from the automotive industry (car manufacturers, their suppliers and logistic companies), characterized by high operational efficiency and a linear approach to the value chain, a very fast-changing telecommunications industry (manufacturers of equipment, software and telecommunications companies) and the health/pharmaceutical industry.

1.2.8.1 Dimensions and Strategies of Competing in Value Grids

The developed model proposes a network approach and offers many new ways to increase efficiency. Pil and Holweg (2006) indicate three dimensions of competition:

1. **Vertical dimension**, in which companies look for non-linear opportunities in their traditional value chain due to connections with new players in the supply chains (upstream) and recipients (downstream).
2. **Horizontal dimension**, in which companies look for opportunities in parallel value chains.

3. **Diagonal dimension**, in which companies use an integrated approach that combines horizontal and vertical dimensions.

These dimensions are illustrated in the diagram below (Fig. 1.4):

1.2.8.2 Competing Within the Value Chain: Vertical Dimension

In the vertical dimension, the authors recommend non-linear thinking.

Effective management of activities within the value chain is one of the sources of competitive advantage. Good cooperation with suppliers can improve the efficiency (cost and time) of the supply chain, and customer relations give effect in the form of greater value offered. However, the distribution of benefits within the value chain strongly depends on the distribution of power between suppliers and producers.

For this reason, companies should focus primarily on opportunities of influencing the upstream (suppliers) as well as downstream (customers) of the value chain. This may lead to:

1. Generating demand among customers by controlling the points and moments of making purchase decisions (which in turn requires an in-

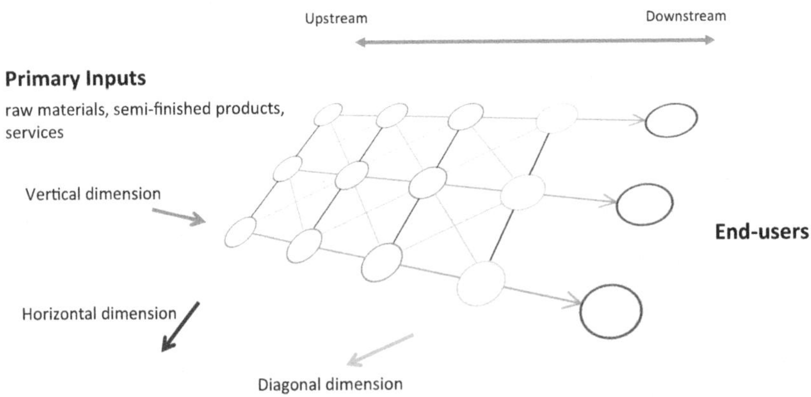

Fig. 1.4 Dimensions of competing in value grids. (Source: Own elaboration based on Pil and Holweg 2006)

depth analysis of the entire value chain in search for decision-making levers). An example of this is the cooperation of pharmaceutical companies with doctors (training, implementation of diagnostic systems, incentive systems, etc.).
2. Designing new products so that they achieve their full potential only in cooperation with existing ones or modification of the market standards in order to support the sale of new products.

In addition, it is advantageous to manage access to information in both directions:

1. Up the value chain:
   (a) Monitoring market conditions of suppliers—price setting mechanisms, competitive environment, legal environment, regulations, layers in value chains.
   (b) Using your own purchasing power to support suppliers—for example, wholesale purchases of steel by car manufacturers selling on preferential terms to sub-suppliers.
2. Down the value chain:
   (a) Obtaining information on the use of products by the users (see also Porter and Heppelmann 2014).
   (b) Loyalty systems.

It is also worth taking advantage of the opportunities resulting from contacts with partners who do not directly cooperate in the value chain. For example, manufacturers of exhaust systems can sell their products not only directly to producers or the secondary market, but also to other segments (layers), for instance, catalysts.

1.2.8.3 Competing in Parallel Chains: The Horizontal Dimension

In the horizontal dimension, Pil and Holweg (2006) recommend the exploration of parallel value chains. The factors differentiating parallel chains are the sources of demand. One of the strategies of searching competitive advantages may be the analysis of the possibility of addressing products to other recipient groups (market segments).

The authors present many potential benefits from exploring opportunities in this dimension:

1. **Improved risk management**: Addressing the product to different target groups can significantly reduce the risk of seasonality and the risk of changes in target markets.
2. **The increase of sales scale:**
    (a) Manufacturers opting for horizontal exploration of the value chain usually **enter other chains, at the same point at which they function in the current chain**. As an example, the authors mention Toyota with its hybrid engines: they are used in the normal way for the production of Toyota cars, but they are also licensed to Ford and Nissan. Another example is the manufacturers of printers and ink cartridges that bring the printer to the market at the lowest possible price to earn later on their own ink cartridges. They can implement two strategies: limit the production to their own printers (then, they remain within the current value chain) or offer their ink containers to other producers (thus going beyond the current chain).
    (b) **Such an approach also poses a threat**. In industries in which companies modulate a particular product or service in the value chain, the risk of implementing substitutes increases.
3. **Integration of various sources of existing values**:
    (a) According to the authors, **going beyond the thinking pattern of a single value chain gives a chance to create new values for end customers**. As an example, they mention the telecommunications industry (as at 2006), under which companies began to integrate various product lines: landline telephony, mobile telephony and the Internet communication. This integration provided the end user with cheaper voice calls: systems could flexibly switch between relatively expensive at that time GSM communication and virtu-

ally free voice communication via the Internet (so-called VoIP: Voice over IP), and telecommunications companies could introduce new packages and price lists that combined these services. A similar trend can now be observed in the multimedia industry. Telecommunications companies now offer not only the Internet access, but also TV networks or video on demand.

(b) **Not only product lines but also industries can be integrated.** Examples of this are the tourist portals (e.g. www.booking.com), where not only can you book a hotel but also rent a car, look for a guide or find airplane connections.

1.2.8.4 Competing in Parallel Value Chains with New Products and Services: A Diagonal Dimension

As for the diagonal dimension, Pil and Holweg (2006) recommend the exploration of various value chains in different layers.

The most universal method of exploring opportunities within the value chain is the analysis of potentials found in various places of different chains. This direction was defined by the authors as diagonal. It comes down to identifying the possibilities of supply chain control (top of the value chain) and discovering new methods of stimulating demand (down the value chain) under non-current value chains.

In their research, the authors identified two strategies used for this purpose:

1. **Pursuing pinch-point mapping**
   - (a) This method should be used in situations where suppliers of key components/services operate simultaneously on other markets.
   - (b) It involves monitoring the situation of key suppliers and providing alternative sources in the case of a breakdown.
   - (c) By "the situation", the authors understand not only the market conditions within their own chain, but also the situation in other markets supported by the supplier. The rapid increase in demand in other markets or failure of a supplier may be a significant risk factor that should be skillfully managed.

2. **Identification of demand-determining factors**. The analysis of value chains in other markets may constitute a chance to use key competitive advantages. For example, shipping companies can not only deliver packages but also handle service requests from large corporations. The Uber company uses a transport network, for example, to transport food, thus creating a platform for the services of other companies.

1.2.9 Value Structures in Service-Dominated Logics

In the part devoted to value networks, a model of value creation proposed by Lusch et al. (2009) was presented. The basis for these conclusions was the research on the value structures in the logics dominated by services. The mechanisms of the service sector functioning are particularly important for research on the impact of AI class systems on value creation.

1.2.9.1 Service-Dominant Logics

Vargo and Lusch (2004) understand service to be the use of own competencies and resources to provide value to external entities and treat it as the basis of economic activity. As a result, service understood in this way is superior to "traditional", measurable and immeasurable products and "services".

This approach constitutes the basis of the service-dominant logic. In this concept "measurable" products are "instruments" of the value supply chain to the customer, while the main function of this chain is to support the processes of creating and supplying value through broadly defined services.

Services understood in this way can be delivered in two ways:

1. **Relieving**: the service provider relieves the customer from the necessity to implement the action;
2. **Enabling**: the service provider strengthens the customer's potential in the implementation of the activity.

Lusch, Vargo and Malter (2006) proposed eight features that characterize companies operating in accordance with service-oriented logic:

1. Focus on the service delivery process, and not on creating products.
2. Concentration on unmeasurable and not on measurable values in the market offer.
3. Focus on creating and using dynamic resources (competencies and knowledge), not consumption and depreciation of material resources.
4. Recognition of the strategic advantage of symmetric access to information over asymmetric access.
5. Transition from propaganda to dialogue.
6. Transition from creating and adding value to proposing and co-creating with the customer.
7. Transition from the transactional model to the relational model.
8. Transition from profit maximization to the "financial feedback" model.

According to the authors, they are the basis of a service-oriented approach and a starting point in the organization's learning model.

1.2.9.2 Value Structures in Service-Dominated Logics

In the model of logic dominated by services, a key role is played by the value network (Lusch et al. 2009). It is understood as being a structure of many loosely connected actors, spontaneously receiving signals and reacting, spanned in time and space. These actors offer various economic and social values, and interact through organizational and technological interfaces in order to (1) co-create valuable services, (2) exchange services, and (3) co-create values.

The supply chain is an element of the broadly understood value network. A company operating in the value chain is often a part of many different supply chains present in it.

It is worth emphasizing that in this approach the value does not replace supply and is not identical with it. The value is generated not so much by the exchange of goods on the market, but by its actual use in a specific context. Only the customer can evaluate it and always co-creates it. The authors illustrate this with an example from the IT market, where the customer does not benefit only from having access to the software, but also from using it for a specific purpose.

As a result, the company can be seen as a set of "business services" integrated to meet the changing needs of customers. This concept illustrates well the trends in the development of IT services and technologies, particularly Service Oriented Architecture (SOA), see e.g. Zhao et al. (2007) (the work devoted to broadly understood IT services, describing concepts such as SOA, SaaS, etc.). It is particularly important in the context of analyses of the business potential of AI class systems, in which modularization of solutions, their standardization and dynamic development of methods facilitating the reuse of intelligent components are observed (e.g. transfer learning).

1.2.9.3 The Learning Model in Value Networks

The main goal of the companies is to integrate and transform competencies into complex values with high market potential. To achieve this, they need to continuously improve their ability to recognize rapidly changing needs and provide services within the network.

Vargo and Lusch (Lusch et al. 2009) propose a learning model of the organization in the network, under which companies

1. develop and strengthen their service orientation,
2. release information from their physical form ("liquify" them),
3. reconfigure resources to maximize network values (increase their "density"),
4. learn by testing various value configurations (hypotheses) on the market and analyzing feedback from customers.

As it can be seen, the information and learning aspects are crucial for generating value in service-oriented companies, which can have considerable consequences for constructing business cases for projects that use AI technologies.

1.2.10 Conclusion

In the above-mentioned value generation models chains, shops, networks and value grids were described. A separate point was devoted to service-oriented logics. These concepts can constitute the basis for creating a model of generating value through solutions using artificial intelligence.

A synthetic summary of the concepts described above is proposed by Stabell and Fjeldstad (1998) (Table 1.1).

By comparing the analyzed value configuration models, they identify key activities that generate value, classify these activities as primary and support activities and analyze factors determining costs and value. The

Table 1.1 Comparison of the value configurations in chains, shops and networks

	Value chain	Value shop	Value network
Value generation logic	Transformation of entrance products into end products	Customer's problem solving	Connecting users
Basic technologies	Chain	Intensive	Mediating
Primary activity categories	Procurement logistics Operations Dispatch logistics Sales and marketing Services	Problem defining Problem solving Solution choice Execution Control and evaluation	Network promotion and contract management Service procurement Infrastructure management
Dominating interactions	Sequential	Cyclic, spiral	Simultaneous, parallel
Relations of primary activities	Connected, sequential	Connected, sequential, mutual	Connected, mutual
Key costs determinants	Scale Possibility use		Scale Possibility use
Key value determinants		Reputation	Scale Possibility use
Business value system structure	Connected value chains	Reference-connected value shops	Connected and layer-ordered value networks

Source: Own elaboration based on Stabell and Fjeldstad (1998)

individual configurations of values differ in terms of primary activities, and they have very similar support activities.

The key criterion for distinguishing individual models is the use of technology in them (see Thompson's (1967) classification). Stabell and Fjeldstad distinguish

1. **sequential technologies,** transforming objects according to a predefined set of ordered activities,
2. **intensive technologies**, which solve customer's problems using a configuration of activities adapted to the needs of the problem,
3. **mediating technologies**, supported by standardized sets of activities at various levels of activity.

Another dimension that differentiates the described value configurations is the level of activity standardization: the level at which technologies are based on standardized or personalized (tailored to the client's needs) combinations of activities.

Different logics of creating values determine different economies of activities in individual structures (Stabell and Fjeldstad 1998). The cost and scale economy is optimal for the value chain (the scale is a factor determining the level of costs). Signaling values (e.g. through reputation) works best in value shops (the scale is, in this case, a factor that influences the signaling of success). The economics of network effects works in the case of value networks (the scale is a factor determining costs and value for the customer).

The quoted authors indicate also that in most organizations there are many different value configurations described. For example, telecommunications companies use mediating technologies in the offer prepared for clients, and sequential technologies in the process of infrastructure production (see also the concept of value constellations by Normann and Ramirez (1993)). In effect, the ability to switch between different value creation logics can be a key competence of modern organizations.

All these conclusions inspire Stabell and Fjeldstad to propose a third (in addition to cost and Porter's differentiation strategies) competition strategy: value configuration.

1.3 The Role of Data, Information and Knowledge in Value Generation

1.3.1 Knowledge as a Key Resource of an Organization

There is a widespread belief in the advent of an economy based on knowledge, in which knowledge is perceived as a key success factor and a source of competitive advantage (Ermine 2013; Foray 2004). Many researchers indicate that knowledge is one of the most important strategic resources of an organization (Davenport and Prusak 2000; Hall 1993; Zawiła-Niedźwiecki 2015a, b), and knowledge representation standards are crucial for expert systems (Abramowicz et al. 2002). The research field focused on the role of artificial intelligence in a knowledge-based economy is also beginning to be noticeable (Mercier-Laurent et al. 2016).

The sources of knowledge found in products and services are primarily the knowledge resources of the organization (Quinn 1992), but more and more often this now includes IT systems, which are an integral part of these products and services (Porter and Heppelmann 2014, 2015). Knowledge management (hereinafter called: KM) is described as a set of strategies, methods and tools enabling management of the intangible resources of the organization's knowledge in order to raise its overall level of competitiveness (Ermine 2013). In the above-presented definition, the key concepts are: "resources", "intangibility" and "knowledge."

One of the biggest challenges of knowledge management today is efficiency measurement. Among the methods of measuring the effectiveness of the KM strategy, it is worth distinguishing the method based on resource theory of competitive advantage (Prahalad and Hamel 1990). In this concept, the prerequisite of gaining competitive advantages is the integration of goals, resources and competencies. The goal of knowledge management is the integration of all resources and knowledge processes that enable the development of such competencies (Ermine 2013).

1.3.2 Data, Information, Knowledge and Wisdom in Knowledge Management

Ermine (2013) proposes a different concept of the knowledge value chain, based on the DIKW model (Data, Information, Knowledge, Wisdom) (see (Rowley 2007) and a very interesting critical review of this approach (Frické 2008).

In this chain, information results from data and information: knowledge is the basis of wisdom. In general: structures at a higher position in the pyramid depend on structures placed in the lower positions, just like in the value chain, they add value to them, which can be illustrated as in the diagram below (Fig. 1.5).

For years, individual concepts from the DIKW pyramid have been widely discussed in the literature (see e.g. Frické 2008). The definitions presented below do not, of course, cover this very rich subject, but they help, though in a simplified way, to organize the concepts used later on.

Data is most often defined as raw facts, accumulated on the basis of observations made either by people or devices. It reaches us in the form of signals that are the result of registration, selection and processing of stimuli from the environment. Therefore, data is the perception of reality through signals from "sensors" (human senses as well as devices) (Ermine 2013).

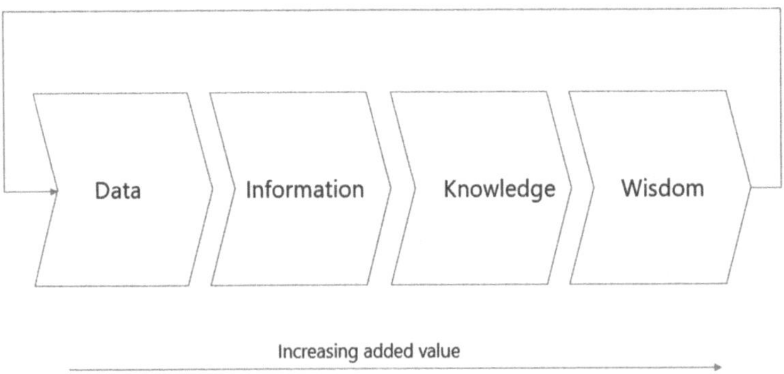

Fig. 1.5 Knowledge Value chain concept according to Ermine. (Source: Own elaboration based on Ermine 2013)

The only unambiguous quantitative definition of information is the probabilistic definition by Shannon and Weaver (1949) (see also Gleick 2011): the entropy concept used in it constitutes the basis for measuring the amount of information, understood as being the amount of uncertainty that has been removed as a result of a message reception. The contribution of Marian Mazur, a Polish scientist, to the information theory needs to be emphasized here. In the 1970s, he created an original theory describing both the quantity and the quality of information (Mazur 1970).

Nonaka (1994) proposed an expansion of the theory of information by adding the semantic perspective. In his opinion, syntactic (quantitative) aspects do not take into account the importance of information in the process of creating knowledge.

In the context of expert systems and artificial intelligence, the third aspect of information is important: its value in the decision-making process. In classical concepts of artificial intelligence—Good Old Fashioned Artificial Intelligence (GOFAI)—it plays a key role in the process of finding solutions in various conditions of uncertainty (see e.g. Norvig and Russell 2016).

Currently, three interrelated information theories are distinguished: statistical-syntactical (related to probabilistic and syntactic aspects of information), semantic (related to meaning) and pragmatic (related to the value of information in the decision-making process).

In the context of the knowledge value chain, Ermine proposes adopting a simple definition of information as data enriched with meaning (Ermine 2013).

According to Rowley (2007), knowledge can be seen as a combination of information, understanding, ability, experience, skills, and values — so, in fact, it is understood very broadly. Le Blanc and Ermine (2011) attempted to quantify this definition by extending Shannon's theory from information to knowledge. In their model, information content is described by Shannon's theory, the meaning by semiotic theory and the context by graph theory. On the basis of these assumptions, the authors introduce the concept of entropy of knowledge, perceiving it as information that has a specific meaning in a given context.

In the knowledge management concepts, the division of knowledge into explicit and tacit is crucial. The explicit knowledge can be codified and archived, e.g. in the form of documents or databases.

The tacit knowledge is available only to people that are in its possession: it cannot be registered and, only to some extent, can be transferred to others.

Knowledge, like information, is now treated as one of the key resources of the organization.

Wisdom is one of the most difficult concepts to define. Ermine describes it as "the ability to use knowledge, in the best possible way, to establish and achieve the desired goals" (Ermine 2013). He operationalizes this definition by distinguishing the individual wisdom (competence) as a combination of knowledge, skills and behaviors conditioning the correct implementation of tasks by a unit and organizational wisdom (capability) as a result of the integration of knowledge with complex and productive team activities conditioning the organization's ability to achieve its goals.

On the other hand, Rowley (2007) proposes several definitions of wisdom, perceiving it to be

1. accumulated knowledge, which enables solving new problems,
2. ability to effectively act in any situation,
3. the use of knowledge and information in practice,
4. ability to assess the situation correctly,
5. the way in which knowledge is used in practice,
6. the ability to choose the best possible actions in a given situation, which take into account the possessed knowledge.

Ermine (2013) identifies wisdom with competencies and proposes a simple definition of competence as knowledge in action. The skills understood in this way mean the ability to use knowledge to improve efficiency, which can be more briefly described as "intelligence."

1.3.3 The Concept of the Knowledge Value Chain

The presentation of the concept of knowledge value chains requires the definition of the following terms: data, information and knowledge management.

The aim of data management is control, protection, distribution and enhancement of data values understood as the organization's resources.

The purpose of information management processes is to give meaning to data in order to support employees and managers in making decisions at operational, tactical and strategic levels (Ermine 2013).

Knowledge management is the process of managing the ability to use the possessed knowledge to achieve goals and improve efficiency at both the individual (competence management) and organizational level (capabilities management) (ibid.).

Ermine (2013) understands the Knowledge Value Chain (KVC) to be a chain of knowledge activities on knowledge resources and the chain of cognitive activities on knowledge management processes. The knowledge value chain defined in this way includes knowledge management processes, which is why KVC is treated as a useful framework for KM processes. In his analyses, the author introduces two dimensions of knowledge management: knowledge value chain and cognitive value chain, as illustrated in the diagram below (Fig. 1.6).

In turn, Wang and Ahmed propose a model of the knowledge chain based on Porter's value chain (Wang and Ahmed 2013) (Fig. 1.7).

As can be seen in the figure above, it is a chain of actions in knowledge resources, divided into "primary" (KM processes) and "support" activities, raising the capabilities of the organization, which in turn raise its competitive advantages (effectiveness and results).

1.3.4 Transformation Processes in the Knowledge Chain

Ermine proposes an interesting concept of transformation processes in the knowledge chains (Ermine 2013). He analyzes them in syntactic, semantic and contextual dimensions – this is illustrated in the figure below (Fig. 1.8).

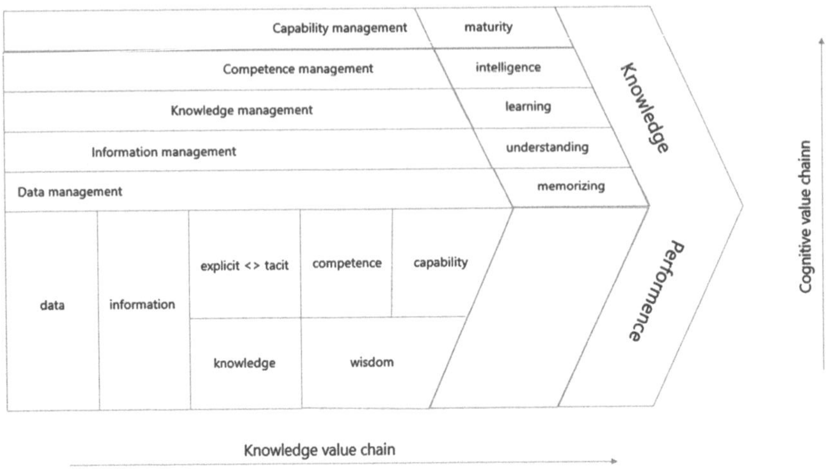

Fig. 1.6 Knowledge value chain and its management. (Source: Own elaboration based on Ermine 2013)

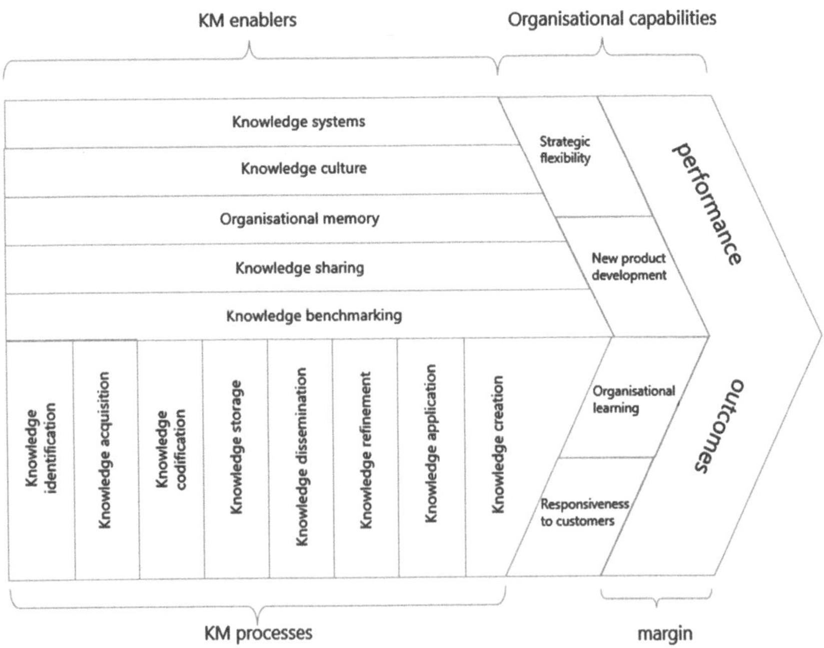

Fig. 1.7 Knowledge chain model according to Wang and Ahmed. (Source: Own elaboration based on Wang and Ahmed 2013)

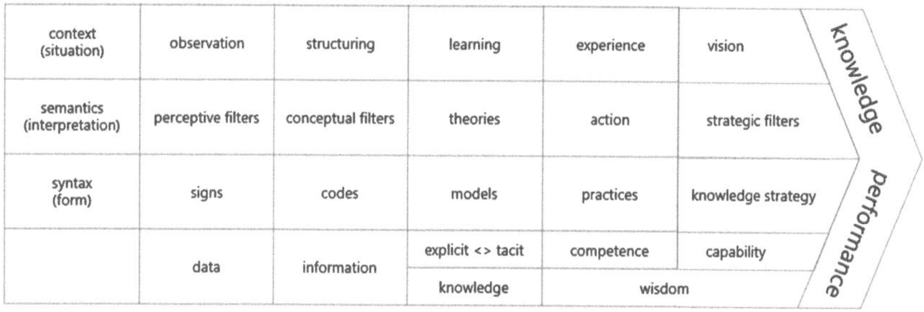

Fig. 1.8 Knowledge transformation processes in value chains according to Ermine. (Source: Own elaboration based on Ermine 2013)

The author divides the transformation processes into two categories:

1. **From reality to explicit knowledge:**
   (a) Objective and measurable, feasible for both human and machine.
   (b) In this category, the role of information technology is considerable.
2. **From information and public knowledge to capabilities**:
   (a) Unmeasurable, subjective, based on beliefs, with greater participation of humans.
   (b) Here the role of information technology can only be supportive.

In syntactic dimension of transformation, the results of its process are explicit.

Due to the cognitive filters that allow interpretation of the results of activities in the process, the semantic dimension supports giving meaning to transformation processes.

The contextual dimension describes cognitive situations in which transformation processes take place.

The result of the author's research is a proposition of a transformation chain in which the following changes take place:

1. **Reality→Data.** Transforming data (signals) through perceptual filters in the observation process.
2. **Data→Information.** Data coding through conceptual filters in which the data is given a structure.

3. **Information→Knowledge**. Building models based on theories in the learning process.
4. **Knowledge→Competencies**. Developing best practices through activities undertaken in experimental processes.
5. **Competencies→Opportunities**. Building strategies for using knowledge by organizing and adjusting goals in vision creation processes.

The systems based on artificial intelligence are inherently characterized by high information saturation, while having more and more opportunities to generate knowledge in various forms. For this reason, the knowledge chain model presented above can be an interesting conceptual framework for further analyses.

1.4 The Influence of Information Technologies on Value Configurations and Competition

The authors of studies on models of value generation in organizations often point to information as one of the main catalysts of these processes. In intelligent systems, information plays a superior role and, therefore, to understand better the mechanisms of creating value in such solutions, the possible impact of information technologies on value configurations and the rules of competition deserve prior analysis.

1.4.1 Liquified Information in the Value Chain

For a long time, knowledge and information technologies have been one of the factors of economic growth (Tunzelmann 2005). In the past, information was inseparable from the matter—paper, stone, wood, and so on. Computerization has enabled the process of "liquifying" information: its separation from the physical medium, duplication, fast transmission and more or less controlled dissemination. This constitutes the foundations of the digital revolution: organizations in the global network economy could adapt better to market conditions and provide better services (Lusch et al. 2007, 2009).

Before the information age, information could move as fast as the matter with which it was associated. IT technologies drastically accelerated its transfer, thus becoming something like the "nervous system" of value chains (Gunasekaran and Ngai 2004). As a result, IT systems have become crucial for receiving information, reacting and learning in the value chain. Organizations have become subjects of learning, while the people and knowledge management systems have become the place of knowledge storage.

One of the consequences is the relative independence of physical and information components in the value chain (e.g. in the supply chain), which consequently means that physical control over resources or their ownership does not condition the possibility of benefiting from them.

As a result, information brokerage industries or data operators were created, and the spectrum of cooperation opportunities between partners within the value chain was widened (Lusch et al. 2009).

1.4.2 Impact of Information Technologies on the Value Chain

There are many studies on the impact of information technology on the value chain. Below, there is a subjective presentation of the most adequate to analyze systems using AI.

According to Porter and Heppelmann (2014, 2015) the development of information technologies increases the digitization of products, due to which they become better platforms for delivering value, foster the development of self-service systems and increases the ability to provide services to other entities (e.g. remote service, consulting, etc.). In turn, the development of communication technologies reduces the need for traditional transport, improves the ability to recognize the needs of suppliers and customers, improves the opportunities for interaction with suppliers and customers, and the effectiveness and responsiveness of cooperation between partners.

The authors claim that information technologies are present in virtually every element of the value chain, both in activities and in connections between them. In particular, activities in the value chain differ in the degree of saturation with physical and information activities. This information saturation concerns both the value chain (and processes) and the products.

Each activity has physical and information components. The physical component contains all the physical activities necessary to carry out the action. The information component includes activities related to obtaining, processing and sending data necessary for the implementation of the action.

In addition, various industries are saturated with information in various ways, and physical products are more and more saturated with information. As a result, IT systems not only affect activities in the value chain and the nature of links between them but also the scope of competition and the way in which products meet the needs of clients.

Porter and Heppelmann (2014, 2015) in the two articles cited above and published in the *Harvard Business Review* at the turn of 2014 and 2015, in a very interesting way, analyze the impact of smart, connected things (products equipped with sensors and communicating with other devices) on the processes of designing, production, logistics, marketing and sales of post-sales security services and human resource management. These analyses will be partly used in the further part of the study as a basis for studying the impact of AI systems on various value generation processes in organizations.

1.4.3 The Impact of Information Systems on Competitiveness and Value Structures

In parallel with the analysis of the impact of information systems on the organization's activity, many studies were conducted in the area of the impact of these technologies on the rules of competition.

The classic item devoted to this issue is the research paper by Porter and Millar (1985). According to the authors, the information revolution affects competitiveness in three ways:

1. **It changes the structure of the industry and, as a result, the rules of competition.** The authors analyze the impact of information on 5 market forces:
   (a) Competition between existing competitors,
   (b) The threat of new players entering the market,
   (c) The threat of introducing new products/services,
   (d) The suppliers' bargaining power,
   (e) The buyers' bargaining power.
2. **It allows creating a competitive advantage by giving rivals new ways to achieve an advantage through:**
   (a) Reducing the costs,
   (b) Increasing diversity,
   (c) A change in the scope of competition (industry, geographical area, market, level of vertical integration).
3. **It affects virtually all functional areas of business:**
   (a) Thanks to information technologies, new business models are becoming feasible,
   (b) These technologies enable generation of new, non-existent needs,
   (c) They also allow you to create new businesses within the existing ones.

Porter and Millar (1985) also created an extremely current (despite the passage of time of over 30 years) set of recommendations for companies interested in using information technologies to achieve competitive advantages. The most important of them are presented below to show how long the conclusions of fundamental research in management sciences may be up-to-date, even in areas with huge dynamics of change (this is the case with information technologies).

1. Evaluate the information saturation:
   (a) Analyze processes in the value chain. Pay special attention to:
      (i) processes that have a large number of suppliers or customers,
      (ii) product line with a large number of variants,

(iii) production process consisting of a large number of steps,
(iv) long-cycle process from the product order to its delivery to the client.

(b) Analyze your products. Pay special attention to a product:

(i) composed of many parts,
(ii) whose production requires the processing of a large amount of information,
(iii) whose sales requires the provision of a large amount of information,
(iv) providing mainly information,
(v) requiring costly training of end users,
(vi) having many alternative methods of application.

2. Evaluate the role of information technologies in the industry structure:

(a) How can information technology affect each of the five forces of competition?
(b) How can they change the boundaries of the industry?

3. How can information technologies create a competitive advantage by influencing:

(a) Reduction of the costs?
(b) The scope of competition?
(c) The opportunity to enter new market segments?
(d) Entering niche markets?
(e) Entering global markets?
(f) Establishing relationships with other industries?
(g) Increasing competitiveness by narrowing the area of activities (concentration)?
(h) Adding more information to the product?
(i) Adding information technology to the product?

4. Evaluate how IT can affect the generation of new businesses:

(a) What information can the company sell (at the moment or potentially)?
(b) What kind of information processing capabilities does the company already have?

5. Create a plan to gain a competitive advantage thanks to information technologies.

The recommendations presented above can be used in the processes of creating business cases for projects that use artificial intelligence to increase the value provided by products and services.

1.5 Value Networks in the Telecommunications and IT Industries

As illustrated in the previous section of this study, for the past few decades the transformation of hierarchically integrated supply chains towards a network of strategic partnerships has been observed (see also Bitran et al. 2007). The catalyst for these transformations are information technologies which, by supporting modularization, dispersion, integration of functional areas and globalization processes, reduce time, spatial and functional constraints of the implemented activities and, as a result, allow radical transformation of traditional business processes (Pagani 2013; Sambamurthy et al. 2003). The dynamic development of these technologies creates the conditions for new, revolutionary business models and the emergence of complex and dynamic ecosystems of innovation (Iansiti and Levien 2004).

1.5.1 Motivation for the Development of New Methods for Assessing Business Potential in the IT and Telecommunications Industries

In 2005, Trossen and Fine (2005) came to the conclusion that in network value configurations, the center-edge topology was not a good model for assessing business potential. When analyzing the example of the telecommunications industry, they stated that in the past, its structure was based on the close integration of telecommunications technologies. The services were provided by a limited number of players providing integrated functionality packages (network core) to end users (network edge). As a result, the control over central (core) technologies provided control over the entire network. In 2005, packet-based technology was increasingly decoupling itself from service and infrastructure layers. In effect, positioning in the network perceived in the topological perspective (core-edge relation) is not so important for the effectiveness of the business model. Therefore, it is necessary to develop alternative methods for evaluating revenue models.

In this way, the authors pointed to the need for a new method of evaluating innovative business models. In their opinion, innovations in the communication industry can appear almost everywhere, at any time and can be introduced virtually by anyone. This is the result of changes in technologies, business models, legal regulations, and particularly, because the barriers to entering the industry are now lower, due to the low costs of access to technology knowledge. This observation is specifically up to date in the area of broadly understood technologies that use artificial intelligence.

The analyses presented above indicate the need to develop new methods and tools for the correct assessment of the innovation business potential. They should not depend on network topology, but rather on functional components and methods of their implementation. Below, the concept of control points and its application to value network modeling in the telecommunications industry is presented.

1.5.2 The Model of Control Points as the Basis of the Business Potential Analysis Method

According to Trossen and Fine (2005), in the assessment of the chances of success of a given innovation, the issue of "control" becomes crucial. The location at any point in the topology of the telecommunications network does not guarantee business success. The identification and control over the control point that allows control over the value network is much more important.

Trossen and Fine define control points as places in the network of values that enable control over a business proposition. Transaction services as well as suppliers or consumers can perform this function. The possible business models can be built by creating various constellations of control points. The structure of these constellations is defined by control structures (methods for the implementation of control points), ensuring the functioning of transaction services and the services implemented in a centralized or decentralized form (Trossen and Fine 2005).

This was confirmed in 2010 by Eaton et al. (2010) who argued that in value networks the profit centers and competitive advantage were accumulated at the points with the highest value and/or advantage (the abovementioned control points); companies that occupy these points have a dominant position in the network, controlling its functioning and redistribution of profits.

Trossen and Fine also note that fast technological changes cause changes in the allocation of these points. Therefore, the key competence is the ability to identify them quickly and to flexibly allocate business models there. The authors propose the following stages of business model analysis in the value networks:

1. **The list of possible business models** and, for each of them, the identification of
   (a) control points;
   (b) actors controlling them;
   (c) their implementation taking into account delivery aspects, service delivery model and methods of managing them.
2. **The analysis of constellations of control points** in the analyzed possible business models.
3. **Evaluation of the value of control points**. The value of the control point is defined by the authors as the product of its profitability (revenues—costs related to a given point) and the demand that can be obtained at this point. The value of the point depends essentially on competitors' ability to create the same point in the value network.

4. **Taking into account the factors of change**
    (a) The changes in the model can be generated by
        (i) technologies,
        (ii) business cycles,
        (iii) regulations,
        (iv) customers preferences,
        (v) capital market,
        (vi) key players' strategies.
    (b) As a result, the list of change factors can be very long. In the example of the Apple iTunes music store analyzed by the authors, there were as many as 80 different variables.
    (c) Each of the factors can generate changes in the network as well as influence other factors. For this reason, it is useful to use maps of the interdependence of individual factors of change.
5. **The identification of the factors crucial for the success of the business model**, among which the authors distinguish:
    (a) **Uniqueness**: how easy is it for other players to create a given control point in the same place of the value network? The higher, the better.
    (b) **Demand**: market share that can be obtained at a given control point. It can be measured in the number of units sold, number of subscribers, sales value, and so on.
    (c) **Value**: specifies the value that a control point or product can generate. It is very difficult to calculate. It depends on many factors, above all, uniqueness and demand.
    (d) **Time**: all the above features of the model change over time, under the influence of the factors described above.
6. **The comparison of various business models** and their success factors, taking into account their evolution over time, which most often requires the use of complex models based on systems dynamics theories.

In their work, the authors illustrate their analysis with the example of the digital music industry (Apple iTunes store); the full description is beyond the scope of the present book, but examining this study is strongly recommended to those who are interested in gaining a more in-depth understanding of the concept of control points.

The model of control points was also used in an interesting way by Eaton et al. (2010) to analyze the business model of Apple Store. They analyzed the interaction of actors with different revenue models in this ecosystem and applied the analysis of control points to identify places where actors can recover value from the network. The use of the concept of economic power (perceived from the perspective of the theory of transaction costs) was a novelty in their approach. The concept was used to identify the best tasks in the network, from which the company can generate the power due to its own uniqueness (tasks that only a company can control) and non-transferability (this advantage can be maintained). In the authors' opinion, these tasks may be identified on the basis of the resources theories and concepts of key competencies (Prahalad and Hamel 1990; Wernerfelt 1984).

1.5.3 The Value Network Models in the Telecommunications and Digital Media Industries

1.5.3.1 Value Networks in the Telecommunications Industry

The value chain model can be successfully applied to the telecommunications industry, largely due to the intensive use of mediating technologies.

An interesting analysis of the value system in this industry is proposed by Cuesta et al. (2010). The value network defines a network of relationships that increases profits (financial and non-financial) through complex, dynamic exchanges. Among the network actors, the authors draw attention particularly to infrastructure providers (Infrastructure as a Service: IaaS), end-user application providers (Software as a Service: SaaS), providers of communication solutions (communication equipment and services) and additional service providers (Value Added Services: VAS; e.g. consultancy, integration, insurance, billing, and so on).

The identification of factors determining costs and value in networks is crucial for studying value network models. Cuesta et al. mention the benefits that individual actors can regain from the network (Cuesta et al. 2010):

1. **Non-measurable benefits** including knowledge (technical, market and strategic), branding, loyalty and trust.
2. **Measurable goods**, including software, hardware and licenses.
3. **Financial benefits**, such as revenues and payments.

In turn, the costs can be divided according to the authors into

1. one-off investments,
2. continuous payments,
3. Pay-Per-Use.

Cuesta et al. (2010) also observe that from the perspective of a network member these relations are dynamic, and for the end user the network complexity is hidden. The above analysis is a good example of the use of value network model to analyze the IT industry—it can be a role model for shaping the impact of artificial intelligence on industries using them.

1.5.3.2 Value Networks in the Media Industry

A very interesting application of the control point method for analyzing value networks in the digital media industry was proposed by Pagani (2013), who identified and analyzed three value networks with different structures: vertically integrated, loosely coupled and a multisided platform.

In her research method, Pagani used the following stages:

1. Breaking the network of values into their functional components to identify the organization of control points and their owners.
2. The analysis of the impact of change factors on the dynamics of these value networks.

3. Creating a value network model as a configuration of control points, containing various transaction services enabling the implementation of functionalities necessary to provide value to the end users. These configurations are described by the author as Control Point Constellations (CPC).
4. The analysis of the ways in which control points create and recover value from the network.

The first result of the research is the identification of control points configuration dependencies on the value network topology.

For a **vertically integrated model**, Pagani (2013) states:

1. A closed, vertically integrated constellation model of control points appears in markets where customers' needs are met only in a limited way.
2. Companies focus on achieving economies of scale in horizontal business models and expanding markets through strategic alliances with other partners.
3. The factors affecting the creation of alliances are:
   (a) The risk of uncertain demand and major changes on the market.
   (b) Market positioning and access to new opportunities.
   (c) The ability to control the customer and increase the share in profits from the sale of products and services.
   (d) Moving to a place in the value chain with higher value added.
   (e) The risk of competing with companies in connected markets.
4. The acquisition of value from the network is controlled by key, vertically integrated players.

In case of loosely related coalitions as the demand for new functionalities and the emergence of incremental innovations decrease (improvements to existing solutions or their reconfiguration to meet new needs), the disintegrated structure of control points divided into horizontal layers becomes the dominant business model, and the acquisition of value from the network is controlled by network operators.

In turn, in the case of multilateral platforms, the biggest mark-ups are generated by companies offering infrastructure (platforms), creating value by reducing distribution costs, transactions and information retrieval by cooperating partners.

According to Pagani, the inter-branch disruptive innovations generate large efficiency gaps in individual markets, which causes their reconfiguration towards vertically integrated constellations of control points. As a result, innovations can affect topologies of value structures within one industry.

The second very interesting conclusion coming from the analyses is the identification of five layers of values in the digital media industry. The author points to:

1. **Value in access to the customer**. It is controlled by companies that have a direct relationship with the end customer. The largest economic value is created at the periphery of the network: this value is generated due to the possibility of high personalization of interaction with the customer.
2. **Value in common infrastructure**. The elements of the infrastructure can be integrated and the access to it can be offered as a service (Software as a Service: SaaS).
3. **Value in modularity**. Due to the modularity and standardization of the device, software, organizational capabilities and business processes will be able to quickly and easily connect with each other and reconfigure. The value will be in the creation of modules that can be incorporated into many different value chains. Companies and individuals will be interested in distributing their opportunities as widely as possible and not just keeping them to themselves.
4. **Value in coordination**. In the era of modularity, the most valuable business skill will be the ability to coordinate the interaction of various modules.
5. **Value in access to content.** The control over access to content is characteristic of the media industry.

The awareness of these layers makes it easier to occupy the optimal place (control point) in the value network, which can bring measurable benefits from the strategic analysis.

1.6 Competencies Necessary to Achieve a Competitive Advantage

The models of value creation presented above result in many interesting recommendations for companies and indications on key competencies necessary to achieve a competitive advantage. These recommendations are in many cases extremely universal and can be a good basis for models of value creation with the use of artificial intelligence.

In the structures for which the value chain is a good model, in addition to Porter's strategy of competing: cost and differentiation, it is worth pointing out two interesting competencies:

1. The ability to optimize the chain, particularly by resolving tradeoffs in optimization processes.
2. The skill to coordinate activities
   (a) within the company chain,
   (b) our own activities and other partners' activities in the industry chain.

The key competencies resulting from the analysis of models of competing in more complex structures than the chain presented above can be divided into three categories: efficiency, creativity and flexibility.

Effectiveness

This competence boils down to the skill of recovering value from network structures.

For Stabell and Fjeldstad (1998), the key is the ability to choose the optimal position in the value structure. To achieve this, the company should be able to:

1. **Choose a place in the value structure** in product, market segment and business value dimensions.
2. **Analyze the potentials in different places of value structures.** This means identifying the ability to control the supply chain (the top of the value chain) and discovering new methods of stimulating demand (the bottom of the value chain) within other than the current value chains.

3. **Evaluate the possibility of addressing your own product to other market segments.**

On the other hand, Pagani (2013) indicates the ability to recover value from the access to customer, common infrastructure, modularity, coordination and content.

Creativity
Creativity, in the context of achieving competitive advantages, often comes down to discovering new methods of creating value. This may require:

1. **The ability to reconfigure roles and relations between partners in order to create new forms of value** (Dyer and Singh 1998; Lusch et al. 2009), particularly:
   (a) The abilities to manage partnerships.
   (b) Identification of information intermediaries that can increase the value of the network.
   (c) The creation of proper architecture integrating those intermediaries with partners in the value network.
   (d) The possibility of the full usage of potential of intermediaries to reconfigure forms, time, place and possession in order to strengthen the value proposition for the customer.
2. **Continuous reconfiguration and integration of own competencies and competencies of customers** (Lusch et al. 2009), especially:
   (a) Reconfiguration of forms
   (b) Reconfiguration of time
   (c) Reconfiguration of place
   (d) Reconfiguration of possession
3. **Complexity management skills.** Network structures are often very complex, so changing their architectures requires competence in the management of complexity (Stanoevska-Slabeva and Talamanca 2007). Modularity in design, competence specialization, decomposition of tasks and technologies, and simplification of interfaces, according to Lusch et al. (2009) should be supplemented by the product life

cycle management model, which divides the stages of material product control into conceptual, development, production and use.

Flexibility

Stabell and Fjeldstad (1998) point to the third strategy of competing through value configurations in addition to cost and the differentiation competitiveness by Porter. It requires flexibility, understood as being the ability to reconfigure relations between actors in different value structures:

1. In case of **value chains**: reconfiguration of sequential relations between suppliers, manufacturers and distributors, adding a specific value in the chain.
2. In the case of **value shops**: reconfiguration of relations in the wheel-with-wheels model as part of problem solving and their implementation (references, sub-outsourcing).
3. In the case of **value networks**: reconfiguration of partner relations by combining horizontal network structures and expanding markets to achieve network effects.

1.7 Summary

The value creations models presented in this chapter, although developed decades ago, turn out to be actually very current. In Chaps. 2 and 3, the basic methods of artificial intelligence and its influence on the creation of value in today's organizations will be described. Then, in Chap. 4, the concepts useful for developing the model of cognitive networks will be presented. Finally, it will be shown how many elements connect business reality of the twentieth century with the newest methods in the twenty-first century.

Notes

1. The distinction between terms "customer" and "client" needs to be emphasized. "Customer" is a person who buys a product or service whereas "client" is a person who obtains advice or customized solutions.

References

Abramowicz, W., Kalczyński, P., & Węcel, K. (2002). Knowledge Representation Standards. In *Filtering the Web to Feed Data Warehouses* (pp. 41–74). London: Springer. https://doi.org/10.1007/978-1-4471-0137-6_3.

Adner, R., & Zemsky, P. B. (2004). A Demand Based View of Sustainable Competitive Advantage. *SSRN Electronic Journal* https://doi.org/10.2139/ssrn.651184.

Bednarz, J. (2011). Klasyczne a nowe teorie przewagi konkurencyjnej przedsiębiorstw. *Prace I Materiały Instytutu Handlu Zagranicznego Uniwersytetu Gdańskiego*, (nr 30), 112–122.

Bitran, G. R., Gurumurthi, S., & Sam, S. L. (2007). The Need for Third-Party Coordination in Supply Chain Governance – ProQuest. *MIT Sloan Management Review, 48*, 30–37.

Bounfour, A., & Edvinsson, L. (2012). *Intellectual Capital for Communities*. London and New York: Routledge.

Bovet, D., & Martha, J. (2000). Value Nets: Reinventing the Rusty Supply Chain for Competitive Advantage. *Strategy & Leadership, 28*(4), 21–26. https://doi.org/10.1108/10878570010378654.

Bowman, C., & Ambrosini, V. (2000). Value Creation Versus Value Capture: Towards a Coherent Definition of Value in Strategy. *British Journal of Management, 11*(1), 1–15. https://doi.org/10.1111/1467-8551.00147.

Bughin, J., Hazan, E., Ramaswamy, S., Chui, M., Allas, T., Dahlstrom, P., et al. (2017). *Artificial Intelligence*. McKinsey Global Institute. Retrieved from https://www.mckinsey.com/~/media/McKinsey/Industries/Advanced%20Electronics/Our%20Insights/How%20artificial%20intelligence%20can%20deliver%20real%20value%20to%20companies/MGI-Artificial-Intelligence-Discussion-paper.ashx

Cuesta, J. C., Luokkanen-Rabetino, K., & Stanoevska-Slabeva, K. (2010). Grid Value Chains – What Is a Grid Solution? In *Grid and Cloud Computing* (pp. 83–96). Berlin/Heidelberg: Springer. https://doi.org/10.1007/978-3-642-05193-7_6.

Davenport, T. H., & Prusak, L. (2000, August). Working Knowledge – How Organizations Manage What They Know. *Ubiquity, 2000*, 2-es. https://doi.org/10.1145/347634.348775.

Dyer, J. H., & Singh, H. (1998). The Relational View: Cooperative Strategy and Sources of Interorganizational Competitive Advantage. *Academy of Management Review, 23*(4), 660. https://doi.org/10.2307/259056.

Eaton, B. D., Elaluf-Calderwood, S. M., & Sørensen, C. (2010). *The Role of Control Points in Determining Business Models for Future Mobile Generative Systems* (pp. 459–463). Presented at the 2010 Ninth International Conference on Mobile Business and 2010 Ninth Global Mobility Roundtable (ICMB-GMR), IEEE. https://doi.org/10.1109/ICMB-GMR.2010.39.

Edvinsson, L., & Malone, M. S. (1997). *Intellectual Capital: Realizing Your Company's True Value by Finding It's Hidden Roots*. New York: Harper Business.

Ermine, J.-L. (2013). A Knowledge Value Chain for Knowledge Management. *Journal of Knowledge & Communication Management, 3*(2), 85–101. https://doi.org/10.5958/j.2277-7946.3.2.008.

Evans, P. B., & Wurster, T. S. (1997). Strategy and the New Economics of Information. *Harvard Business Review, Sept–Oct*, 70–82. Harvard University.

Foray, D. (2004). *Economics of Knowledge*. Cambridge: MIT Press.

Frické, M. (2008). The Knowledge Pyramid: A Critique of the DIKW Hierarchy. *Journal of Information Science, 35*(2), 131–142. https://doi.org/10.1177/0165551508094050.

Gebhart, M., Giessler, P., & Abeck, S. (2016). Flexible and Maintainable Service-Oriented Architectures with Resource-Oriented Web Services. *Emerging Trends in the Evolution of Service-Oriented and Enterprise Architectures, 111*(1&2), 23–39. https://doi.org/10.1007/978-3-319-40564-3_3.

Gleick, J. (2011). *The Information: A History, a Theory, a Flood*. New York: Pantheon Books.

Godlewska-Majkowska, H., Łyciuk-Bzdyra, M., Wodecki, A., Zarębski, P., & Zarębski, K. (2010). Atrakcyjność inwestycyjna polskich regionów w 2007 roku. *Studia I Analizy Instytutu Przedsiębiorstwa, Innowacyjność jako czynnik wzrostu atrakcyjności inwestycyjnej polskich regionów w latach 2002–2007*, 55–234.

Gunasekaran, A., & Ngai, E. W. T. (2004). Information Systems in Supply Chain Integration and Management. *European Journal of Operational Research, 159*(2), 269–295. https://doi.org/10.1016/j.ejor.2003.08.016.

Hall, R. (1993). A Framework Linking Intangible Resources and Capabilities to Sustainable Competitive Advantage. *Strategic Management Journal, 14*(8), 607–618. https://doi.org/10.1002/smj.4250140804.

Hoyt, J., & Huq, F. (2000). From Arms-Length to Collaborative Relationships in the Supply Chain. *International Journal of Physical Distribution & Logistics Management, 30*(9), 750–764. https://doi.org/10.1108/09600030010351453.

Iansiti, M., & Levien, R. (2004). *The Keystone Advantage*. Boston: Harvard Business Press.

Le Blanc, B., & Ermine, J.-L. (2011). A Shannon's Theory of Knowledge. In *Creating Collaborative Advantage Through Knowledge and Innovation* (Vol. 5, pp. 51–67). World Scientific. https://doi.org/10.1142/9789812707482_0004.

Li, Y., Roy, U., Shin, S.-J., & Lee, Y. T. (2015). *A "Smart Component" Data Model in PLM* (pp. 1388–1397). Presented at the 2015 IEEE International Conference on Big Data (Big Data), IEEE. https://doi.org/10.1109/BigData.2015.7363899.

Lippman, S. A., & Rumelt, R. P. (2003). A Bargaining Perspective on Resource Advantage. *Strategic Management Journal, 24*(11), 1069–1086. https://doi.org/10.1002/smj.345.

Lusch, R. F., Vargo, S. L., & Malter, A. J. (2006). Marketing as Service-Exchange: Taking a Leadership Role in Global Marketing Management. *Organizational Dynamics, 35*, 264–278.

Lusch, R. F., Vargo, S. L., & O'Brien, M. (2007). Competing Through Service: Insights from Service-Dominant Logic. *Journal of Retailing, 83*(1), 5–18. https://doi.org/10.1016/j.jretai.2006.10.002.

Lusch, R. F., Vargo, S. L., & Tanniru, M. (2009). Service, Value Networks and Learning. *Journal of the Academy of Marketing Science, 38*(1), 19–31. https://doi.org/10.1007/s11747-008-0131-z.

MacDonald, G., & Ryall, M. D. (2004). How Do Value Creation and Competition Determine Whether a Firm Appropriates Value? *Management Science, 50*(10), 1319–1333. https://doi.org/10.1287/mnsc.1030.0152.

Mazur, M. (1970). *Jakościowa teoria informacji*. Warsaw: Wydawnictwa Naukowo-Techniczne.

Mercier-Laurent, E., Owoc, M. L., & Boulanger, D. (2016). In E. Mercier-Laurent, M. L. Owoc, & D. Boulanger (Eds.), *Artificial Intelligence for Knowledge Management* (Vol. 469). Cham: Springer. https://doi.org/10.1007/978-3-319-28868-0.

Min, S., Mentzer, J. T., & Ladd, R. T. (2007). A Market Orientation in Supply Chain Management. *Journal of the Academy of Marketing Science, 35*(4), 507–522. https://doi.org/10.1007/s11747-007-0020-x.

Nonaka, I. (1994). A Dynamic Theory of Organizational Knowledge Creation. *Organization Science, 5*(1), 14–37. https://doi.org/10.1287/orsc.5.1.14.

Normann, R. (2001). *Reframing Business*. Chichester: Wiley.

Normann, R., & Ramirez, R. (1993). From Value Chain to Value Constellation: Designing Interactive Strategy. *Harvard Business Review, 71*(4), 65–77.

Norvig, P., & Russell, S. (2016). *Artificial Intelligence: Modern Approach* (3rd ed.). Upper Saddle River: Prentice Hall.

Pagani, M. (2013). Digital Business Strategy and Value Creation: Framing the Dynamic Cycle of Control Points. *MIS Quarterly, 37*, 617–632.

Pil, F. K., & Holweg, M. (2006). Evolving from Value Chain to Value Grid. *MIT Sloan Management Review, 47*, 72–80.

Porter, M. E. (2008). *Competitive Advantage*. New York: Simon and Schuster.

Porter, M. E., & Heppelmann, J. E. (2014). How Smart, Connected Products Are Transforming Competition. *Harvard Business Review, 92*, 64–88.

Porter, M. E., & Heppelmann, J. E. (2015). How Smart, Connected Products Are Transforming Companies. *Harvard Business Review, 93*(10), 96–114.

Porter, M. E., & Millar, V. A. (1985). How Information Gives You Competitive Advantage. *Harvard Business Review, 63*(4), 149–160.

Prahalad, C. K., & Hamel, G. (1990). The Core Competence of the Corporation. *Harvard Business Review, 68*(3), 79–91.

Quinn, J. B. (1992). *Intelligent Enterprise*. New York: Simon and Schuster.

Ransbotham, S., Kiron, D., Gerbert, P., & Reeves, M. (2017). Reshaping Business with Artificial Intelligence. *MIT Sloan Management Review*.

Rószkiewicz, M., Węziak, D., & Wodecki, A. (2007). Kapitał intelektualny Lubelszczyzny – Propozycja operacjonalizacji i pomiaru. *Studia Regionalne I Lokalne, 2*(28), 59–88.

Rowley, J. (2007). The Wisdom Hierarchy – Representations of the DIKW Hierarchy. *Journal of Information Science, 33*(2), 163–180. https://doi.org/10.1177/0165551506070706.

Sambamurthy, V., Bharadwaj, A. S., & Grover, V. (2003). Shaping Agility Through Digital Options – Reconceptualizing the Role of Information Technology in Contemporary Firms. *Management Information Systems Quarterly* https://doi.org/10.2307/30036530.

Shannon, C. E., & Weaver, W. (1949). *The Mathematical Theory of Information*. https://doi.org/10.1234/12345678.

Shoham, Y., Perrault, R., Brynjolfsson, E., Clark, J., & LeGassick, C. (2017). *Artificial Intelligence Index* (pp. 1–101). Retrieved from https://aiindex.org/#report

Simon, H. A. (1977). *The New Science of Management Decision* (Rev. ed.). Englewood Cliffs: Prentice Hall.

Stabell, C. B., & Fjeldstad, Ø. D. (1998). Configuring Value for Competitive Advantage: On Chains, Shops, and Networks. *Strategic Management Journal, 19*(5), 413–437. http://doi.org/10.1002/(SICI)1097-0266(199805)19:5<413::AID-SMJ946>3.3.CO;2-3.

Stanoevska-Slabeva, K., & Talamanca, C. (2007). Development of a Generic Value Chain for the Grid Industry. *Grid Economics and Business Models: 4th International Workshop, GECON 2007, Rennes, France, August 28, 2007, Proceedings* (pp. 44–57).

The Effect of Acceleration Techniques on Product Development Time J. Zirger and Janet L. Hartley, IEEE Transactions on Engineering Management (May 1996). pp. 143–152. (1996). *Journal of Product Innovation Management, 13*(6), 555–556. https://doi.org/10.1016/S0737-6782(96)89830-4.

Thompson, J. D. (1967). *Organizations in Action*. New York: McGraw Hill.

Trossen, D., & Fine, C. (2005). Value Chain Dynamics in the Communication Industry. MIT Communications Future Programme, MIT.

Vargo, S. L., & Lusch, R. F. (2004). Evolving to a New Dominant Logic for Marketing. *Journal of Marketing, 68*(1), 1–17. https://doi.org/10.1509/jmkg.68.1.1.24036.

Vargo, S. L., & Lusch, R. F. (2008). Service-Dominant Logic: Continuing the Evolution. *Journal of the Academy of Marketing Science, 36*(1), 1–10. https://doi.org/10.1007/s11747-007-0069-6.

von Tunzelmann, N. (2005). J. Mokyr, The Gifts of Athena – Historical Origins of the Knowledge Economy, Princeton University Press, Princeton and Oxford (2002). *Information Economics and Policy, 17*(2), 271–273. https://doi.org/10.1016/j.infoecopol.2004.10.001.

Wang, C. L., & Ahmed, P. K. (2013). The Knowledge Value Chain: A Pragmatic Knowledge Implementation Network. *Handbook of Business Strategy, 6*(1), 321–326. https://doi.org/10.1108/08944310510558115.

Wernerfelt, B. (1984). A Resource-Based View of the Firm. *Strategic Management Journal, 5*(2), 171–180. https://doi.org/10.1002/smj.4250050207.

Woodward, J. (1970). *Industrial Organization Behavior and Control*. Oxford: Oxford University Press.

Zawiła-Niedźwiecki, J. (2015a). Structuring Knowledge Management – Classical Theory, Strategic Initiation and Operational Knowledge Management (Part I). *Foundations of Management, 7*(1). https://doi.org/10.1515/fman-2015-0041.

Zawiła-Niedźwiecki, J. (2015b). Structuring Knowledge Management – Levels, Resources and Efficiency Areas of Knowledge Management (Part II). *Foundations of Management, 7*(1). https://doi.org/10.1515/fman-2015-0042.

Zhao, J. L., Tanniru, M., & Zhang, L.-J. (2007). Services Computing as the Foundation of Enterprise Agility: Overview of Recent Advances and Introduction to the Special Issue. *Information Systems Frontiers, 9*(1), 1–8. https://doi.org/10.1007/s10796-007-9023-x.

2

Artificial Intelligence Methods and Techniques

Artificial intelligence (AI) is a fascinating concept whose origins can be found in the mid-twentieth century. It is an interdisciplinary field, integrating the efforts of logicians, mathematicians, computer scientists, psychologists and, more recently, managers and ethicists. Developing dynamically in the dimension of methods as well as technology, on the one hand, raises many hopes; on the other hand, it raises many fears and controversies (compare e.g. Bostrom 2014), particularly among investors who are interested in ventures with high development potential, yet they are afraid to invest in projects they simply do not understand.

In this chapter, the basic concepts and methods of artificial intelligence are presented. The introduction describes the various aspects of Big Data and shows how it is crucial for the implementation of AI solutions. Next, the various definitions, methods, learning mechanisms and technologies used to create intelligent systems are discussed. The final section explains how cognitive computing IT solutions are exerting an increasing influence on the development of the whole field of AI.

A. Wodecki, *Artificial Intelligence in Value Creation*,
https://doi.org/10.1007/978-3-319-91596-8_2

2.1 Data, Information and Knowledge in Contemporary Information Systems

One of the objectives of the presented research was to assess the potential of using global projects in the area of machine learning and artificial intelligence (AI). Among 323 analyzed enterprises (companies at various stages of development, research projects or social initiatives), the vast majority offer systems introducing new quality to the areas of business information systems. Due to the limited volume and strictly defined research goal, only models and solutions that could significantly contribute to the development of AI class systems and corporate transformation towards cognitive organizations are presented.

After a short presentation of Porter's concept of "smart, connected products" and its technological foundations, new sources and forms of data, and methods for its storage and processing that are important for the implementation of AI class solutions are indicated. In the next step, the examples of new values that can be submitted to different groups of activities within the organization's value chain are presented and the trends in building and updating knowledge structures are described. Finally, new information architectures that can significantly affect the scale and speed of AI class implementation in organizations are presented.

2.1.1 Smart, Connected Products

Under the concept **"smart, connected products"** Porter and Heppelmann (2014) understands the systems in which individual products used by end users can communicate with the environment and thus significantly improve the processes of designing, personalizing, updating and servicing devices. In a simplified way, one can imagine such a system as a set of devices connected remotely to a central server as well as to each other, exchanging data such as information about current usage, context or packages with software updates.

According to Porter, intelligent things have three key components: material, "smart" and communicative.

Material components are physical and electronic parts.

Smart components are elements that aim to digitally increase the value of physical components. These include sensors, microprocessors, storage locations, software (drivers, operating systems, databases) and user's advanced interfaces.

Communication components, most often, enable mutual communication of the product with the background: other products, user, producer, business partners or the immediate environment. The purpose of this communication may be a simple data exchange, or a more advanced remote access for the user to functionalities unavailable on the device itself, but available on remote systems with which the item is connected.

Porter distinguishes three types of communication: 1-to-1 (e.g. a product with a user or producer), 1-to-many (e.g. a manufacturer with many devices, an example of which is the software upgrade of products already provided to users), and many-to-many (the network of devices that communicate with each other, e.g. in a smart farm). The telecommunications infrastructure implemented in such solutions usually constitutes various types of communication ports, antennas and digital communication protocols.

The implementation of such a system requires many investments to be incurred. At the infrastructure level, Porter uses here the concept of technology stack. It includes:

1. Product, with its material (hardware) and digital components (software).
2. Telecommunications infrastructure (communication protocols, network infrastructure, etc.).
3. Central solutions: infrastructure defined by Porter as a "product cloud", which includes in particular:

(a) Databases collecting data about products and their use.
(b) Flexible platforms for creating new applications (appropriate PaaS layers—Platform as a Service—in Cloud Computing class solutions).
(c) A database of business rules and analytics, responsible for generating, storing and population of intelligent algorithms and business rules for products as well as necessary for their proper functioning of the infrastructure.
(d) Intelligent product applications enabling management of monitoring, control, optimization and autonomous product operation processes.

4. Security systems.
5. Reports of communication with the background.
6. External data sources.

In this chapter it will be shown that the architecture proposed by Porter is similar to the model architecture of solutions using artificial intelligence. Porter puts a stronger emphasis on products as data sources (and here he transfers the burden of his analyses), while the research on AI solutions focuses on the value generated by systems analyzing information from these products. This distinction is crucial for further research. The very interesting conclusions made by Porter regarding the possible impact of smart, connected products on the organization's value chain and the rules of competition on the market can be complemented with many qualitatively new observations resulting from the research on the impact of class systems on markets and management. To put it simply: changing the research perspective from the analysis of final products to AI class systems generates qualitatively new hypotheses.

2.1.2 Data Sources

Among over 323 projects analyzed in the research process, nearly 30% of them offered various solutions in the field of obtaining, processing and analyzing data, often in a very innovative way.

The following are the most interesting solutions that can play an important role in the implementation of artificial intelligence systems.

2.1.2.1 Data from Internal Sources

For most organizations, internal business information systems are still the primary source of data. Integrated ERP (Enterprise Resource Planning) class systems provide information from various functional areas such as finance, human resources, production, logistics or customer and partner relationship management within the supply chain management.

In the context of the implementation of AI class systems, it is worth paying attention to the new trend of creating IT applications based on data from sensors in industry.

Companies such as Predix[1] (www.predix.io, part of the General Electric group) or C3IoT (www.c3iot.com) offer advanced solutions combining the Internet of Things infrastructure with data communication systems and solutions enabling the creation of applications that use them. As a result, companies (mainly manufacturing and energy sector) have the opportunity to create advanced solutions, not only analytical (including forecasting), but also applications that enable management of single devices or a production line. These solutions can obviously be integrated with an already existing ERP system. The development of applications based on the Internet of Things infrastructure may indicate the emergence of a new class of business information systems.

2.1.2.2 Data on the Use of a Product

One of the most important data sources for AI systems are the products used by a consumer. These can be physical products (machines, mobile devices and even clothes) as well as digital products (e.g. applications or websites).

Data from these sources are most often obtained via sensors and directly from devices that use electronic communication protocols.

In the area of medicine, an interesting example is the Proteus system (www.proteus.com), enabling remote monitoring of the digestive system status based on data transmitted through the sensor, placed in the stomach, to the mobile application and then to the central server. Sentrian (www.sentrian.com), in a similar way, enables remote monitoring of health status and vital parameters of patients, while Preact (www.preact.com), based on data collected in such a way, predicts the future health of patients and recommends optimal strategies to involve them in the therapeutic process.

The data acquired from interfaces constitute a separate category. The popularity of personal digital assistants is slowly increasing, allowing simple tasks to be given to systems or asking questions, most often via voice commands. The most advanced solutions in this category are offered by Amazon (Amazon Alexa and Echo solution), Google (Google Now), Apple (Siri) and Microsoft (Cortana). These systems offer direct help and use commands issued by users to create their behavioral profiles and improve their own algorithms, for example, speech recognition. As a result, not only do they have vast knowledge about the current needs and interests of their clients but also are continuously learning and improving their own efficiency.

A particularly interesting new form of communication is user interaction with bots: computer programs that can conduct conversations on various topics, most often in the text form on the instant messaging. The Kik company (www.kik.com) offers producers the opportunity to create their own bot, which, for example, on behalf of a clothing manufacturer, will recommend clothes and encourage young people (a typical communicator Kik user) to shop. Such conversations consolidate the brand image, lead to transactions as well as generate many valuable data about the user's preferences.

Another interesting source of data are users' interactions with other people and the content from websites and social networks. These types of systems have very extensive analytical capabilities and because of that they are able to create advanced profiles not only of individuals but also whole social groups (e.g. in the form of diagrams describing the network of relations).

The source of data, which is worth pointing out in the context of the development of AI class systems, is also information about users' contacts with customer service offices or sellers. Chorus systems (www.chorus.ai), TalkIQ (www.talkiq.com) or GridSpace (www.gridspace.com)

enable transcription of traditional conversations (in the form of audio, e.g. via telephone or the Internet) to the text form, and then, by using Natural Language Processing (NLP), they allow identification of key moments of conversation (e.g. interest, question about a product, fear, indication of competition, etc.) and its effects (the realization of conversation goals, customer satisfaction). This enables the identification of the best practices and creates and updates, for example, call schemes in the customer service center.

2.1.2.3 Data from External Sources

Finally, the huge amount of data from external sources cannot be neglected. External data can be available publicly or offered by companies specializing in it.

Public data sources are a very good source not only for strategic analysis but also as a resource enabling the development of machine learning systems or artificial intelligence.

Among external, commercially available data sources, it is worth drawing attention to the solutions of companies offering access and analysis of satellite images (e.g. Planet.os or CapeAnalytics), aggregation of data (concerning customer behavior or markets) from millions of external sources (DataSift and Bottlenose) and systems enabling automatic content analysis of websites (import.io and DiffBot). Managers of modern companies should consider such solutions in the spectrum of their analytical tools, while cheaper and easier access to them may be one of the sources of competitive advantage of the organization.

2.1.3 Data Complexity

Numerous sources, large volumes of data, the multitude of its form, and uncertainty about the quality makes the systems using AI naturally related to the concept of Big Data. The most important features of Big Data in the context of research on AI are presented below—understanding these elements makes it easier to deduce the possible impact of AI class systems on management.

The word "Big" in the term "Big Data" usually refers to four of its features: volume, velocity, variety and veracity.

2.1.3.1 Volume

According to IBM (Big Data infographics 2016) humanity generates approx. 2.5 × 10 ^ 18 of data per day.[2] It is forecasted that by 2020, we will have created approximately 40 × 10 ^ 21 of data, that is, about 300 times more than in 2005. Most data is generated in the manufacturing, public, telecommunications, financial and health sectors (see Bughin et al. 2017).

Such large amounts of data are a challenge primarily for the infrastructure providers (telecommunications, data storage and processing) and software developers (the need to invent more and more efficient algorithms that allow the processing of such a gigantic amount of data).

2.1.3.2 Velocity

Data is not only generated in large quantities, but also often at a huge pace. It is estimated (see e.g. Nelson 2016), that autonomous vehicles will generate about 4 terabytes (4 × 10 ^12 bytes) of data within eight hours of driving, that is, approximately 500 gigabytes per hour. The New York Stock Exchange generates approximately 1 terabyte of transaction data in one session. This data must be intercepted and transmitted to servers at the right pace, without losses or error, which requires continuous development of telecommunications infrastructure as well as dedicated software.

2.1.3.3 Variety

Data can be generated in various forms. Visual forms (video and images) predominate, often recorded in industry-specific formats (e.g. images from magnetic resonance in medicine). The other form is the text, both in the form of documents and unstructured statements on discussion forums or in social media. Also, the following forms need to be mentioned: audio records, data from industrial sensors, "personal" (e.g. body state monitors) or home appliances, non-text interactions between users on the Internet (e.g. likes in social networks) or reports (logs) from user behavior in digital media. Such a variety of forms are yet another challenge for the creators of AI class systems; it forces the creation of their new classifications and the design of solutions that enable the generation of value from data in a finite time and with regard to infrastructural constraints.

2.1.3.4 Veracity

The magnitude of the information generated in the world naturally lowers confidence in it. The doubts may result from various causes: purely infrastructural (errors in the generation of data by devices, improper data transfer or reading/reading from archiving systems), the suspicion of an unintentional human error (e.g. mistakes when entering data or using incorrect statistical procedures in the process of their analysis) or intentional manipulation (e.g. to achieve marketing or political goals). The flood of information at a fixed level of human processing capacity causes a reduction in the ability and determination to deepen its analysis and verification of reliability. In connection with the possibilities of advanced systems in the field of identifying behavior profiles of consumers, there are growing concerns about the credibility of information, which in gigantic amounts, pace and diversity appear in the digital reality.

2.1.4 Data Processing Methods

To release the potential hidden in the collected data, it should be processed and analyzed. This can be achieved by many different solutions: from pure programming to Business Intelligence class systems. Interestingly, the most advanced of them are offered for free under the Open Source licenses, while the knowledge necessary for their effective use is also often available for free in the form of manuals or even professionally prepared electronic courses. As a result, this increases the chances of companies that do not have large budgets to compete with large, affluent organizations in the field of AI systems. The awareness of the existence and possibilities of the solutions presented below is, therefore, one of the key managerial competencies.

2.1.4.1 The Systems That Increase the Efficiency of Information Processing

The first category of IT systems supporting data management are the systems supporting managing its stream (e.g. Flume, https://flume.apache.org/), storage in the form of non-relational databases (e.g. Cassandra, http://cassandra.apache.org/ or HBase, https://hbase.apache.org/), very fast statistical analysis (e.g. Spark http://spark.apache.org/) and parallel processing (e.g. Hadoop, http://hadoop.apache.org/), or programming languages that enable the creation of super-efficient applications based on large data (e.g. Scala https://www.scala-lang.org/). These systems are successfully used by the world's biggest developers of large IT systems, while being available in most cases for free under the Open Source license as part of the Apache project.

Interestingly, prestigious world universities provide high-quality free online courses on the use of these systems, such as the Spark course offered by Berkeley (https://www.edx.org/course/introduction-apache-spark-uc-berkeleyx-cs105x), the Hadoop course offered by the University of California San Diego (https://www.coursera.org/learn/hadoop) or the five-module programming specialization in the Scala language offered by Écolc Fédérale Polytechnique de Lausanne (https://www.coursera.org/specializations/scala). If we add to it a large amount of guides, books and expert discussion forums, it turns out that system developers have free access not only to IT solutions but also to sources of knowledge about their correct and effective use.

2.1.4.2 Environments and Statistical Libraries

Another class of IT systems supporting data processing and its analysis are the environments enabling the creation of analytical applications or machine learning and the libraries used by them with statistical procedures.

The machine learning algorithms used in AI systems often use neural network methods (Deep Learning). The creation of such solutions is supported by (free) systems such as the one developed by Google Tensorflow (https://www.tensorflow.org/), the Theano project initiated at Universite de Montreal (http://deeplearning.net/software/theano/index.html), or created by the Torch community (http://torch.ch/). One cannot forget about the systems created by global corporations providing IT solutions such as Microsoft's CNTK (https://github.com/Microsoft/CNTK) or DSSTNE from Amazon (https://github.com/amznlabs/amazon-dsstne). On the other hand, the creation of applications based on advanced statistical analyses (i.e. not only neural networks) is possible within a very popular R environment (https://www.r-project.org/).

The environments supporting the creation of AI systems complement libraries of statistical procedures, among which the most important is SciPy (www.scipy.org), Scikit-Learn (http://scikit-learn.org) or the Mahout library provided as a part of the Apache project (http://mahout.apache.org/).

2.1.4.3 Environments for Developers

The solutions described above require the knowledge of statistical procedures as well as some programming skills (mainly in Python and Java). For creators and teams that do not have such technical skills, solutions for creating advanced applications without the need to write computer programs are provided. However, such comfort is not for free any more.

The environments for developers can be divided into

- solutions supporting the implementation of R&D projects, particularly enabling advanced data mining or testing of various hypotheses, but also supporting the management of Data Science projects and the cooperation of scientists;
- systems enabling the creation of industrial AI class applications;
- environments that support application development within existing AI class ecosystems.

This classification is somewhat arbitrary (many of the solutions described below may be assigned to more than one of the proposed categories), but it was adopted to simplify further analyses.

2.1.4.4 Solutions Supporting the Implementation of Research Projects

A very popular free solution is the Weka system developed by the University of Waikatoo (http://www.cs.waikato.ac.nz/ml/weka/index.html). This seemingly simple window environment offers the opportunity to create and test very advanced models, and for this reason it enjoys growing popularity. The didactic framework, particularly, the high-quality online course and a modern, frequently updated textbook presenting the most important methods and techniques of Data Science with a large number of examples and sets of real data are a huge added value. As a result, Weka is not only a starting point in the career for many specialists in the field of Data Science but also a tool used in further professional practice.

While Weka is a typically academic project, three consecutive solutions presented below have already been developed by companies with a clearly defined business model. RapidMiner (https://rapidminer.com/), H2O (www.h2o.ai) and DeepLearning4j (https://deeplearning4j.org/) are fully professional environments enabling the creation of advanced solutions in the areas of Data Science and machine learning and the integration of these solutions with the ones already existing in the organization, or published in generally available repositories. These solutions address today's serious problem of identifying experts, who would combine technical skills (e.g. programming highly efficient industrial applications), with scientific expertise (the knowledge of advanced statistical methods). In the above-mentioned environments, technological difficulties (e.g. programming or optimization of a solution in terms of efficiency) were reduced to a minimum, enabling the users to focus on data analysis and the research work. It is also important that these systems are offered in a *freemium* model: basic, fully functional versions are offered for free, the fee is charged only for functions that enable industrial applications of the work results. These features, and a rich didactic framework, make RapidMiner and H2O particularly popular among Data Science teams in many organizations.

The third interesting category is created by solutions that increase the effectiveness of Data Science projects. Among them, there are: Domino Data Lab, SigOpt, Dataiku and DeepSense. In addition to typical solutions for advanced data analysis, they provide advanced environments enabling the implementation of research projects, including process design and group work. In this way, they complement the portfolio of key tools for the functioning of each of the professional R&D departments of modern organizations.

2.1.4.5 Environments That Enable the Creation of Industrial Applications

Another class of solutions for the creators of AI systems are environments dedicated to creating professional Data Science applications. Among them, it is worth mentioning: Cycorp (http://www.cyc.com/), DataRobot (https://www.datarobot.com/), Yhat (https://www.yhat.com/), BigML (https://bigml.com), Seldon (https://www.seldon.io/), Bonsai (https://bons.ai/) and Spark Beyond (http://www.sparkbeyond.com/). The detailed presentation of the capabilities of these systems goes beyond the scope of this book; however, in the context of the challenges faced by managers responsible for the full use of the data held by the organization, mentioning them seems necessary.

2.1.4.6 Application Development Environments Within Existing Ecosystems

The third category of solutions constitutes the environments of large companies developing full ecosystems around their own AI systems. Currently (2018), the market leaders in this field are: Amazon, Google,

Microsoft, IBM and Apple. Each of these companies offers their own comprehensive environments for application developers using the capabilities of their proprietary solutions. Amazon supports Alexa's system programmers (https://developer.amazon.com/alexa-skills-kit), Microsoft developers of applications using Cortana (https://developer.microsoft.com/pl-pl/cortana), IBM supports Watson's programmers (https://www.ibm.com/watson/developercloud/), while Apple supports Siri's programmers (https://developer.apple.com/sirikit/). Each of the above systems offers technological solutions as well as the training materials and community support. The goal is to popularize our own solution and, as a result, to further develop the ecosystem: these companies are fully aware that nowadays their own solutions need to be developed on the basis of the community—their own resources are no longer fully sufficient. In this context, Google's approach to the development of the TensorFlow environment is slightly different, (https://www.tensorflow.org), as it is not directly related to Google's systems; nevertheless, in a sense, the company strengthens its position as the leader of AI solutions.

2.1.5 Conclusion

2.1.5.1 The Potential of New Data

Porter (Porter and Heppelmann 2014) in an interesting way indicates the impact of smart, connected products on the role of data in generating value.

Once, the main source of data was the organization's own operational data (obtained e.g. from production systems or ERP) and the data exchanged within the value chain (orders, interactions with suppliers, systems supporting customer relationship management, research, etc.). This data was processed within organizational silos, often with limited exchange between departments, and after often-costly integration, provided knowledge about customers, product demand or costs. Yet, the possibility to obtain information on how to use the products themselves and their actual value for the customer was limited.

Now, data is delivered directly by a product, becoming a resource in itself, on equal terms with people, technology and capital. At the same time, data acquires full value in context: the value increases exponentially as they are integrated/collated with other data such as service history, warehouse location, resource prices, weather or other external conditions.

As a result, it can be said that nowadays one of the sources of competitive advantage is the ability to unleash the full potential of both existing and external data. Today's data can be compared to steam in the times of the industrial revolution: it was a cheap and widely available resource, but organizations that could convert thermal energy into mechanical energy gained a huge advantage. Today, data is becoming a universally available good: the ability to use it to improve products or services will decide about the advantage.

2.1.5.2 Challenges

The new quality and the amount of data, information and knowledge that can be generated from them, is the source of opportunities as well as challenges.

The large amounts of data, available in various forms, coming from various sources and generated at high speed, cause difficulties in assessing its credibility, business potential and the possibility of using it. On the other hand, a wide spectrum of potential applications makes concentration difficult in the choice of strategic goals and their consistent implementation.

The high dynamics of the existing evolution and the emergence of new solutions supporting the creation of AI class systems raises the complexity of the processes of creating data processing strategies and designing these system architectures. Breaking down the barriers connected with creating advanced class solutions affects the acceleration of development in virtually all industries, which increases competitiveness and reduces the problems with new, more flexible competitors entering the market (see e.g. Nokia's failure with the Israeli Waze start-up in the area of navigation systems).

In order to be able to take advantage of opportunities and meet the challenges related to the increasing access to data and tools enabling its effective processing, managers should develop:

1. the awareness of data generated by already owned systems in various elements of the value chain;
2. the ability to identify business potential inherent in internal, external and customer-generated data;
3. the ability to use AI class systems to assess the reliability of data, especially from external sources;
4. the ability to create solutions based on data streams available in near-real time, and not just historical data;
5. the ability to identify and quickly implement solutions drastically simplifying the creation of AI class systems.

2.2 Concept and Basic Methods of Artificial Intelligence

2.2.1 Definitions of Artificial Intelligence

For hundreds, if not thousands of years, people have tried to understand the way they perceive, understand and act on the reality that surrounds them. Starting from early philosophical reflections, through the beginning of psychology to contemporary methods of cognitive neuropsychology, they have developed both the tools of this metacognition and extended the scope of knowledge in that area.

The knowledge about one's cognition creates the temptation to try to create structures that would work like a human being, and maybe even better. This need is fundamental for the research on artificial intelligence.

In the efforts to create intelligent structures, people have tried to design solutions that would most accurately reflect the way they think and work. Reflections of philosophers (see e.g. Dennett 2014) and the results of psychological tests (see e.g. Kahneman 2011; Nisbett 2015) showed, however, that in many situations people think and act irrationally. There was a natural temptation to create a structure that would behave "rationally"—whatever that meant.

Norvig and Russell (2016) ordered the definitions of Artificial Intelligence (AI) in the above-mentioned dimensions: (1) thoughts and behaviors, and (2) their effectiveness: human level (burdened with errors) and rational (ideal).

2.2.1.1 Thinking like a Human

At the heart of the systems trying to "think like a human" there are the discoveries in the science of cognitive psychology, which examines the processes of perception (sensory perception, object recognition), attention, memory (short-term and permanent), abstract thinking, goal-oriented actions (decision-making, initiating and monitoring actions), emotions, social relations, awareness and free will. Cognitive psychology is now an interdisciplinary field: it combines "classical" psychological research with neurological research (cognitive neuroscience) and computer modeling (computational cognitive neuroscience). The discoveries and models of psychology have initiated attempts to reproduce and simulate cognitive architectures (see e.g. ACT-R system: http://act-r.psy.cmu.edu/about/) and cognitive functions of the brain based on its neuronal substrate (see e.g. emergent simulator developed at the University of Colorado: grey.colorado.edu/emergent/index.php/Main_Page). Research on artificial intelligence is naturally inspired by discoveries of cognitive science, but also more often help psychology to explain the mechanisms of brain activity (Hassabis et al. 2017).

The result of these interdisciplinary efforts are systems that "think" like a human being—capable of receiving signals from the environment through various "senses," interpreting these signals, analysis and reasoning, making decisions and learning on the basis of the analysis of relationships between activities and their effects. These systems, often referred to as *cognitive computing*, are presented in more detail later in the study.

2.2.1.2 Acting Like a Human

Modeling of AI systems to make them operate inspired by the functioning of the brain constituted a means to create solutions that behave like a human being. One of the classic examples of the quality assessment criteria for AI is the one proposed by Turing (1950). His goal was to propose an operational definition of artificial intelligence. In the original version, Turing suggested that instead of examining whether a machine can think, one should check whether it can behave like a human. The test consists, in a simplified way, in conversation (in real time) of a machine with a person, whose task is to assess whether they are talking to a machine or another human being. If a machine manages to deceive a person more than 30% of the time during the conversation, we can say that the system is intelligent (it passed the Turing test). Modern versions of tests extend the original proposal for the possibility of testing image perception (video transmission) and for transmitting physical objects for assessment.

There are some other interesting "intelligence tests" for machines, for example:

1. Woźniak test: *The robot is intelligent, if it can enter the average home and make itself a cup of coffee* (Wozniak n.d.).
2. Goertzel test: *The system is intelligent, if it is able to enroll in studies, approach and pass courses and obtain a diploma* (Goertzel 2017).
3. The Nilsson test: *The system is intelligent, if it is able to work equally as or better than a man in an economically important position* (Nilsson 2005).

In order to successfully pass the above-mentioned tests (and in effect behave as a human being), the system should have at least the following options (Norvig and Russell 2016):

1. **Natural language processing**: reception, interpretation and formulation of statements, both in the form of audio and text.
2. **Knowledge representation**, to be able to collect the acquired information and generated knowledge.

3. **Automatic reasoning**, to identify patterns in the recorded information and to use the accumulated knowledge to answer questions and generate new applications.
4. **Machine learning**, to learn from its own experiences and adapt to new conditions.
5. **Image analysis**, in order to recognize and identify the location of objects.
6. **Manipulation** of physical objects.

The above-mentioned areas of "competence" of intelligent systems are the foundations of modern AI methods and technologies. It turns out that in many cases, machines constructed by engineers have already such capabilities that far outweigh the capabilities of humans (so-called "narrow" artificial intelligence). Achieving an advantage in Artificial General Intelligence, although still beyond the reach of technology, is the subject of intensive research of many scientific and industrial teams.

2.2.1.3 Rational Thinking

The laws of logic are the basis of rational thinking and have been discovered and developed for thousands of years by the most eminent human minds. The works on logic, initiated independently in India (Medhatithi Gautama and his school of Anviksiki, VII BC), China (School of Moists, fifth century BC) and Greece (Aristotle, fifth century BC) to develop rules of correct thinking and ordering arguments, continued beyond the Middle Ages and flourished in the nineteenth century, when a precise notation was developed for claims about various objects and relations between them.

The results of these studies are fundamental for the logical tradition in the development of AI systems, successfully used up till now in expert systems recommending, for example, optimal routes in transport. Despite their successes, the limitations of this class of solutions are visible in situations in which we deal with the "hidden" knowledge (informal, unstructured) and burdened with uncertainty, for example, in the area of data generated by sensors or possible unpredictable phenomena in the background. In addition, the requirement for a full analysis of all available facts and options makes calculations practically impossible to perform due to the limited computing power.

As a result, AI systems based solely on the laws of logic currently have relatively narrow applications, which does not mean that they are not used in more complex systems, as a complement to other methods.

2.2.1.4 Rational Actions

As already mentioned, the dream of creating systems that are not burdened with their "human" irrationality has become the basis of the trend in artificial intelligence oriented around the so-called rational agent. A detailed description of this concept goes beyond the scope of this book (the interested reader should go to a very good analysis of Norvig and Russell (2016)), so here only its most important assumptions will be presented.

The agent concept means an object that takes action (*agent* comes from the Latin word *agere*: to act). A computer agent (that is, a program running on the computer) is expected to receive and interpret signals from the environment, act autonomously, sustain action over a longer period of time, adapt for changes and formulate and achieve its goals.

The agent operates in a certain environment: it has some knowledge about the background, given explicitly (e.g. by a "teacher") or accumulated as a result of past experiences. Thanks to the data from the sensors, it also records information about the current state of the background. It can take specific actions at a given moment (*spectrum of possible actions*). It has also a specific *measure of efficiency* allowing the assessment of the degree of success.

Rational agent is an agent that behaves rationally. The rationality of behavior at a given moment depends on (Norvig and Russell 2016)

1. **measures of efficiency** defining the criterion of success,
2. agent's **knowledge about the background**,

3. **actions** that the agent may take up at the moment,
4. **sequences of information about the environment (precepts)** that the agent has acquired so far.

Norvig and Russell define a rational agent in the following way:

For each possible sequence of precepts, a rational agent should choose the action that most likely maximizes its effectiveness function, taking into account the acquired information about the state of the environment (percepts) and possessed knowledge about this environment.

There are many important conclusions that result from the above definition of rationality:

1. The agent should have **clearly defined measure of effectiveness**:
   (a) **The effectiveness of undertaken activities** will be judged on the basis of how much they have brought the agent closer to achieving this measure—hence the need for a clear, measurable definition.
   (b) **The measure of effectiveness is defined by the creator**. This is a fundamentally important issue. It seems to be natural (the machine should achieve the goals set by the designer), but in many cases it turns out that the "designer" is not aware or cannot clearly define the goals (e.g. the consumer on the Internet). Then, the system should be able to independently determine effectiveness measures, e.g. based on the analysis of user behavior, but always within certain security frameworks (Ng and Russell 2017).
2. When assessing the rationality of the agent's behavior the **consequences of its behavior** should be taken into account:
   (a) The agent **takes action sequences** based on perceptions and knowledge about the environment.
   (b) These activities **change the state of the environment**.

    (c) If these **changes in the environment maximize the measure of effectiveness**—then we say that the agent behaves rationally.
    (d) **The assessment of rationality is not affected by the change in the agent's status.** In other words, we do not assess the rationality of behavior on the basis of the agent's opinion of its own effectiveness. The complacency of the actions carried out or the conviction of good intentions of the situation when they have not affected the improvement of the environment is not taken into account (which is often the case when assessing human activities).

3. **The correctness of reasoning is not the basic criterion for an evaluation** system—as it was in the case of logic systems:

    (a) In some situations **there is no way to logically prove that** an action undoubtedly leads to the goal. However, it is necessary to make a decision—in such cases, one cannot be guided solely by the laws of logic.
    (b) Rational actions (the ones undertaken to achieve the desired goal in the best possible way) can be sometimes taken without logical inference. An example is reflex action, for example, to move away from a fire.

The rationality of behavior defined above is universal (guided by the laws of logic, it allows uncertainty and approximation) and is probably the basis for most of the current projects in the field of artificial intelligence, particularly machine learning.

2.2.2 Classification of Environments

One of the goals of research on artificial intelligence is to create an agent which will be able to behave rationally in its environment. Its architecture and operating model will naturally depend on the characteristics of this environment. Below, the classification of environment features is presented and it will later serve to organize various methods of artificial intelligence (Norvig and Russell 2016).

2.2.2.1 Observability: Fully Observable—Partially Observable

The agent, thanks to its sensors, can collect information about the current state of the environment. If its sensors give the opportunity to gather a full set of information relevant to the activities undertaken in the environment at all times, we say that its environment is fully observable. Relevance depends on the adopted measure of effectiveness. Otherwise, we are dealing with the environment partially observable.

2.2.2.2 Number of Agents: Single-Agent and Multi-Agent

If the agent is the only entity operating in the environment, we say that the environment is single-agent. Otherwise, we are dealing with the multi-agent environment. In the cases when we are not sure if the other object operating in the vicinity is an agent, we need to check it and if the agent is present its measure of effectiveness should be examined. If this measure is related in some way to the agent's measure, then the environment is multi-agent. This connection can be competitive (if the maximization of the target function of the second agent is associated with the minimization of our agent) or cooperative.

2.2.2.3 Determinism: Deterministic—Stochastic

The environment is deterministic if the next state of the agent is determined only by its current state and the action taken. If, however, there are other (than the current state and operation) factors affecting the next state of the environment (e.g. other agents)—we are talking about the stochastic environment.

2.2.2.4 Episodicity: Episodic—Sequential

Episodic environment is when the agent's experience can be divided into single, "atomic" episodes. In each of these episodes the agent receives some information about the state of the environment (percepts) and takes up some actions. The next episode does not depend on the actions taken in previous episodes.

In sequential environments the current state is conditioned by the actions taken in the previous steps, and the current decision may affect future decisions.

2.2.2.5 Dynamics: Static—Dynamic

Environment is

1. **static** when the environment does not change its state while the agent makes a decision;
2. **half-dynamic** when the environment does not change when making decisions, but its effectiveness measure changes;
3. **dynamic** if the environment can change its state at the time the agent makes a decision.

2.2.2.6 Continuity: Discrete—Continuous

Classification in this dimension applies to the state of the environment, dynamics of changes in time and percepts and activities of the agent. Each of these areas can be discreet or continuous.

For example: chess game has a discreet environment, discrete changes in time and discreet perceptions and actions. In the case of driving a car, each of these elements is continuous.

2.2.2.7 Knowledge: Known—Unknown

The environment is known if the agent knows the laws prevailing in it, which in particular means that it knows its consequences for every action (the impact on the environment).

Otherwise, the environment is unknown: the agent does not know the laws in it and does not know what are the consequences of the taken actions. With time, however, on the basis of the acquired experiences, it can gain such knowledge (e.g. due to the reinforcement learning mechanisms).

The quality and level of complexity of artificial intelligence methods are directly related to changes in the described characteristics of the environment, sometimes referred to as relaxation of limits.

2.2.3 Solving Problems by Searching

2.2.3.1 Classical Search

Environment

The term "classical search" is understood as being a set of methods for solving problems in environments fully observable, discrete, deterministic and known (Fig. 2.1).

Such "friendliness" (observability and predictability) of the environment has enabled the development of many effective methods of solving problems, using mainly algorithmic methods, without having to refer to the probability theory. Classical search methods, intensively developed since the mid-twentieth century, were limited mainly by the small computing power of computers available at that time. Searching is the process of constructing a sequence of actions that, under conditions of full observability and determinism, maximize the measure of effectiveness, for example, by finding the shortest way to the goal.

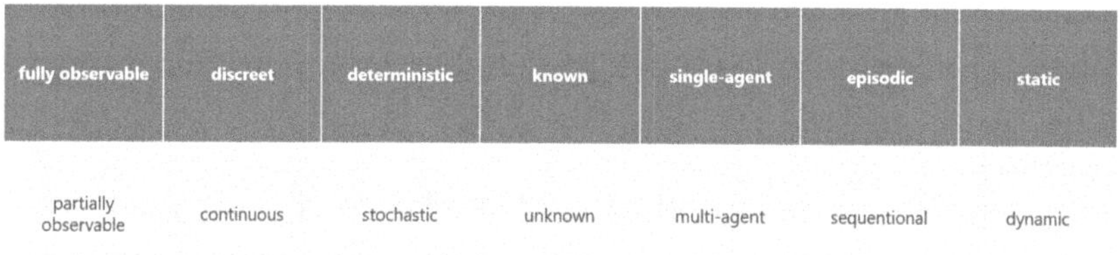

Fig. 2.1 Characteristics of environment in classical search. (Source: Own elaboration)

The examples of problems are

1. searching for the shortest routes on the map;
2. traveling salesperson problem: a conditionally imposed route (a city can only be visited once);
3. distribution of elements in an integrated circuit with the condition of minimizing surfaces, delays in signal communication or production costs;
4. robot navigation: movement in continuous space, not discrete (as on a map);
5. identification of assembly sequence of a complex product.

Methods and Algorithms

The first steps in the classical search method are (see e.g. Norvig and Russell 2016)

1. the formulation of the goal that the agent has to achieve;
2. defining the problem, which includes:
   (a) **the initial state,**
   (b) **the set of possible actions,**
   (c) **transition models** determining the results of each of these activities,
   (d) **the objective function** making it possible to check whether the intended goal has been achieved (and whether it is possible to terminate the search).

Solving a problem is the path that passes through the state space from the initial state to the target state (the states do not have any internal structure).

The most important algorithms used to solve the classical search problem are searching trees—including all possible transition paths from initial to final, and graph searching—searching trees that ignore unnecessary paths. Their quality is assessed taking into account completeness, optimality, time and spatial complexity.

The strategies of searching for solutions depend on whether the agent has access to broader information about the environment, most often in the form of the heuristic function, or does not have such information.

Agents who have access only to the elements included in the problem definition apply strategies without information. The most important of them are

1. **breadth-first search**, which in the first place explores the shallowest branches of the decision tree;
2. **uniform-cost search**, exploring the branches with the lowest cost;
3. **depth-first search**, first exploring the deepest paths in the decision tree;
4. **iterative-deepening search**, which raises the method of searching deeper with the increasing parameter of the deepening until the solution is found;
5. **bidirectional search**, searching for a solution starting from the goal and gradually moving to the initial state.

Agents with access to heuristic function enabling the evaluation of the cost of a solution from a given point to the target use informed strategies, yet the quality of their algorithms depends on the quality of the heuristic function. The most important of them are

1. **best-first search**, which selects the branch in the decision tree on the basis of the objective function defined in the definition of problem;
2. **first, greedy best-first search**, which develops branches with the minimum heuristic value;
3. **A* search**, expanding paths with the minimum value of the sum of the objective and heuristic functions.

2.2.3.2 The Classical Search Extension

In the real world, environments that are perfectly observable and predictable are rare. It is necessary to develop methods of rational action in less "comfortable" environments. The first attempts to extend the classical search addressed environments in which two criteria were "loosened": observability and determinism (see e.g. Norvig and Russell 2016) (Fig. 2.2).

The local search method is used in situations where the path leading to the destination is not important (as it is, for instance, in the identification of routes), it is only important to reach the final state (e.g. a specific spatial configuration of elements). The choice of a particular strategy is determined at the same time by the continuity of spatial dimension

1. in **discrete** environments hill climbing, simulated annealing, local-beam and genetic algorithms are most often used;
2. in **continuous** environments linear programming, convex optimization and genetic algorithms are used most frequently.

In partially observable environments due to the lack of certainty about the current situation, it is necessary to use the concept of belief states: a set of possible states in which an agent may be at a given moment. Standard algorithms for searching solution space are used to solve the problem, yet the most effective are the so-called incremental algorithms, which create state-by-state solutions.

In environments where observation is not possible, the exploration solutions are applied, such as online search, which is based on creating maps and attempts to identify goals (if there are any) and heuristics upgrade (methods of conduct) along with the process of gaining experience.

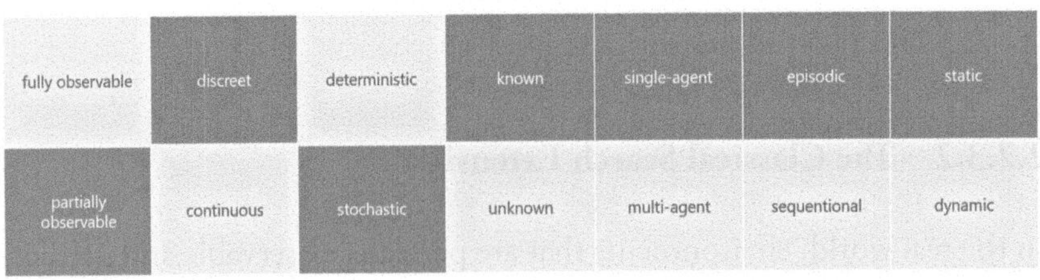

Fig. 2.2 Characteristics of environment in extended classical search. (Source: Own elaboration)

2.2.3.3 Search in Competitive Environments

Competitive environments are those in which other agents have an objective function, the maximization of which is associated with the minimization of the measure of "our" agent's effectiveness.

These types of environments are multi-agent, may be fully observable (as in chess) or partially observable (as in bridge) and most often discrete, static, deterministic and known (Fig. 2.3).

Games are an example of such situations. When undertaking activities, the agent must take into account the actions of other players whose goals are contrary to its intentions.

The game is defined by

1. its **initial state,**
2. for each state: a **set of allowed activities,**
3. for each activity: **its result** (impact on the environment),
4. a test to determine the end of the game (final state),
5. an objective function assigned to the final state.

Problem-solving algorithms, that is, identifying the best possible actions that maximize the objective function, depend on the degree of environmental observability.

In the case of games with excellent information (fully observable, e.g. chess, checkers) the most popular are

1. **minimax** used in two-player games, choosing optimal moves based on the depth-first search strategy;

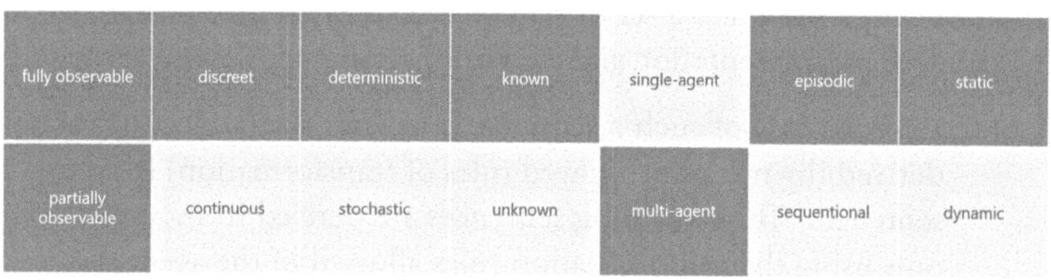

Fig. 2.3 Characteristics of competitive environments. (Source: Own elaboration)

2. **alpha-beta** operating as minimax, but with the elimination of unnecessary movements;
3. algorithms using the heuristic function to limit the space of potential solutions.

In games of imperfect information (partially observable, such as poker or bridge), it is necessary to deduce the current and future probable belief states, which requires solutions using methods from the probability theory. In the newest solutions, these algorithms are supported by a system that predicts human behavior, which enabled the defeat of the world's best poker players (Moravčík et al. 2017).

2.2.4 Knowledge and Planning in Certain Situations

Intelligence can be defined as a rational action based on reasoning processes that operate on the internal representations of knowledge, not on reflexes. The reasoning should be implemented in accordance with the rules of logic, for example propositional logic or first-order logic. Agents taking action in accordance with these rules are called agents based on knowledge.

2.2.4.1 Agents Based on Knowledge

Knowledge-based agent plans and works on the basis of internal representations of knowledge and rules of correct thinking. The model architecture of such an agent includes (see e.g. Norvig and Russell 2016)

1. **knowledge base**, i.e. a set of sentences expressed in the language of knowledge representation and containing statements about the world:
   (a) a special case of such a sentence is **axiom**: a sentence that is not derived (by means of allowed rules of transformation) from other sentences. The remaining sentences are derived from a set of axioms using the transformation rules allowed in the agent system;

   (b) before taking action, the agent has only **background knowledge**. Its knowledge base is being enriched as new experiences are gained.

2. **rules of inference**, that is, the rules for deriving new sentences from existing ones;
3. **sensors** collecting information about the state of the environment;
4. **actuators** enabling taking actions that change the surroundings.

Once launched, the agent works most often in the following way:

1. it records information about the state of the environment (percepts);
2. it transfers them to the knowledge base and asks it for recommendations for action to be taken;
3. the knowledge base:
   (a) carries out the process of analysis and inference, particularly examining the possible consequences of actions in a given state of the environment;
   (b) recommends the best possible actions.
4. the agent:
   (a) implements these activities;
   (b) analyses the consequences of actions (reflection): registers and provides information to the knowledge base about the consequences of actions taken (their impact on the environment and the measure of effectiveness);
   (c) updates the knowledge base: the implemented learning mechanisms extend it with the gained experience.

2.2.4.2 Classical Planning

The main limitation of the above-described classical methods of finding solutions is the number of possibilities they generate, which should be analyzed, significantly exceeding the available computing powers. One solution to this problem is specialized heuristics, and based on the logical structure of the problem, they help to significantly reduce the search space. Planning based on the identification of this type of heuristics is called classical planning. They are used, for example, to identify optimal routes (logistics) or to plan the optimal sequence of activities (e.g. during assembly).

Classic planning usually deals with problems in the environment that is single-agent, observable, static and deterministic. The goal is to develop an action plan that leads to the intended goal. Planning systems use for this purpose algorithms operating on logical sentences describing states and relations between states and actions (Fig. 2.4).

Planning Domain Definition Language (PDDL) enabled the unification of the representation scheme of possible actions and their results (i.e. the representation of a planning problem). The description of initial and final states as products of logical symbols and representation of actions in terms of initial states and their effects allowed generating effective heuristics and, as a result, significant limitation of the space of possible states, improving the quality of algorithms and reducing the number of necessary calculations so that they would be realizable by the available computers. It is worth emphasizing that at the very foundations of these algorithms there are the rules of propositional calculus and first order logic: Aristotle would probably be surprised to see the practical application of his rights in, for example, planning aircraft routes.

Searching the solution space can be done "forward" (progression) or "backward" (regression). At the same time, heuristics can be generated by assumptions about the interdependence of partial objectives or reducing the constraints imposed on solving the problem. The most common algorithms used in classical planning are: planning graph, deduction based on the first order logic and direct search of the partially ordered plans space.

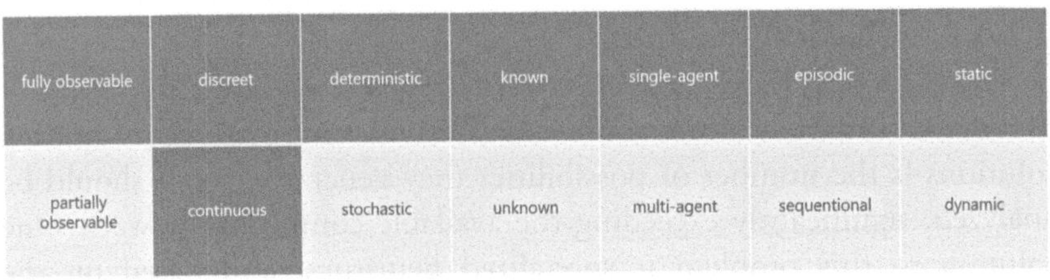

Fig. 2.4 Characteristics of environment in classical planning. (Source: Own elaboration)

2.2.4.3 Planning and Acting in the Real World

As already mentioned, subsequent approximations to real conditions rely on the abolition of further restrictions characterizing the environment in which the agent operates (Fig. 2.5).

Planning activities in environments partially observable, multi-agent, dynamic and stochastic is very complicated; particularly, it is necessary to extend the language of state description and impact on the environment. It also requires

1. taking into account resource constraints (e.g. financial, energy, material, human) and time constraints (time in planning is treated as a specific resource);
2. working out methods of constructing hierarchically organized plans;
3. planning activities in uncertain situations (with limited information);
4. taking into account other agents' activities, often with other objective functions.

Among the most commonly used methods for planning in such conditions, the following are worth mentioning:

1. **hierarchical task network** consisting in cascading plans from higher to lower (operational) levels;
2. **contingent planning**, making the choice of the next sequence of actions dependent on the current state;
3. **multi-agent planning** necessary when there are many agents in the environment.

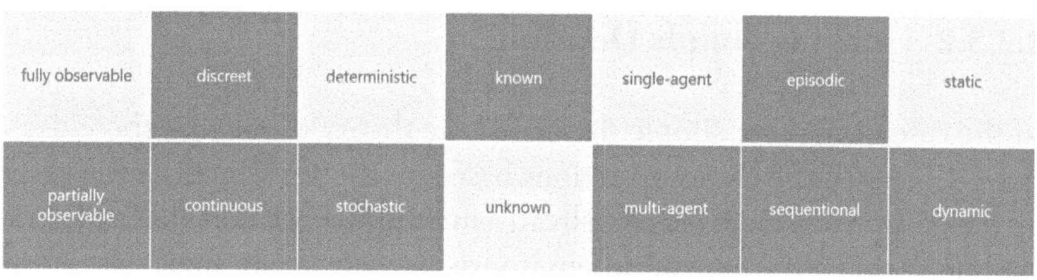

Fig. 2.5 Characteristics of near-real environments. (Source: Own elaboration)

2.2.5 Knowledge and Planning in a State of Uncertainty

2.2.5.1 Motivation

In the real world, agents must often act in a situation of uncertainty. Its most common sources are incomplete state observability, unpredictability of the environment or combination of all of them. Such environments are partially observable and stochastic.

In such an environment, the agent does not know exactly what state it is in, and it is not sure what the consequences of its actions will be. It must operate with the concept of convictions that are only likely to relate to actual states. The theory of decision combines the agent's beliefs and goals, defining the optimal action as the one that maximizes the function of the objective.

The following methods of probabilistic reasoning are most commonly used to solve problems in such situations:

1. **Bayes network** representing conditional relations in the environment in the form of acyclic graphs, whose branches correspond to random variables. The inference in these networks consists in calculating the probability of distribution of variables explained with the assumption of explanatory variables;
2. **Stochastic approximation** methods, particularly the likelihood weighting method, the Mark Carkolo chain method and the Relational Probability Models;
3. For **processes running over time**: hidden Markov models, Kalman filters and dynamic Bayes networks.

2.2.5.2 Making Simple Decisions

In the case of making simple decisions, the theory of making these decisions deals with the choice of actions based on the assessment of the value of their immediate effects. As already mentioned, in non-deterministic and only partially observable environments, an agent may not know exactly what its current state is. As a result, it cannot precisely determine the consequences of the action taken in a given state, but only operate with the probability that it will be in a given condition assuming that it has performed it.

In such situations, the agent's preferences are measured by the utility function that assigns a certain value to a given state. The expected usefulness of the action is defined as the average of the utility function of the results of activities, weighted by the probability of occurrence of possible states. A rational agent should take actions that at that very moment maximize the utility function defined in such a way.

To develop a decision-making strategy in such environments, the following theories are used:

1. **Probability theory** describing what the agent should believe in on the basis of the environment perception.
2. **Usability theory** describing what it should want to achieve at the moment.
3. **Theory of decision** combining these two theories to identify the optimal activities at the moment.

2.2.5.3 Making Complex Decisions

Complex decisions are those decisions that are made in partially observable, multi-agent, sequential, dynamic, stochastic and unknown environments (Fig. 2.6).

As a result, these are some of the most difficult to imagine conditions, however, occurring very often in the real world.

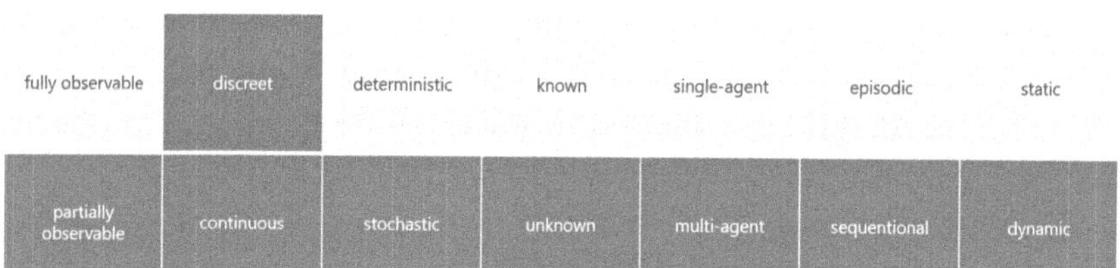

Fig. 2.6 Characteristics of environments in taking complex decisions. (Source: Own elaboration)

Sequential decision problems in partially observable environments (also known as Markov Decision Processes—MDPs) are defined by transition models defining the probabilities of results of actions and reward functions describing the prize in a given state. The solution to Markov Decision Process is the strategy assigning everyone a specific decision. The optimal strategy is a strategy that maximizes the usefulness function of the sequence of states resulting from the actions taken.

Partially Observable Markov Decision Processes (POMDPs) are definitely more difficult to solve than the classic MDPs. To solve them, dynamic decision networks are used to represent transition models and game theory to describe rational agents operating in multi-agent environments in which agents interact with each other.

2.2.6 Learning

The ability to learn is crucial to maintain autonomy and ensure artificial intelligence (AI) systems development. Acquired, cleaned and organized data are transferred to algorithms of machine learning, which is usually divided into three categories (see e.g. Raschka 2015): supervised learning, reinforcement learning and unsupervised learning.

To put it simply, supervised learning is learning from examples. The system analyzes many examples (usually in the form of pairs: question-answer provided in the training set) and modifies its structure in such a way (mapping of input data—questions—to output data—responses) as to provide the best solutions to the problems given in the training set. In the next step, the effectiveness of the learning process is verified on the test set: the system solves problems that have not yet been answered, and the person (or algorithm) verifying the quality of learning compares these answers to the real ones that are part of the test set. If the results are satisfactory, the AI system is allowed to solve real problems (i.e. problems that have not been solved by the system nor the user).

Supervised learning is most often used in classification problems (binary or multidimensional classification) and regression analyses. In the first case, the goal is to find a link between the set of features on the input with a discrete solution (in the case of a binary classification, most often

YES or NO, and for a multidimensional classification, e.g. a finite set of features). An example may be the diagnosis of a disease based on the image or recognition of the object in the picture.

In the case of regression, the task of the algorithm is to create a link between the set of features and a continuous variable on the output. An example of this is an attempt to forecast property prices (price as an output variable) based on the history of prices from a given period.

Reinforcement learning is a special case of supervised learning. The difference is that the system is taught on the basis of the feedback from the background (evaluation of the correctness of the solution to the problem), and not the previously prepared training set of question-answer pairs. Thus, it is an example of learning through action, or, referring to the neurocognitive analogy, error-driven learning, which is one of the basic mechanisms of human learning (especially the acquisition of tacit knowledge, e.g. cycling).

In very simple terms, the reinforcement learning looks like this:

1. The system receives a task to do;
2. It formulates a hypothesis and accomplishes the task;
3. It receives information from the background about the degree of correctness of the result (usually in the form of an error understood as the difference between the effect of the action and the correct solution);
4. Another hypothesis (and action) is directed to minimize the error;
5. It receives a reply again… ;
6. … (more iterations)…;
7. This process is continued until a satisfactorily low error level is obtained. An error close to zero stops the learning process.

The essence of support in the concept of *learning with support* is to "promote" (by choice) those activities which in effect generate a minimal error. Basically, it distinguishes the learning process of machines from the animal (and humans) rewarded training; in the latter case, the reward is usually the introduction into the state of pleasure, and the punishment for error is pain. Machines do not feel pleasure (yet), nor probably pain (though recent research indicates behavior similar to aggression in multiagent systems—see e.g. Leibo et al. 2017).

Reinforcement learning works best in situations where the system must perform sequences of actions, and the complexity of input parameters prevents the creation of reliable test sets. The examples of this are autonomous vehicles, ground as well as air, or computer games (e.g. Go).

The aim of unsupervised learning is to discover completely new patterns and not to identify rules in training sets as in the case of supervised learning. The system is not supported by any training set or a feedback on the correctness of actions or responses. The learning process uses, for example, cluster analysis (when grouping of similar objects is recommended) or Markov models (when analyzing time series, e.g. human speech).

Unsupervised learning is most often used in situations where the user cannot give examples or correct behaviors that could be the basis for learning the system. It may be related to a high level of complexity of the background (e.g. too many factors to be included in the analysis) or the lack of knowledge about the data structure. The example of application is the need to identify people whose behavior in the crowd is unusual, on the basis of the analysis of images from the monitoring system. The system must first identify the "actors", then their behaviors, and finally classify them and indicate the most unusual one.

Another case is when new patterns appear faster than humans can identify them, which in turn makes it impossible to prepare training sets and supervised learning. This concerns IT security systems that need to analyze huge amounts of data from IT systems in real time, identify anomalies in it and react to it very quickly. In addition to the network security, the examples of the use of this learning mechanism include bioinformatic support for gene or protein sequencing.

The last interesting method of intelligent systems learning is transfer learning. It uses the knowledge acquired during the solving of one problem to the solution of other problem. In the case of AI, most frequently, this method is implemented in two ways:

1. Algorithms are taught in virtual environments (simulators, see e.g. Brockman et al. 2016), and then they are implemented in solutions operating in natural environment (e.g. robots).

2. To create a neuronal network that can solve new problems, another part of the network, good at solving similar problems, is applied. An example of this could be the construction of a network recognizing specific images (e.g. dog breeds) with the use of internal layers of network, recognizing other objects exceptionally well (e.g. ResNet50), supplemented with layers of high abstraction enabling recognition of specific breeds.

Transfer learning is an innovative method, which often drastically accelerates the quality and speed of neuronal network learning and as a result it becomes a significant component of value structures applying artificial intelligence.

2.2.7 Perception, Communication and Action

To be able to operate effectively in the environment, the system must be capable of collecting information about the environment (by using sensors), communication (both receiving and sending messages) and actions (using actuators). The quality (e.g. precision) and effectiveness (e.g. efficiency or speed) of these processes are critical to the effectiveness of the operation: they reduce uncertainty and increase the efficiency of impact on the environment.

It is no wonder that many of current AI trends are focused on improving technologies which support perception, communication and agents' activities.

In the area of perception, the research is focused on image recognition, both static and video. Among the algorithms used for this purpose, different architectures of deep learning dominate, particularly convolutional networks, such as capsule networks. Their effectiveness increases year by year: according to the AI Index report (Shoham et al. 2017), since 2010, the image labeling error rate has dropped from 28.5% to below 2.5%, overcoming human capabilities (error of 5%).

It is worth emphasizing here that the image recognition algorithms do not only serve agents, but are also used in many systems supporting people in their daily activities. And this is not only about image recognition, but also, for example, intelligent auto-focus and background blur in cameras, (semi-)automatic correction of images, automatic description and classification of photos or frames in video films supported by AI.

In the area of Natural Language Processing (NLP) deep network methods are also used; this time, however, due to the sequencing of a signal with slightly different architectures (mainly different types of recurrent neural networks), especially with Long-Short Term Memory (LSTM). The AI Index report (Shoham et al. 2017) shows that the ability of AI class systems to recognize human speech, for example, in the process of converting speech to text, has already exceeded human capacity (in 2017), and the ability to understand human speech is gradually improving. Also in this case, there are a lot of applications other than just the support of agents in the operation: from automatic text corrections (spelling, but also style and grammar) by reducing the cognitive load (highlighting the most important parts or automatic summaries of longer texts) to support of programmers in the software development process (fault identification, programming style corrections, etc.).

The systems supporting physical impact on the environment are the domain of robotics. They combine many other technologies: from the interpretation of data from the environment, through planning to interaction, for example, manipulation of objects. The programs controlling robots as well as their physical structures— including entirely new methods of movement, see the projects implemented by Boston Dynamics: https://www.bostondynamics.com/—are constantly being improved. The implementation of reinforcement learning mechanisms enables practically continuous self-improvement of these solutions and, as a result, a gradual overcoming of human limitations (strength, speed, precision).

2.2.8 Creative and Prognostic Capabilities

2.2.8.1 Creative Capabilities

When presenting various methods and possibilities of modern AI systems, their creative capabilities should be mentioned. The dynamic development of such solutions is possible thanks to the GAN class methods (Generative Adversarial Network), in a sense, using game mechanisms.

The idea behind it is as follows:

1. The aim of the process is to create an agent capable of "perfect counterfeiting" of a certain class of objects.
2. The object generated by the agent ("cheater") will be "perfectly counterfeited" when another agent ("expert") specializing in the identification of a given class of objects (e.g. images, sounds, melodies, texts) will not be able to check whether things that need to be assessed are original or generated by "cheater."
3. The function of the target (the measure of effectiveness) of the "cheater" agent is in effect maximization of incorrect assessments of "expert" (statements that "counterfeit" objects are original).
4. The teaching process is as follows:
   (a) "Cheater" agent (usually a neural network) generates the first object based on the so-called hum (a set of random signals at the entrance).
   (b) "Expert" agent assesses to what extent the product is original.
   (c) Information about this assessment returns to "cheater."
   (d) "Cheater" changes the methods of generating its products and reintroduces it to "expert" until it reaches the desired measure of effectiveness.
5. The effect of many iterations of this process is the agent (neural network) that can very well generate new objects, which are remarkably similar to the original one.

This technology can be used in many different ways. The most interesting ones concern image generation. For example (all images for Zhu et al. n.d.):

1. The style transfer allows presentation of a given photo as if it was painted by a specific painter.
2. The inverse operation makes it possible to recreate an object (e.g. a landscape) that the artist actually could see.

3. The transferred "style" is not necessarily the painter's style, but for example the time of year.

The readers interested in this subject are encouraged to examine (Zhu et al. n.d.), in which there are very attractive visualizations of the mechanisms described above.

The GAN method can be used to generate artificial, but extremely realistic-looking faces (see e.g. Karras et al. n.d.). A very interesting application of artificial intelligence methods is the attempt to generate a video (the speech of President Barack Obama) solely based on the commonly available audio file (Suwajanakorn et al. 2017).

It turns out that generative possibilities can also be applied to sounds, human voices and text. Google launched the Magenta project in 2016 (https://magenta.tensorflow.org/), in which AI systems compose music. In turn, the company Lyrebird (https://lyrebird.ai) on the basis of the sent samples of real people is able to generate statements from the written text sounding almost as if it was said by the person it wants to imitate. The next Narrative Science system (narrativescience.com) allows the generation of interpretations of data provided in the form of spreadsheets. Obviously, the possibilities of using such solutions are very wide.

2.2.8.2 Predictive Capabilities

Time series forecasting was one of the first goals of AI. The eternal dream of predicting, for example, share prices, has driven the development of various techniques, from regression models to LSTM neural network architectures.

Vondrick and others (Vondrick et al. 2016) used the GAN method to forecast situations that will happen in the future only on the basis of the scene presented in one picture. The system, after processing nearly 2 million videos from youtube.com, can generate several seconds of video material being the "future" of the situations shown in the pictures.

Another very interesting area is predicting human behavior. In the above-cited work (Moravčík et al. 2017) the system successfully used it in the game against professional poker players. In turn, Hartford and others

(Hartford et al. 2016) have successfully applied AI systems to predict behavior of people in behavioral games.

It turns out that forecasting may concern not only stock-exchange listings. Recursive neural networks can, for example, successfully "predict" another word in a longer sequence of text. If they can predict the word, why would not it be possible to "forecast" the entire paragraph? Or maybe a whole chapter? Or books? The attempts that have been made are quite promising—see e.g. the "new" volumes of *Game of Thrones* generated by artificial intelligence (https://github.com/zackthoutt/got-book-6/tree/master/generated-book-v1). As it can be seen, human fantasy is unlimited.

2.2.9 Summary

The purpose of the research on artificial intelligence is to create systems (agents) that operate at least as good as humans. Agents can operate in different environments, with different levels of predictability and complexity.

To be able to operate effectively, the system must have

1. a defined objective function:
    (a) the ability to perceive the environment and one's own state,
    (b) built-in or expandable behavior rules,
    (c) the ability to take actions affecting the environment.

The degree of difficulty of the task and the associated level of complexity of the algorithms is strongly dependent on the predictability of the environment and agent's perceptive abilities. Current AI methods to a large extent contribute to reducing these uncertainties. These methods

1. reduce uncertainty associated with preceptor registration (image, text and speech recognition algorithms);
2. reduce uncertainty associated with the dynamics of environmental changes (predictive algorithms);

3. reduce uncertainty associated with the assessment of the consequences of actions taken (machine learning methods, precise motor solutions);
4. broaden the ability to react correctly (new forms of knowledge representation, methods of gathering experience and studying the impact of activities on the environment).

Among the new trends expanding the described applications, particular attention should be paid to

1. generation and transformation methods (e.g. GANs),
2. creating AI systems explaining their operation rules and methods of inference Self Explainable AI),
3. systems that independently identify target functions (Ng and Russell 2017).

2.3 The Most Important AI Technologies

2.3.1 Classification of AI Technologies

There are many different technologies supporting the implementation of Big Data projects, machine learning and artificial intelligence (see e.g. Zilis and Cham 2016). The so-called landscapes are helpful in the classification of these solutions as they are constantly updated and published on the Internet by domain experts.

For example, Matt Turck on his portal (www.matturck.com) in April 2017 published the following summary of Big Data solutions. According to the author, these systems can be classified as follows (Fig. 2.7):

For the purpose of this study, approximately 400 different projects in the area of artificial intelligence were analyzed. The result of this analysis, carried out in terms of various mechanisms of value generation, is the following classification of AI projects (Fig. 2.8):

A brief description of individual technological categories is presented below. A somewhat deeper description will be found in Section 4: Cognitive Computing Systems.

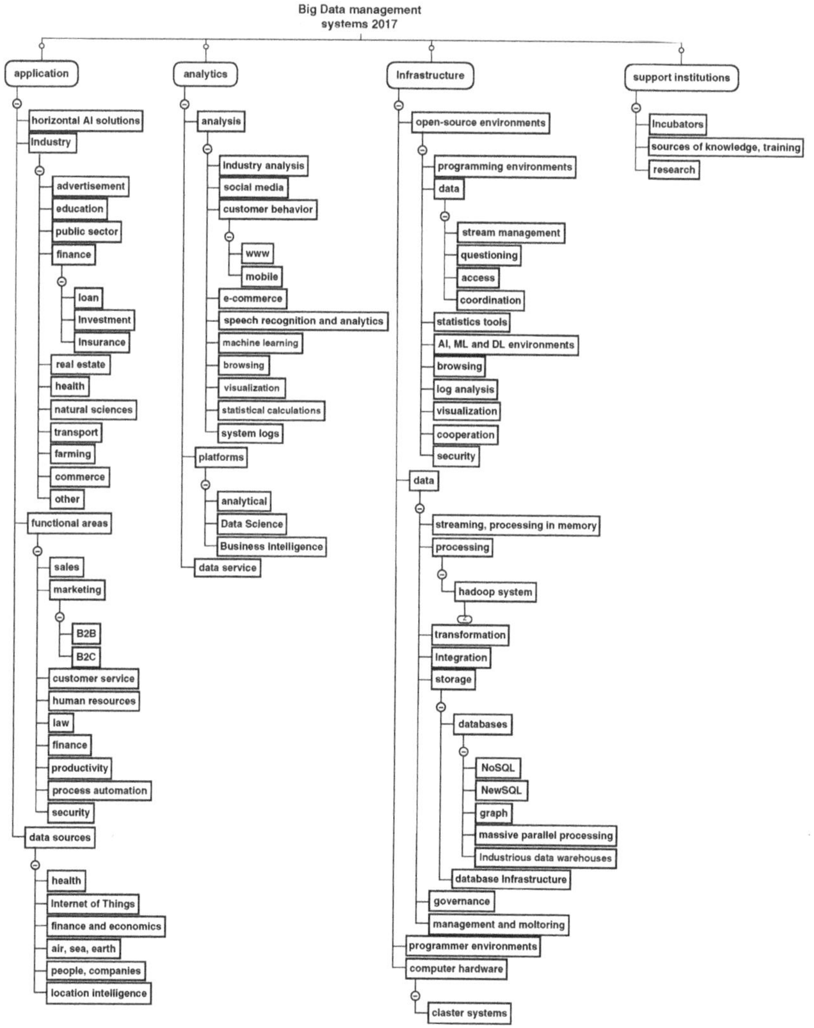

Fig. 2.7 Classification of systems supporting Big Data management. (Source: Own elaboration based on www.matturck.com)

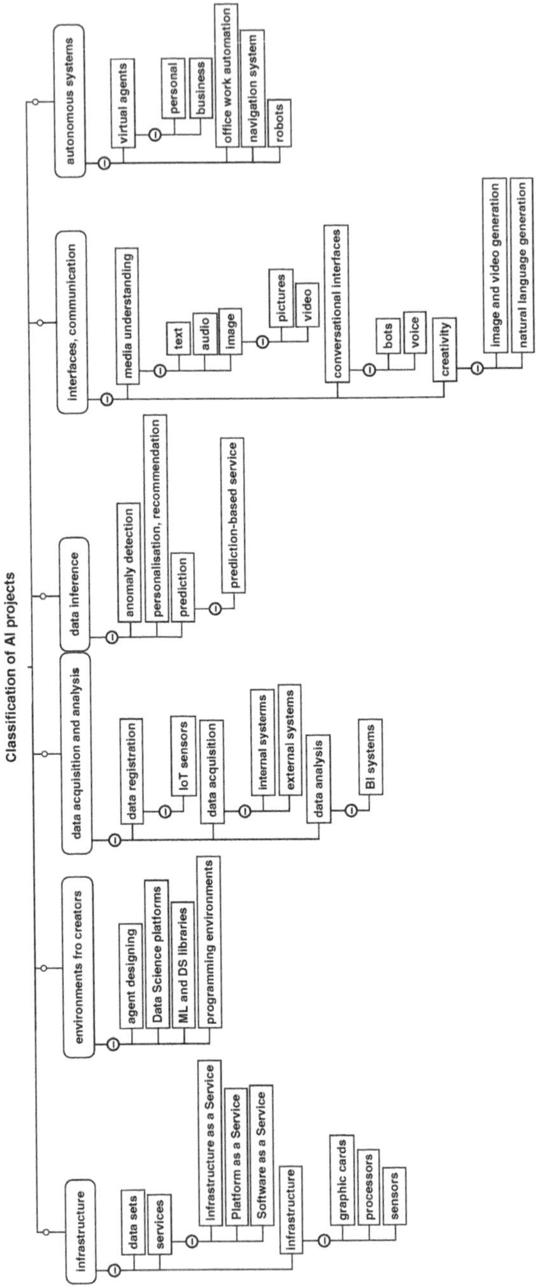

Fig. 2.8 Classification of systems supporting AI solution design. (Source: Own elaboration)

2.3.1.1 Infrastructure

Infrastructure projects constitute the core of solutions enabling the creation of AI systems. These include electronic circuits enabling the generation of computing power (e.g. processors or Graphic Processor Units (GPU)—intensively used in the calculation of neural networks) and recording of data from the environment (sensors used, for example, in the Internet of Things solutions).

The next layer consists of services available through "cloud computing," particularly providing Infrastructure as a Service (IaaS), Platforms as a Service (PaaS) and Software as a Service (SaaS).

A separate category of "infrastructure" is data sets, which can be not only a valuable source of information, but also a good base for the development and testing of AI algorithms.

2.3.1.2 Environments for Developers

These environments allow developers to create AI solutions. Among them, it is worth distinguishing a wide range of systems made available as open source— constituting probably the majority of industrial solutions, professional libraries supporting statistical calculations, machine learning and creation of AI systems, advanced Data Science platform, simplifying the processes of obtaining and preparing data, designing, testing and implementing production algorithms, and effective group work of machine learning and AI specialists. A separate category consists of the systems enabling the creation of assistants (bots), both business and personal.

2.3.1.3 Acquiring and Exploring Data

The next class includes the systems enabling data capture (sensors with the right software), their acquisition (software and telecommunications infrastructure and enabling effective management of large data streams), and their registration and analysis. These systems are often divided into acquisition and processing support systems of their own or external data (when integration with the environment is necessary).

2.3.1.4 Inference from Data

The data obtained and analyzed are the basis for the systems whose purpose is to reason and recommend solutions. Three categories of solutions dominate in this area: predictive, personalizing and detecting various anomalies. Very often, these are dedicated systems for strictly defined industries: the source of efficiency of individual algorithms is a very good knowledge of the specificity of the industry.

2.3.1.5 Interfaces, Communication

The next class of systems currently undergoing a renaissance are the systems enabling effective communication with users. They are based on advanced algorithms of media understanding (image and video recognition, processing and natural language generation). These algorithms are implemented in the conversational interfaces enabling direct communication with the user, mainly voice and text (so-called bots). The last, relatively new, category contains the generative systems, enabling the creation of new content (e.g. data interpretation in the form of narration) or multimedia (images, films, spoken words or music).

2.3.1.6 Autonomous Systems

The last and probably the most advanced group, are autonomous systems. Among them, there are virtual agents (autonomous systems representing the company, e.g. in customer service processes), personal assistants (supporting users in everyday activities) and systems that automate office work (e.g. automatically classifying invoices in accounting systems).

A separate, "industrial" category consists of autonomous transport systems (car, air —mainly drones—and transport in warehouses), navigation systems supporting them and the very dynamically developing area of industrial robots.

2.3.1.7 Summary

The landscape of systems supporting the creation, management and development of AI class systems is very complex. What's more, due to the very effective connection of education, research and industry (see e.g. Shoham et al. 2017) this sector is developing very dynamically. The solutions that have been perceived until recently as pure technologies (such as blockchain) are becoming the basis for revolution in the area of management (decentralization), trust (dispersed books) or financial markets (cryptocurrencies).

If you add to it growing investments in systems that are often incomprehensible to investors, it is difficult to predict how this landscape will look in a few years. Therefore, it is worth developing possibly universal methods of recovering values from AI systems.

2.4 Cognitive Computing Systems

The term "cognitive computing" (hereinafter CC) is relatively new. It was first used by software development companies such as IBM or Hewlett Packard at the beginning of the twenty-first century as a term describing autonomous learning systems based on large amounts of data, applying to a goal function and interacting with people in a natural way.

John E. Kelly (2015) indicates the year 2011 as the boundary date between the "programming era" (from 1950 until now) and the "cognitive" era. The creators of the IBM Watson project illustrate the most important mechanisms of CC systems with the Watson system, which after a spectacular victory in the game show Jeopardy in 2011 (see e.g. Gabbatt 2011) became a symbolic step towards information systems with artificial general intelligence (AGI). To win the quiz show, IBM Watson had to be able to hear the question, interpret it correctly, and on the basis of the information gathered in local resources (without Internet connection) put forward a lot of hypotheses that could be the basis for the correct answer. In the next steps, it had to assign a confidence level to each of the hypotheses, select the most accurate hypothesis, assess the risk of reporting an answer (the correct answer is rewarded, the error is penalized by negative points), and finally answer the question. And all this in the time of one second. Even a cursory analysis of this process demonstrates similarity to the way a human works—hence there is the word "cognitive" (cognition) in the term cognitive computing.

Cognitive Computing Consortium (https://cognitivecomputingconsortium.com/), founded by companies and institutions such as SAS, Hewlett Packard, Nara Logics or Customer Matrix, specifies the definition of the concept by indicating four key features of CC class systems: contextuality, ability to update the state, adaptability and interactivity. This approach, due to its universal and comprehensive nature, has been adopted as the basis for the definition of cognitive computing systems in the research presented below.

2.4.1 Features of Cognitive Computing Systems

According to the Cognitive Computing Consortium (see e.g. "Cognitive Computing Defined" n.d.) cognitive computing (CC) systems are characterized by the ability to "understand" the context, the ability to self-update the state, adaptability and interactivity (see e.g. Hurwitz et al. 2015). These features will be described in detail below as a starting point for analysis of the architecture and functions of CC systems.

2.4.1.1 The Ability to "Understand" the Context

The contextuality of CC systems is explained as the ability to understand, identify and acquire contextual information from the background such as the meaning, syntax, time, location, the domain of knowledge, regulations, user profile, process, task or goal. CC systems identify and separate from the context such features as time, location, task, history or profile in order to create the best set of information necessary for the correct implementation of the task. It also means the ability to obtain this information from qualitatively different digital sources, structured as well as unstructured: texts, images, films, sensors or databases. CC systems have also access to high computing performance, which allows searching for patterns in the data obtained in this way for its later use when solving the problem.

2.4.1.2 The Ability to Update the State

Another feature of CC systems is the ability to acquire independently information necessary to solve the problem, formulating and addressing questions or acquiring additional information sources. This is one of the conditions of autonomy; in the case of uncertainty, these systems can independently turn to the background for the missing information, and in this sense they are self-directed. To maintain the continuity of these systems, it is also necessary to be able to remember previous states and interactions in the ongoing process.

2.4.1.3 Adaptability

The ability to adapt to new conditions is one of the most important distinguishing features of the CC systems, probably the ones that approach them most closely to human intelligence (specifically fluid intelligence, understood as the ability to behave effectively in new situations). A measure of adaptability is also the ability to solve ambiguous problems, assess the significance of often-conflicting signals and tolerance towards the lack of predictability. With such capabilities, the CC systems can suggest the "best" answers in a given situation rather than "real" answers, which distinguishes them from "traditional" computer programs. The basis of adaptability is learning while acquiring new information and depending on the changing goals. Also, the ability to learn on the basis of one's own experience (in particular from the mistakes) and to obtain and process information in real time, or close to real, is crucial.

The process of designing CC solutions will be described in more detail below. For the moment, the important role of humans in the "teaching process" of such systems needs to be emphasized. After creating the knowledge corpus (based on information obtained from various sources, in particular from the domain experts) CC systems are trained by providing a series of pairs of "questions" and "answers", and then periodically checking the correctness of new solutions for the problem system. The knowledge created in this way is then strengthened by the interaction with people who review the quality of the response and its reaction in new situations. The role of people at this stage (and further stages) of operation of CC class solutions is very important. It will be crucial in the analysis of their possible impact on the management of organizations.

2.4.1.4 Interactivity

The last feature of CC systems indicated by the Cognitive Computing Consortium is their interactivity, understood as being the ability to interact with other systems (in particular with people) in a way that is natural for them.

As a result, users have the opportunity to express their expectations in a simple and comfortable way, and the feedback provided by the system is understandable for them and adapted to the current context. Similarly, CC class systems are able to exchange information with other systems (devices, programs, services, databases, etc.) in their physical environment as well as in the "cloud." This requires the use of advanced technologies, namely, from the area of natural language processing (NLP) and its natural language generation (NLG), both in audio and text form, or the implementation of many different digital communication protocols with external systems. The research results presented in the further part of the study indicate an intensive development of this class of solutions, which will significantly contribute to increasing the potential of CC class systems.

2.4.2 Components and Principles of Cognitive Computing Systems Design

In order to fulfill the tasks set before them, the requirements for CC class systems should have (Hurwitz et al. 2015)

1. **communication interfaces** enabling the processing and the correct interpretation of a user's questions;
2. the so-called **corpus** or **corpora**: knowledge structures that are sufficiently large and credible to enable the system to formulate and test hypotheses based on background data and continuous learning;
3. **algorithms** enabling the formulation and assessment of hypotheses in order to answer questions, solve problems or formulate new conclusions.

Below, the individual stages of designing CC class systems, their operation mechanisms and model architecture will be presented. This scheme will facilitate the classification of projects and ventures in the areas of artificial intelligence and machine learning in Chap. 3.

2.4.2.1 Designing a CC System

The process of designing CC systems (see e.g. Hurwitz et al. 2015) is usually distinguished by three stages: building the knowledge corpus, supplying the system with data and implementing machine learning mechanisms.

Building the Knowledge Corpus

The corpus is a possibly complete representation of knowledge from the area in which the CC system operates. It allows for answering questions, discovering patterns, relationships and formulating new conclusions.

The data and knowledge are obtained from various sources, in various forms and at various stages of the system's operation. Due to the huge amount of data and the limited processing capabilities (determined e.g. by the computer performance, the available capacity of the archivers or the bandwidth that connects data), during the design process of the corpus, special attention should be paid to

1. the scope of data and information contained in the corpus:
   (a) too narrow will limit the system's ability to make conclusions;
   (b) too broad will extend the processing period or prevent its effective use;
2. organization of this information, which also has a significant impact on the quality and speed of inference.

Therefore, in the process of creating the corpus, the domain experts are most often employed, as they are able to indicate not only reliable but also useful sources and ranges of data for solving a given class of problems.

During the process of corpus design, apart from the information itself, the so-called taxonomies (describing hierarchical relationships between objects and their features) and ontologies (defining more complex relations, e.g. between symptoms and disease diagnoses, often developed by industry groups, e.g. supported by Google, www.schema.org) are created.

Data Input

The basis for correct behavior and effective problem solving by CC class systems is data.

As in the case of sensory reception processes in humans, the CC system can obtain information from the background (via various sensors and communication protocols) and from its own resources (corpus, but also from e.g. internal diagnostic processes). In the case of external sources, it is necessary to evaluate the information periodically or continuously: its quality, relevance and other parameters crucial for the problem-solving process.

After obtaining data and information from external and internal sources, the system should have the ability to integrate it and, when necessary, to obtain additional information from the background.

At the architecture level, two layers are responsible for acquiring and pre-processing information: data-access layer and feature-extraction layer.

The data access layer is to obtain data from various sources and in various formats (e.g. text, audio, video, data from sensors, etc.), its pre-processing and entering on database systems. To handle these processes, the tools of the ETL class are used: Extract-Transform-Load.

The feature-extraction layer is responsible for (see e.g. Hurwitz et al. 2015)

1. identification of data, whose analysis will be important for solving the problem;
2. abstraction and cleaning of this data for machine processing;
3. transformation of data into representations, i.e. identification of its key features so that it can be better processed by machine learning algorithms.

It is worth emphasizing that CC systems should be able to dynamically select data sources that, at a given stage of analysis, add the highest value to the problem-solving processes, both their selection and filtering.

Another step after obtaining and transforming data is most commonly the data analysis. It results in showing the most important characteristics and relationships within the data sets, descriptive or predictive analyses. It is particularly important to identify the most important patterns in the data. Objects within a pattern may have a similar structure (e.g. shapes in images), values or other form of similarity. Information about these similarities plays later an important role in the selection of appropriate machine learning algorithms.

Machine Learning Algorithms Implementation

Acquired, cleaned and organized data are transferred to the algorithms of machine learning: supervised, reinforcement or unsupervised learning. Their effective implementation supports the autonomy and development of CC class solution on the basis of the acquired experiences and as a result, it constitutes a critically important component of the whole solution.

2.4.3 CC Systems as a New Quality in Management

2.4.3.1 CC Systems and "Traditional" Business Information Systems

CC class systems introduce a new quality to the "landscape" of business information systems. The features mentioned below distinguish them from "traditional" information systems (see e.g. Kelly 2015).

The first feature that distinguishes CC systems from "traditional" computer programs is probabilistic, and not deterministic character.

Traditional computer programs

1. operate on the basis of predefined rules;
2. conclude on the basis of mostly structured data from well-defined sources. They cannot conclude on the basis of unpredictable or unstructured data and cannot independently select the best new sources of data and information in a given context;
3. most often they offer precise, definitive answers or solutions to problems.

In contrast, CC systems:

1. go beyond the given rules and programs, they can adapt to the environment and modify their algorithms accordingly;
2. they can use complex, unpredictable or unstructured data. They analyze and interpret images, films, human speech or data from various sensors. They can explain their meaning;
3. they do not offer final answers. They can assess the validity and reliability of data sources, formulate and evaluate many different hypotheses and present their results by determining their level of confidence.

With such capabilities, CC class systems generate hypotheses, the arguments supported by facts and recommendations concerning large and complex data sets, and do not provide simple solutions to computational problems. They can extract meaning from unstructured data, which is around 80% of the world's data, and due to this, they can cope with the size, complexity and unpredictability of information generated by modern information systems.

Another factor that distinguishes CC systems from "traditional" systems is their ability to infer and act on the basis of the generally formulated objective functions. In order to do it effectively, these systems learn and conclude on the basis of interaction with the background and not on programs previously prepared by their creators.

2.4.3.2 The Potential of CC Systems in the Design of New Services and Management

A detailed analysis of the possible impact of CC solutions on the elements of the value chain in an organization will be presented later in this book; here, only their potential in designing new services and management is to be outlined.

The Ability to Solve a New Class of Problems

As described above, CC systems have the ability to solve complex problems in different situations characterized by ambiguity, uncertainty and fast variability, described by large sets of information, in which users' goals change as new information is acquired and the learning is constantly happening. This potential greatly broadens the spectrum of applications of information systems, which is obviously a source of new opportunities, but also risks or challenges.

Equipping Products and Services with "Intelligence"

The solutions described below and used by many companies allow equipping products and services with "intelligence." An example of this might be autonomous vehicles, robots or so-called digital agents representing people or organizations on the Internet.

The Increase of Business Processes "Intelligence"

The CC solutions based on the Internet of Things such as the Predix.io system, enable "equipping with intelligence" the entire business processes, making the concept of the Industrial Revolution 4.0 more realistic. The processes improved in such a way can use internal and external data better, due to which organizations have a better insight and understanding of workflows, context and business environment. As a result, they are constantly learning, are better in predicting and have better operational efficiency.

These abilities are at the heart of the concept of cognitive organization presented at the end of this book. This is an organizational structure, which has created "sensory", "intelligent" and "executive" layers from many different subsystems, and as a result, has become a system of cognitive computing class on a macro scale (at the organizational level).

Improving the Exploration and Discovering Processes

One of the foundations of competitive advantage in fast-changing environments with high information saturation is the organization's ability to quickly identify patterns, anomalies and trends in its environment, and effectively use this knowledge to understand reality and accurately predict an increasingly complex and unpredictable future (see e.g. Kelly 2015).

Such potential is particularly important in industries in which strategic decisions are subject to high risk, such as pharmacy (drug design), finance (investments), and production of modern materials or sophisticated start-ups. Skillfully used CC class systems facilitate functioning in such a reality, helping to discover new relations and patterns, identify opportunities or present hypotheses explaining the reality.

Redefinition of the Role of a Man

CC systems have a significant impact on human relations with the environment (not only digital), and sometimes they redefine their role. They can act as personal assistants, and even trainers or coaches, support decision-making and recommend optimal solutions for the user in a given context.

When interacting with a user, CC systems base their recommendations on the history and behavior patterns (behavioral profiles), the current context (place, task, and even an emotional state), drawing data from various sources for this purpose, such as purchase history, medical files or data generated by the sensors of the Internet of Things. At the same time, they are improving themselves: human choices are "training sets" for their machine learning algorithms, due to which their effects significantly improve over time, increasing the user's satisfaction and, what is a threat, making them addictive.

CC systems at the level of the organization scale and raise the level of expert knowledge. The rate of knowledge growth in practically every field exceeds the possibilities of its acquisition by experts.

CC systems enable the aggregation of a large amount of information and support of their activities. The trend of the increasing role of experts in the CC system implementation processes presented in Chap. 3 also points to the opposite trend: the total use of the potential of these systems will only be possible if their capabilities are combined with human knowledge and intelligence.

The last trend that should be signaled here is the impact of CC systems on reallocation and modification of decision-making processes. The number of areas in which important decisions are (or will soon be) taken by IT systems is growing. These are, for example, systems reactions to threat states (industrial failures or IT attacks) and investment decisions taken up by algorithms (see e.g. HFT: High Frequency Trading). This phenomenon, often forced by the characteristics of the business environment, can significantly affect the role of human in the decision-making process: from the person making decisions based on the analysis of source data to someone who only designs and monitors the function of the intelligent system efficiency.

2.5 Summary

The above-presented outline of the basic AI methods and technologies obviously does not exhaust the topic. However, it is satisfactory as for the general understanding of the influence that these systems might have on contemporary organizations. The next chapter will be devoted to the presentation of the ways in which AI solutions can change management methods of companies, competing and building competitive advantages on the current and future markets.

Notes

1. The complete list of analyzed projects, companies and organizations along with the appropriate addresses of web pages are set out in Appendix 3 of Chap. 5. There, detailed and up-to-date information can be found on the offered products and services, operational or business models. For ease of reading, on the following pages there will be only the names of projects given, without reference to online resources.
2. Due to the different scales (short and long) used in the terminology of numbers that are powers of 10, the use of terms such as "trillion" or "quintillion" was abandoned. The Anglo-Saxon countries use a short scale, while the European, the long one, which can sometimes lead to misunderstandings. For example, a quintile denotes the number of 10^18 in a short scale, and in the long scale: 10^30.

References

Bostrom, N. (2014). *Superintelligence*. Oxford: Oxford University Press.

Brockman, G., Cheung, V., Pettersson, L., Schneider, J., Schulman, J., Tang, J., & Zaremba, W. (2016, June 5). OpenAI Gym. arXiv:1606.01540

Bughin, J., Hazan, E., Ramaswamy, S., Chui, M., Allas, T., Dahlstrom, P., et al. (2017). *Artificial Intelligence*. McKinsey Global Institute. Retrieved from https://www.mckinsey.com/~/media/McKinsey/Industries/Advanced%20Electronics/Our%20Insights/How%20artificial%20intelligence%20can%20deliver%20real%20value%20to%20companies/MGI-Artificial-Intelligence-Discussion-paper.ashx

Cognitive Computing Defined. (n.d.). *Cognitive Computing Defined*. Retrieved January 31, 2018, from https://cognitivecomputingconsortium.com/resources/cognitive-computing-defined/

Dennett, D. C. (2014). *Intuition Pumps and Other Tools for Thinking*. New York: W.W. Norton & Company.

Gabbatt, A. (2011, February 17). *IBM Computer Watson Wins Jeopardy Clash*. Retrieved January 31, 2018, from http://www.theguardian.com/technology/2011/feb/17/ibm-computer-watson-wins-jeopardy

Goertzel, B. (2017, September 5). *What Counts as a Conscious Thinking Machine?* Retrieved December 26, 2017, from https://www.newscientist.com/article/mg21528813.600-what-counts-as-a-conscious-thinking-machine/

Hartford, J. S., Wright, J. R., & Leyton-Brown, K. (2016). *Deep Learning for Predicting Human Strategic Behavior. Generating Videos with Scene Dynamics.* Presented at the 30th Neural Information Processing Systems (NIPS), Barcelona.

Hassabis, D., Kumaran, D., Summerfield, C., & Botvinick, M. (2017). Neuroscience-Inspired Artificial Intelligence. *Neuron, 95*(2), 245–258. https://doi.org/10.1016/j.neuron.2017.06.011.

Hurwitz, J., Kaufman, M., & Bowles, A. (2015). *Cognitive Computing and Big Data Analytics.* Indianapolis: Wiley.

Kahneman, D. (2011). *Thinking, Fast and Slow.* New York: Farrar, Straus and Giroux.

Karras, T., Aila, T., Laine, S., & Lehtinen, J. (n.d.). *Progressive Growing of GANs for Improved Quality, Stability, and Variation.* Retrieved December 28, 2017, from http://research.nvidia.com/publication/2017-10_Progressive-Growing-of

Kelly, J. E. (2015). *Computing, Cognition and the Future of Knowing.* Retrieved January 31, 2018, from https://www.research.ibm.com/software/IBMResearch/multimedia/Computing_Cognition_WhitePaper.pdf

Leibo, J. Z., Zambaldi, V., Lanctot, M., Marecki, J., & Graepel, T. (2017, February 10). *Multi-agent Reinforcement Learning in Sequential Social Dilemmas.* Retrieved from https://arxiv.org/abs/1702.03037

Moravčík, M., Schmid, M., Burch, N., Lisý, V., Morrill, D., Bard, N., et al. (2017). DeepStack: Expert-Level Artificial Intelligence in Heads-Up No-Limit Poker. *Science, 356*(6337), 508–513. https://doi.org/10.1126/science.aam6960.

Nelson, P. (2016, December 7). *One Autonomous Car Will Use 4,000 GB of Data Per Day.* Retrieved January 20, 2018, from https://www.networkworld.com/article/3147892/internet/one-autonomous-car-will-use-4000-gb-of-dataday.html

Ng, A. Y., & Russell, S. (2017, August 17). *Algorithms for Inverse Reinforcement Learning.* Retrieved December 27, 2017, from http://bair.berkeley.edu/blog/2017/08/17/cooperatively-learning-human-values

Nilsson, N. J. (2005). Human-Level Artificial Intelligence? Be Serious! *AI Magazine,* Winter, *26*(4), 68–75. https://doi.org/10.1609/aimag.v26i4.1850.

Nisbett, R. E. (2015). *Mindware.* New York: Farrar, Straus and Giroux.

Norvig, P., & Russell, S. (2016). *Artificial Intelligence: Modern Approach* (3rd ed.). Upper Saddle River: Prentice Hall.

Porter, M. E., & Heppelmann, J. E. (2014). How Smart, Connected Products are Transforming Competition. *Harvard Business Review, 92*, 64–88.

Raschka, S. (2015). *Python Machine Learning*. Birmingham: Packt Publishing Ltd.

Shoham, Y., Perrault, R., Brynjolfsson, E., Clark, J., & LeGassick, C. (2017). *Artificial Intelligence Index* (pp. 1–101). Retrieved from https://aiindex.org/#report

Suwajanakorn, S., Seitz, S. M., & Kemelmacher-Shlizerman, I. (2017). Synthesizing Obama: Learning Lip Sync from Audio. Retrieved December 28, 2017, from http://grail.cs.washington.edu/projects/AudioToObama/siggraph17_obama.pdf

The Four V's of Big Data. Retrieved May 18, 2018, from http://www.ibmbigdatahub.com/infographic/four-vs-big-data

Turing, A. M. (1950). Computing Machinery and Intelligence. *Mind, LIX*(236), 433–460. https://doi.org/10.1093/mind/LIX.236.433.

Vondrick, C., Pirsiavash, H., & Torralba, A. (2016). *Generating Videos with Scene Dynamics*. Neural Information Processing Systems Foundation, Inc. Presented at the 30th Neural Information Processing Systems (NIPS) 2016, Barcelona.

Wozniak, S. (n.d.). Wozniak: Could a Computer Make a Cup of Coffee? Retrieved December 26, 2017, from https://www.fastcompany.com/1568187/wozniak-could-computer-make-cup-coffee

Zhu, J.-Y., Park, T., Isola, P., & Efros, A. A. (n.d.). *Unpaired Image-to-Image Translation Using Cycle-Consistent Adversarial Networks*. Retrieved December 27, 2017, from https://arxiv.org/pdf/1703.10593.pdf

Zilis, S., & Cham, J. (2016, November). The Competitive Landscape for Machine Intelligence. *Harvard Business Review*. Retrieved from https://hbr.org/2016/11/the-competitive-landscape-for-machine-intelligence

3

Influence of Artificial Intelligence on Activities and Competitiveness of an Organization

The previous chapter was devoted to the most significant concepts, methods and technologies of artificial intelligence (AI). This gives grounds for the presentation of influence which these systems might have on the contemporary organizations and markets.

In this chapter, the impact of intelligent systems on the organization's activity and competitiveness is presented. Firstly, the results of research on the adoption of AI solutions in companies are set out. The chapter shows the characteristics of the organizations that implement them successfully, describes key success factors and the most important barriers. Later, on the basis of many case studies, it describes the way AI systems change activities in the value chain (including design, production, logistics, sales and marketing, service, human resources and knowledge management). Finally, the chapter shows how smart solutions can change markets and competitiveness, and influence the role of human in the organization.

A. Wodecki, *Artificial Intelligence in Value Creation*,
https://doi.org/10.1007/978-3-319-91596-8_3

3.1 Objectives, Subject, Method and Quantitative Analysis of Research Results

3.1.1 Objectives and the Subject of Research

Applications of artificial intelligence (AI) and cognitive computing (CC) systems in business are becoming more and more popular. They bring a lot of hope, but also fears. Companies are trying to implement such solutions with a greater or lesser understanding of the methods of operation of AI (Ransbotham et al. 2017).

The general goal of this study is an assessment of the possible impact of AI solutions on companies and markets and a development of a value generation model in structures (organizations and networks).

To achieve this, the following specific goals were formulated:

1. Indication of the most important methods and possibilities offered by AI class systems from the perspective of industrial deployments.
2. Identification of the possible impact of these technologies on the primary and support activities of the organization.
3. Evaluation of the possible impact of AI technology on the value creation logic.
4. Evaluation of the possible impact of AI technology on the rules of competition on the markets.
5. Identification of key competencies, human and organizational, necessary to achieve competitive advantages in markets saturated with AI class solutions.

3.1.2 Research Methodology

The research process has been divided into the following stages:

1. Analysis of value generation models in management sciences.
2. Analysis of literature sources concerning the impact of AI class systems on generating value in companies and rules of competition on the markets.

3. Identification of almost 400 companies and an in-depth analysis of 323 companies and projects using artificial intelligence to increase the value of products and services.
4. Identification of possible impact of smart technologies on the operation of organizations and markets.
5. Formulation of the value generation model with the use of intelligent solutions and cognitive network concepts.

In the process of identification of nearly 400 researched projects using AI class systems, market reports concerning the investments in this class system, articles from management periodicals and many publications of specialists in this field were used.

Then, from nearly 400 projects, 323 projects were selected, eliminating inactive or poorly documented ventures. Each of the projects was analyzed on the basis of the information obtained from the websites of suppliers and customers, as well as the reports available on the Internet. After several iterations, 85 criteria for the classification of each project were proposed, and then an appropriate classification was made in the scale of "apply" or "does not apply." The final list of criteria is shown in the diagram below (Fig. 3.1).

Next, based on the information obtained during the analysis process, the database underwent a statistical analysis and an attempt was made to answer the research questions.

Observation results were the basis for formulation of the value generation model using intelligent systems (see Chap. 4). In the process of its formulation, the case-based reasoning method was used. This method, having its origins in the field of AI (see e.g. Kolodner 1992), is based on the use and/or the adaptation of existing experiences to understand and solve new problems. The application of this approach consisted of:

1. Searching for "classical" models (described in Chap. 1) of value creation that could be used to develop a value generation model using intelligent solutions ("retrieve" phase).

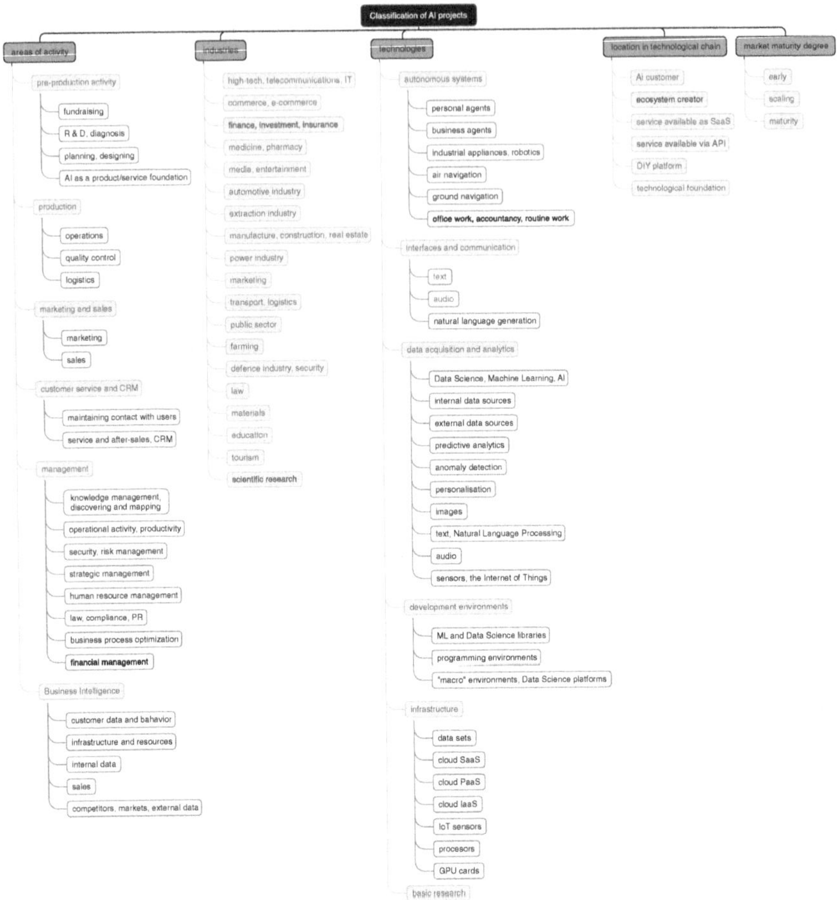

Fig. 3.1 The dimensions of the AI project classification used in the research. (Source: Own elaboration)

2. Identification of solutions in these models (including strategic options and questions) the most adequate for new phenomena connected with the use of intelligent systems ("ballpark solution" stage).
3. Adaptation of the solutions identified in this way for describing new phenomena ("adaptation" stage).
4. Application of these solutions and critical analysis of their effects ("justification and criticism" step).

5. Development of a new solution (model of cognitive networks) based on conclusions from critical analysis (the equivalent of the "evaluation" and "memory update" stages).

As a result, "classical" models of value creation in organizations (e.g. chain, grids or value networks) were used to develop proposals for a value generation model in structures saturated with AI class solutions.

3.1.3 Detailed Analysis of Value Offered

Among 323 of analyzed cases, the vast majority offers solutions for high technology industries (in particular telecommunications and IT), commerce and e-commerce, finance and health. This is in line with the observation of McKinsey's experts (Bughin et al. 2017), who similarly point out these industries as those that absorb AI solutions most intensely.

The second group of industries is media, entertainment, marketing, industry (in particular power industry), transport/logistics and the public sector. Slightly less numerous, but also popular, are the solutions for farming, the defense sector, education or tourism (Fig. 3.2).

Another dimension of the analysis was the application of AI systems to specific areas of the organization's activities (Fig. 3.3).

As can be seen, solutions supporting design and pre-production activity prevail, particularly research on products, markets, customer potential, and so on. The solutions supporting marketing and sales, production and service are slightly less numerous (Fig. 3.4).

Among AI solutions that contribute to support activities, solutions focused on knowledge management (including exploring and mapping knowledge) dominate. Subsequently, there are systems supporting operational activity and productivity, security and management as well as strategic management. Also present, although slightly fewer, are HR, financial and legal systems (Fig. 3.5).

An in-depth analysis of the number of systems supporting data analysis is interesting. It turns out that the most numerous are forecasting systems, slightly less numerous, but also very popular systems supporting the work of data engineers (including Data Science platforms and

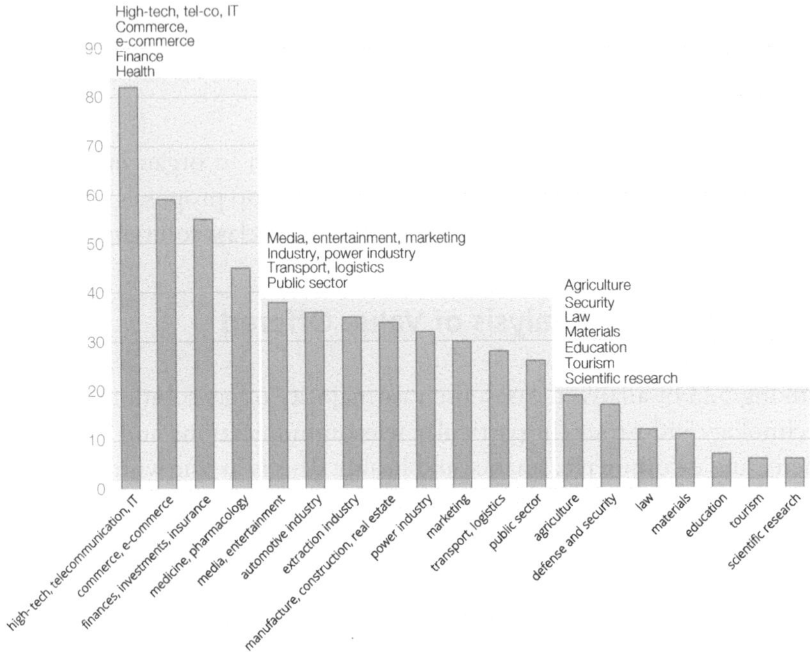

Fig. 3.2 The number of companies in given industries as identified in the research. (Source: Own elaboration)

solutions enabling creation of AI solutions), followed by solutions aimed at obtaining and analyzing data coming from within or outside the organization, and only then the recommendation systems, analyzing images, texts, audios or detecting anomalies. The results of these studies are similar to the data from reports showing the landscape of investments in AI systems (see e.g. Bughin et al. 2017), where machine-oriented solutions dominate (that is, support platforms data analysis), and with a slightly smaller contribution of image recognition systems or natural language processing (Fig. 3.6).

Another dimension of the AI system classification was their location in the technology chain. The following categories are distinguished here:

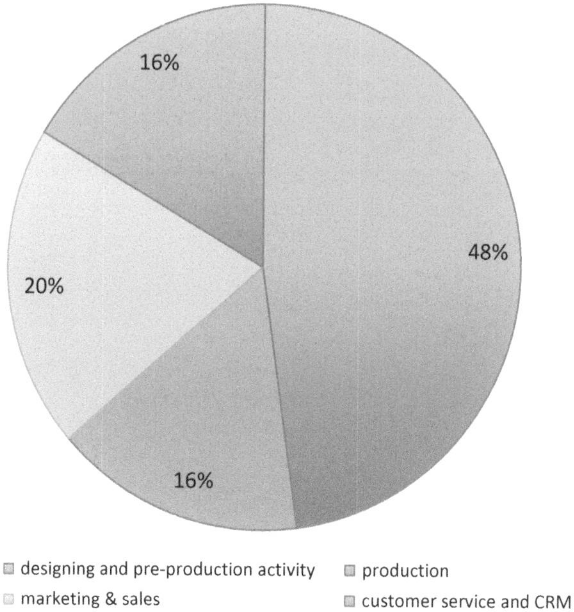

Fig. 3.3 The number of AI solutions supporting primary activities of the organization. (Source: Own elaboration)

1. **Fundamental systems**, enabling, for example, the implementation of basic research in the area of AI or the creation of advanced, proprietary solutions. This category includes, for example, libraries enabling the creation of AI systems or companies dealing with general artificial intelligence.
2. **Platforms** enabling independent, relatively simple creation of AI solutions.
3. Providers of intelligent services that enable access to their solutions or via a cloud (**SaaS**) or programming interfaces **API**. This category of systems is particularly important in the context of the development of cognitive networks.
4. **Companies using AI solutions.**
5. **Creators of ecosystems** intensively using AI solutions.

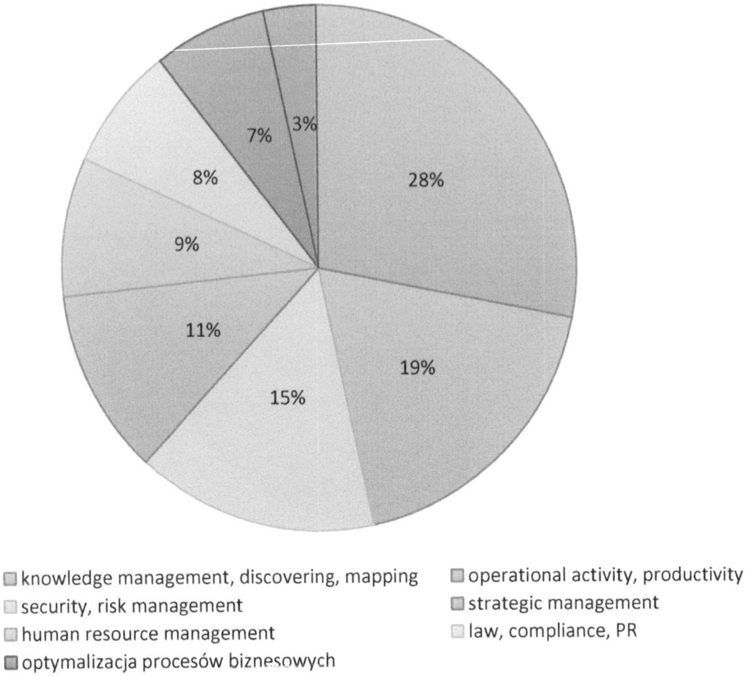

Fig. 3.4 AI solutions contributing to support activities in the value chain. (Source: Own elaboration)

The results of the research show that smart solutions available in the SaaS model or through APIs dominate (in total, they constitute 63% of all solutions). Slightly less numerous are fundamental solutions and DIY platforms (a total of 31%), while the least numerous are beneficiaries of these solutions (end clients and creators of ecosystems).

Summing up the quantitative analyses presented above, the following conclusions might appear:

1. **The AI branch** is just developing: technical and service infrastructure is already available; adoption in practice is still at a relatively low level.

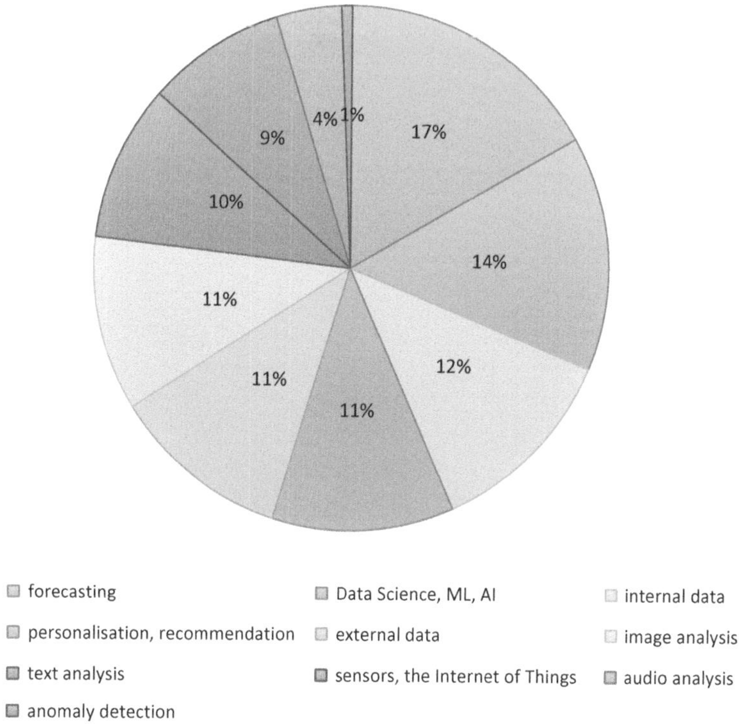

Fig. 3.5 AI systems supporting data analysis. (Source: Own elaboration)

2. **AI class solutions are more and more affordable for companies**: the solutions available in the SaaS or API model dominate, which minimizes costs and drastically reduces the implementation time in business practice.
3. **Companies interested in creating AI systems independently have virtually all tools at their disposal:** from free, constantly developed libraries to very easy to use Data Science platform.
4. AI systems contribute to the **renaissance of knowledge management methods**, offering qualitatively new sources and types of data, methods for their analysis, interpretation and visualization.

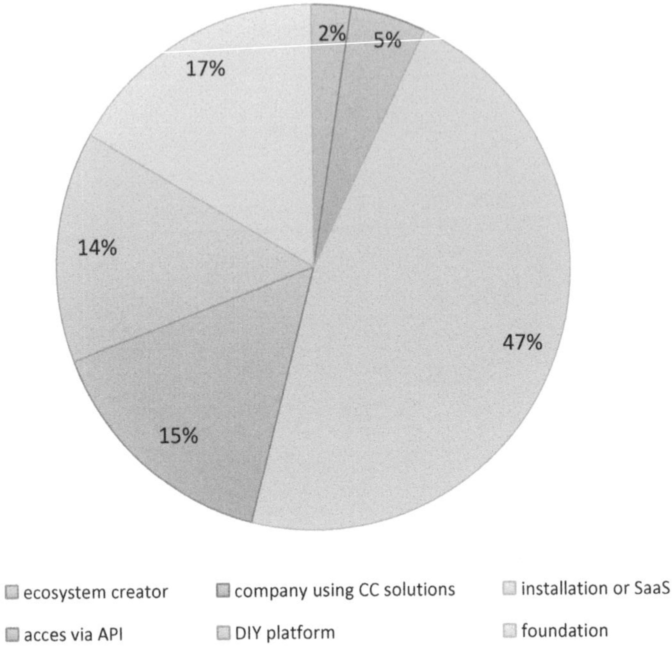

Fig. 3.6 Classification of AI systems according to the location in the technological chain. (Source: Own elaboration)

5. More and more systems are oriented towards automation and optimization of relations between **activities at the edge of the value chain:** data integration from sales processes, marketing and service with product and service design systems. In a sense, it causes a symbolic "closure" of the value chain into a "loop."

As can be seen, in the case of better accessibility to smart solutions, the basis for success in their implementation is managerial knowledge (e.g. the ability to form a good business case), not just the knowledge of technologies or AI methods.

3.2 Adoption of Artificial Intelligence Systems in Contemporary Organizations

3.2.1 Investments in AI and Adoption of This Class of Solutions

3.2.1.1 Stimulants of Investments in Digital Technologies

There are many different factors motivating the company to invest in information technologies. The Bloomberg company in its report on the impact of digital technologies on the energy sector (*Digitalization of Energy Systems* 2017) organizes them into the following categories (for simplicity, the list below omits factors directly related to the energy industry):

1. Economic factors:
   (a) reduction of operating costs,
   (b) higher revenues due to the reduced failure rate,
   (c) higher revenues due to the sales market expansion.
2. Technological advantage:
   (a) resource efficiency increase,
   (b) greater stability and predictability,
   (c) lower error costs:
      (i) better responsiveness,
      (ii) better detection of errors.
3. Income sources:
   (a) products and services,
   (b) new payment models,
4. Changes in regulations:
   (a) regulations for the protection of personal data GDPR,
   (b) change of ecological norms and goals,
   (c) development and modernization grants,
   (d) new security and integration requirements and standards.

5. Individual customer:
    (a) pressure,
    (b) resource owners,
    (c) governments,
    (d) regulators.
6. Industry pressure:
    (a) competition strategies,
    (b) regulatory pressure,
    (c) increase in resource costs.

An interesting stimulus of investment in the AI industry is the relation of the industry with education and research indicated in the AI Index report (Shoham et al. 2017). The authors of the report are interested in the relation between the intensity of research (measured by the number of publications devoted to AI), the number of students participating in AI courses and investments of venture capital funds in such solutions. It turns out (in great simplification and after normalization of these factors) that the increase in research intensity stimulates the increase in the number of students enrolled in the relevant courses, which is almost immediately followed by the increase in investment in AI. As can be seen, these three "worlds" are linked with each other: research stimulates the development of human resources, which then can develop business systems, which in turn stimulates further research.

Many of the above-mentioned factors motivate companies to implement artificial intelligence systems—the current state of these investments is presented below.

3.2.1.2 Investments in Artificial Intelligence Systems

According to the AI Index report quoted above (Shoham et al. 2017), in the United States since 2000, the number of AI startups has increased 14 times and is today (at the beginning of 2018) close to 700. At the same time, annual investments in such companies increased six times.

The McKinsey company in its report *Artificial Intelligence. The Next Digital Frontier?* (Bughin et al. 2017) estimates that investments in AI are currently dominated by the largest technology companies and in 2016 amounted to around USD 20–30 billion, 90% of which was spent on system development, and 10% on acquisitions of external companies. The largest companies investing in AI are IT companies (Google, Baidu, IBM, Facebook, Amazon, Apple and Salesforce), companies in the automotive industry (BMW, Tesla, Toyota) and broadly understood industry (ABB, Bosch, General Electric and Siemens). Investments of the investment funds were also significant, but much lower (USD 6–9 billion). Broadly understood technologies of machine learning had the greatest number of investments. The most popular narrow applications are computer vision, natural language processing, autonomous transport, robotics and virtual assistants. Mergers and acquisitions were motivated mainly by the desire to acquire talent rather than by economic criteria. Even the notion of acqui-hiring was being used meaning acquisition in order to gain experts. Interestingly, with the annual demand for AI specialists estimated at 10,000, the average "valuation" of the expert acquired in the acquisition process ranged between USD 5 and 10 million.

3.2.1.3 Characteristics of Companies with the Highest AI Adoption

Another interesting issue, in addition to the investments themselves, is **an implementation of AI solutions in practice**. In the cited study, McKinsey examined 3000 managers aware of the potential of AI solutions, from 10 countries and 14 industries, analyzing 160 different use cases. It turns out that only 20% of them have implemented AI solutions, while only 12% of 160 use cases are commercially implemented.

What does adoption of artificial intelligence look like in various industries? The greatest number of implementations of AI is in the digitally "saturated" technological industries: high technology and telecommunications, automotive and industrial, financial services, public utilities (e.g. energy), media, consumer packaged goods, transport and logistics as well as in trade. It turns out that the level of adoption correlates with the industry's digitalization index (in the McKinsey research, the MGI Digitization index was used for this purpose).

What is interesting and very important, the leaders of the AI implementation ranking invest the most in these technologies. This means that pioneers, who already have more experience than companies that do not use AI, definitely put more resources and efforts into these technologies. It can be expected that the "distance" in the adoption of AI will increase, and soon we will have to deal with a new division, not so much digital as "intelligent."

AI solutions are most often implemented in practice by big companies with higher capital (which is often associated with greater risk acceptance), good quality data and access to talented AI experts, both technological (programmers, Data Science specialists) and managers (aware of AI, able to create a good business case and implement such a solution).

These companies also have aggressive investment policies, wide (many different technologies) as well as deep (the same technology in many areas of activity). The factor that distinguishes these "pioneers" is also a high level of business complexity, both geographically and operationally. Their efficiency is largely determined by the quality of forecasting, accuracy and the speed of decisions and personalization of interaction with clients.

3.2.2 Key Success Factors

The creators of the McKinsey report cited above (Bughin et al. 2017) indicate five factors determining the effective transformation of the organization towards AI: good business case, solid data ecosystem, access to good AI techniques and tools, adaptation of business processes to the capabilities of AI and favorable organizational culture. Below, the most important of them are briefly described.

3.2.2.1 Business Cases

The ability to construct a good business case is, for many reasons, a critical determinant of the company's success in implementing AI.

First, it helps convince decision-makers to invest in this type of enterprise. AI technologies are difficult to understand, so when recommending a project to business sponsors, it is better to focus on potential benefits and costs rather than on the details of technologies and implementation methods.

Secondly, formulating project goals in business terms forces the implementation team to focus on the company's values and not just launching an attractive technology for engineers. In other words, the success of the project is measured by the benefit of the organization, not by technical parameters. This is particularly important for such risky and expensive projects as AI projects; therefore, flexible management methodologies are recommended, in which projects are implemented in small stages (sprints) focused on further increases in business value.

At the end, the first, even small, successes of AI projects with a good business case encourage further attempts. As a result, new ventures are easier to compete (at the stage of portfolio planning) with other projects in the organization.

The analyses of experts from the McKinsey company indicate that companies successfully implementing solutions of artificial intelligence focus on using its capabilities in activity groups close to the center of the value chain (i.e. more on design and production than e.g. marketing and service services). This is a significant difference compared to more generally understood digital projects, where client-oriented IT projects continue to dominate.

The main motivation of companies implementing AI in practice is the increase of revenues, market shares, profits, and not the reduction of costs.

For example (Bughin et al. 2017):

1. The French Airbus manufacturer implemented AI systems to support engineers in quick diagnosis and finding solutions to problems on the production line. The system has an ordered database of historical events (problem, its context, diagnosis, solution) and when a new problem occurs, it supports the employees by recommending them, in near-real time, the most probable solutions: this is possible in 70% of cases. As a result, the time to solve the problem is shortened, which

in turn results in reduced repair time and increased efficiency of the production process.
2. A similar solution is applied by British Petroleum. BP engineers have access to systems that in near-real time recommend optimal parameters of engineering works, such as machine settings, drilling parameters, and so on. This significantly increases the efficiency of work; by taking advantage of the best practices from the past, it shortens the time and increases the quality of activities.
3. Amazon, after the acquisition of the Kiva robot manufacturer, uses robots to automate transport and packaging in its warehouses. This results in shortening the packing time (so-called "Click to ship") from 60–75 min to 15 min, so even by 5–6 times, the increase in storage capacity by 50% (the use of the space, which has been reserved for people so far) and reduction in operating costs by 20%.
4. The German online store Otto.de uses predictive systems to forecast the level of demand for its goods: AI systems can predict the demand for the next 30 days with the 90% accuracy. This enables earlier, automatic ordering of goods from suppliers. Benefits: shortening the delivery time to the end customers (and, as a result, improving their satisfaction and company's competitive advantage), reducing transaction costs with suppliers (process automation, smaller share of human work).
5. Ping An, one of the largest insurance companies in China, uses face and voice recognition systems to support the lending process (as part of its scoring system). Thanks to this, the time is shortened and the quality of this process is improved.

As can be seen, the above examples of AI implementation projects bring tangible business benefits.

3.2.2.2 Transformation Strategy

The commitment of decision-makers, a good implementation strategy and a robust data ecosystem are the foundations necessary for the successful implementation of AI projects.

An interesting conclusion from McKinsey's research is that there a strong relationship between a company's determination to implement AI, and declared profit from operating activities. The "determination" of AI was described on the basis of the assessment of compliance with the statements such as: *Disrupting our industry using AI technology is at the core of our strategy, We have changed our longer-term corporate strategy to address the AI threat or opportunity disruption,* or, *We have developed a coordinated plan to respond to the longer-term corporate strategy.*

It turns out that the differences in the average profits of companies not implementing AI and companies with proactive AI strategy ("determined"), depending on the industry, range from 5 to even 20 percentage points (the largest differences can be observed in the healthcare industry, financial services and high technology). There are no grounds to look for cause-and-effect relations. For example, it may turn out that the side variable (mediator) is, for example, a high level of education and openness of decision makers to changes; nevertheless, this observation is certainly inspiring and gives a lot to think about).

The research conducted by MIT Sloan and the Boston Consulting Group indicates the need to develop a robust data ecosystem (Ransbotham et al. 2017). Efficient infrastructure and high quality processes data acquisition, storage, organization (integration, cleaning, enrichment) and analysis constitute the key conditions for the success of AI projects. It is worth emphasizing that in Data Science projects the time spent on collecting, organizing and preparing data for analysis may, according to various estimates, constitute 50 to 80% of the entire project; compare e.g. Lohr (2014).

Another factor of success is working out effective strategies for generating and implementing AI solutions. The purchase and "installation" of the AI solution do not guarantee the recovery of value from such a system. It is crucial to adjust (practice) the algorithms in their own context and on their own data, which, first of all, requires a straight information ecosystem and secondly, the ability to supervise and control the quality of the process of "training" algorithms.

For example: predictive service systems (recommending the optimal moment of repair of devices) depend heavily on the specifics of the use of the equipment. Agricultural tractors work differently and in different conditions than sports cars; it is practically always necessary to adapt AI algorithms to specific conditions. And this in turn requires an understanding of decision-makers, access to experts and implementation projects.

The strategies of acquiring the system (and, more generally, the outsourcing policy) are another important element of the AI strategy. One should be wary of the often used strategy for AI systems: "First check whether you can buy, then implement ready-made, and only if impossible: create your own." A lot of AI solutions are available "remotely" in the Software as a Service (SaaS) formula or via Application Programming Interface (API), which creates the temptation of quick and cheap implementation in order to quickly and cheaply check the business case. Although, this situation is quite common, a company should be aware of:

1. The fact that ready-made solutions of a given class (e.g. virtual agents supporting customer service) may not work in a given organization. A company should not discount such usage scenario solely on the basis of an initial bad experience: it may turn out that the same technology, after adapting to the specifics of the company's operation, will start to work very well.
2. There are many disadvantages to maintaining external AI services, for example, related to data security and operational risk (see e.g. Zawiła-Niedźwiecki and Byczkowski 2009), transfer of knowledge about customer behavior of the solution provider, lack of competence development in a company, and so on.

In the area project management methodologies, the creators of the MITSloan and BCG report (Ransbotham et al. 2017) recommend agile methodologies. This is related to the high level of uncertainty of such ventures:

1. There may be many unexpected problems at various stages of the project, which makes long-term planning of deadlines and budgets very difficult.

2. The same is true for the scope of the project: in the implementation process, some functionalities may be impossible to implement, but unexpected opportunities may also appear.

As a result, agile management methodologies (such as Scrum) in which projects are implemented in short, goal-oriented (business or functional scope) stages work best. The culture of openness to unexpected events and risk acceptance is also very important.

3.2.2.3 Adaptation of Processes and Development of Necessary Competencies

AI systems affect not only products and services, but also the processes of their delivery (basic and supporting activities in the value chain). For this reason, companies interested in maximum value recovery from AI implementations should skillfully adopt their own processes and organizational structures within them. Naturally, it also requires developing new competencies.

The key competencies for AI implementations will be described later in this study, here only the most important ones will be mentioned:

1. **The intuition of AI's capabilities among the management**, especially understanding the impact of this class of solutions on the company and its environment and understanding the role of data, algorithms and teaching processes.
2. **AI and Data Science skills**, namely, knowledge of AI methods and algorithms and the ability to design, test and implement production of such systems.
3. **Technical skills**, particularly the skill of programming such solutions and the management of appropriate infrastructure.

3.2.2.4 Managing Relations with Customers, Partners and Competitors

AI systems have an impact not only on the products and processes of their delivery, but also on the broadly understood company environment.

The organization implementing AI solutions should have developed management strategies in this area of relations with customers, partners and competitors.

In the case of customers, the key is ensuring trust (see Grudzewski et al. 2008). The vast majority of AI systems intensively use data on customer behavior, not only about customers' activities on websites, in social media or the use of mobile devices, but also the way of using different "things"—home appliances, cars, life-monitoring devices, televisions, and so on—and even identifying their emotions or intentions and affecting shopping behavior.

These are often very sensitive data: it is necessary to take care not only about the comfort of customers (e.g. by informing them about how this data is processed, stored or made available to external entities or giving the opportunity to view and edit this information), but also about the compliance with legal regulations (e.g. new very restrictive Personal Data Protection Regulation—GDPR, which has just entered into force in the European Union).

The key is also the strategy of relations with business partners. AI systems can be a threat to them, for example, by allowing them to be eliminated from the company's value chain. For this reason, it is very important to inform the partners early about the company's plans and their possible consequences and to support them in the transformation processes. It's not just about broadly understood social responsibility—partners are often a key element in the organization's value chain, they are not only dependent on cooperation with a given company, and changes that are too rapid can simply destroy the basics of traditional business (e.g. distribution or service).

Interestingly, AI systems make new forms of cooperation with competitors possible. This particularly applies to more and more integrated industry systems, for example, supporting intelligent farms. Companies that compete with each other must cooperate, for example, on the level of the data exchange standards development. As can be seen, AI favors the so-called coopetition and requires the development of the ability to create strategic alliances in new "smart" conditions.

3.2.2.5 Organizational Culture and Organizational Skills Conducive to the Implementation of AI Solutions

As already mentioned, companies with successful implementation of artificial intelligence solutions should have a specific organizational culture and specific skills. McKinsey experts (Bughin et al. 2017) have identified eight factors that distinguish AI's "pioneers":

1. Ability to cooperate effectively.
2. Openness to changes and new ideas.
3. Boards with vision and the desire for leadership necessary to manage in times of constant change.
4. Analytical skills better than the competition's.
5. Vision and planning in the long run.
6. Business strategy related to the technology strategy.
7. The ability to change existing products and services to maximize the value of new technologies.
8. Good and effective data governance.

As can be seen, in addition to technical capabilities, the support of decision-makers, strategic management and innovation-friendly organizational culture are very important for the success of AI.

3.2.3 Barriers and Risk Factors

3.2.3.1 Barriers to AI Adoption

AI implementations are of high risk. As it turns out, these factors strongly depend on the level of "maturity" of AI—the level of implementation of these solutions in a given organization.

MIT Sloan researchers and the Boston Consulting Group (Ransbotham et al. 2017) conducted research on 3000 managers from companies at various levels of adoption of AI solutions. Within this group 85% of managers believe in the potential of artificial intelligence, 25%

implement it in their companies, only 5% use it intensively and less than 39% have an AI strategy.

The authors of the report divided the surveyed companies into groups considering two dimensions: a degree of understanding of the possibilities and methods of AI and the level of their implementation. As a result, they identified four groups:

1. Pioneers (19% of respondents): companies that **understand and implement AI**.
2. Researchers (39% of respondents): companies that **understand, but do not implement AI**.
3. Experimentalists (13% of respondents): companies that **do not understand, but implement AI**.
4. Passive (36% of respondents): companies that **neither understand, nor implement AI**.

A small share of pioneers and a large share of passive companies is noteworthy. Experimentalists (who do not understand but implement) are a very interesting group.

The authors of the report identified the following barriers to the implementation of AI systems:

1. Difficulties in acquiring and developing talents.
2. Competing of AI projects with other projects in the company.
3. Safety aspects of systems using AI.
4. Cultural barriers in the AI adoption.
5. Limited (or lack of) technological capabilities (analytical, data management, IT, etc.).
6. Lack of leadership support for AI initiatives.
7. Unclear or lack of business cases for this type of projects.

The barriers mentioned above were ordered according to the significance for particular groups identified in the study: very important factors for pioneers and rarely indicated by "passive" group were placed on the top, while the factors important for "passive" and meaningless for pioneers were located on the bottom.

These observations can be treated as a foundation for the organization's AI maturity model.

For mature companies, such factors as clear business cases, support for leaders, capabilities and access to technology or cultural acceptance are not a major problem (in fact, these organizations have appropriate competencies in this area). The high weight of these factors for "passive" companies indicates, in turn, their deficits in these areas.

Passive companies, in turn, do not see problems with factors such as security aspects, attracting talents or cultural acceptance—this can most probably be justified simply by the lack of practical experience. For experienced companies (pioneers), implementing new projects and investing more and more intensively in AI—compare the report by Bughin et al. (2017)—the most important barriers are access to talents, competition with other projects and security.

3.2.3.2 The Risk of AI Projects

In addition to barriers to AI adoption, the analysis of risk factors related to the implementation of this class of projects is also important.

Ransbotham (2017) indicates the danger associated with hasty implementation of immature solutions. In his opinion, organizations will add complexity to their AI systems faster than they regain their value before they reach production readiness. As a result, AI systems will require greater involvement (service, management, etc.) than the current efforts of the employees they are to replace (e.g. imperfect solutions in customer service or dynamic pricing). In other words: the costs of handling immature solutions (training, assist, quality control, error correction) will be higher than the benefits of implementing them. Therefore, Ransbotham recommends caution in the form of

1. implementation of many mechanisms controlling the effects of AI;
2. AI testing and gaining experience in areas that are not risky and ensure quick and simple success;
3. high levels of thoughtfulness in the implementation of AI in areas where trust and reputation are important: it is easy to lose them, and it is difficult to recover them later (see Grudzewski et al. 2008).

Other risk factors identified by experts include mentioned earlier managers' conviction that the purchased solution is ready for use (no training required) or the risk of impairing the key competencies of the organization as a result of assigning relevant activities to AI systems (e.g. the knowledge about customer needs, security monitoring or broadly understood reactivity and flexibility). A separate category consists of the factors related to hazards in workplaces or the loss of customer trust.

3.2.4 Summary

The study "Five Management Strategies for Getting the Most From AI" (2017) summarizes the key success factors of AI projects in the following manner, based on the results of Bughin et al. (2017):

1. Orientation on growth rather than on cost cutting.
2. Investment in talent, both managerial and technical.
3. Openness to the revision of company's strategic goals: not only to protect what is already there, but also to design new business models and new products and services.
4. Relying on a solid digital basis (Data Governance).
5. Initiating, supporting and creating local AI ecosystems.

When deciding to launch the first AI projects, it is also worth conducting a multidimensional audit of the company's readiness for AI, trying to identify company's place in the classification proposed in the MIT Sloan and BCG report (Ransbotham et al. 2017) and addressing possible barriers and risk factors early enough.

3.3 The Impact of AI Systems on Activities in the Value Chain

3.3.1 Design

The development of advanced, intelligent technologies causes changes in expectations towards products created with their use. One of the results of the conducted research is the identification of possible changes in the design processes. The most important conclusions are presented below. They are divided into areas of expectations towards products and design methods, testing, modification and updating.

3.3.1.1 New Requirements for Products

Modern technologies and AI class systems allow for equipping products with intelligence, quality development of new interfaces, design of autonomous solutions that interact with the environment and constantly improve themselves and, as a result, enable the creation of new ecosystems and business models. Below, the most important areas where new design requirements may appear are briefly described.

Equipping Products with Intelligence

One of the most obvious expectations towards AI class systems is the addition of "intelligence" to products manufactured with their participation. Approximately 25% of the analyzed solutions offer technologies that enable the addition of intelligent functions.

The first group consists of companies offering components that form the foundation for autonomous systems. Among them, the solutions from the following areas can be mentioned:

1. Ground navigation (e.g. nuTonomy, Drive.ai, AiMotiv, MobileEye).
2. Air navigation (e.g. Skydio, Shield AI, Pilot.AI).
3. Sensors and image analysis (e.g. Chronocam, Pilot.AI, Lunit).
4. Advanced microscopes (e.g. Nanotronics).
5. Systems that adapt to the environment learn and interact with each other (e.g. Rethink Robotics, Osaro).

Image recognition systems constitute another category dedicated to various industries:

1. Automotive (e.g. Algocian, DriveAI, AdasWorks, MobilEye, nuTonomy, Nauto, AImotive, Chronocam).

2. Marketing, media and entertainment (e.g. Netra, CrowdFlower, Diffbot, Import.io, Affectiva).
3. Medical (e.g. Oncora, Arterys, Butterfly Network, Enlitic, Imagia, Chronocam, Lunit Inc., Nanit, Zebra Medical Vision).

The growing popularity of conversational interfaces stimulates the development of solutions enabling speech recognition, for example, Gridspace, Talkiq, Nexidia, Capio, MindMeld, Clover, Qurious AI, Clarabridge, CrowdFlower, Deepgram and Snips.

The category of solutions integrating data from various sources (e.g. Twillio) and platforms enabling building comprehensive AI systems for various industries (e.g. Sentient or Predix.io) are also worth distinguishing.

Qualitatively New Interfaces

Advanced image and speech recognition systems enable the creation of new communication interfaces both at the level of user interaction with a product and an organization itself. This area is a very good example of "coupling" of technology development with changing consumer habits.

One of the strongest current trends is the development of the conversational interfaces. They enable communication of the end user with the system via a natural language, and what happens even more often, with the use of the audio channel. The most advanced solutions of this class can be found in Amazon products (e.g. Amazon Echo, using Alexa's technology), Apple personal assistants (Siri), Google and Microsoft (Cortana).

One of the motivations for the development of these types of solutions for the largest global companies is the strive to create an ecosystem of services based on a single, user-friendly interface. However, it turns out that companies that do not have such ambitious aspirations can also create their own solutions using the technologies of companies such as Twilio, Capio, MindMeld or Mobwoi.

More advanced interfaces use technologies of virtual or augmented reality. In the case of virtual reality, the users do not have direct contact with the physical environment in which they are located, which is most often possible due to the use of glasses completely cutting off the image from the environment. An example of this is the Oculus VR system. On the other hand, the solutions of augmented reality impose a digital layer for the real image, enriching in this way the user's experience. One of the first solutions of this class was the Google Glass system, and currently (2017) Microsoft is starting to become the leader with the HoloLens solution.

Augmented reality can have a huge impact on the development of methods of designing and manufacturing products and, more generally, on the evolution of future occupations. Challenges related to the huge dynamics of development of AI class systems and their impact on the role of human in a society will be addressed later in this chapter, but here, it should be emphasized that one of the possible options will be cohabitation of people with machines: a form of cooperation in which intelligent systems "learn" from people, and people increase their abilities, thanks to machines. Such processes are already taking place on production lines, where human workers are supported by cobots (collaborative robots) and augmented reality.

For example, solutions of HoloLens support design processes (through visualization of the designed solutions in reality and simulations of their operations), production or service (e.g. through remote monitoring and control). In addition, they can be used in education or to ensure security. As a result, they can contribute to the dissemination of AI class solutions due to drastic improvement of the quality of interaction between people and machines.

Another class of solutions in the area of new interfaces comprises business agents. While personal assistants (e.g. Amazon Alexa, Google Now or Apple Siri) support the user in their daily life, personal agents constitute an interface between the client (usually an individual) and the organization. It is also worth mentioning technologies enabling independent creation of business agents like Semantic, Snips. Kitt.ai, Kasisto and selected IBM Watson services.

The last trend that is worth mentioning in the context of new interfaces is replacing physical components with digital elements. Such solutions can be found more and more often, for example in cars, where traditionally mechanical elements of the desktop (e.g. speedometer or tachometer) are replaced with digital displays. This approach is not only cheaper, but gives designers a much greater opportunity to update and personalize the product. For example, as the system is improved, the car manufacturer can remotely update the interface software or adjust the range of displayed information to an individual user preferences (so-called adaptive interfaces).

Continuous Self-Improvement

It can be expected that another new requirement for the designed products will be their ability for continuous self-improvement. This is related to the development of methods in the area of unsupervised learning, especially as to the ability to dynamically adapt learning strategies to the current context (predictive learning).

To achieve this, in the design process, it is recommended to plan to equip products with communication interfaces for algorithms marketplaces (e.g. Algorithmia) and the ability to select and implement the best structures of knowledge and algorithms in a given context.

As a result, the product will be able to continuously update its knowledge on the basis of its own experience as well as to use global libraries of algorithms generated by the community and other machines connected to the system.

Interactions with Other Machines

The ability of continuous self-improvement described above, due to the integration with external knowledge bases and communication with other machines, indicates another desirable feature of all ecosystems: the ability to maximize the network effect through continuous exchange of "experiences." The architecture of the AI class solution (understood as a system of communicators) should enable continuous learning of the entire system on the basis of the experience of individual devices.

The growing skills and autonomy of AI class solutions can lead to increasing competencies. In the so-called programmatic marketing, the systems representing companies interested in broadcasting advertisements online can buy advertising spaces in the advertising marketplaces (e.g. Google Ad Exchange). On the other hand, companies interested in broadcasting advertisements on their own websites may order them to be sold to IT systems representing them in such marketplaces. As a result, in the virtual space, the transaction is concluded between two machines representing their employers. Similar processes take place on the financial and even recruitment markets (e.g. Wade and Wendy).

Therefore, the development of methods from the area of machines marketing should be expected. Since the algorithms are more and more often responsible for purchasing processes, in order to be able to sell successfully, it is recommended to develop individual algorithms that can effectively sell products to buyer algorithms. For this reason, another desirable feature of new products may be the ability to identify the current needs of algorithms operating on stock exchanges and inference based on the acquired knowledge about the current intentions of organizations using them. It is possible to use methods from the area of behavioral profiling of people for this purpose; in this case, however, the purchase needs profiles of algorithms to some extent reflect the intentions of their clients.

The development of this class of solutions is possible due to the achievements of a mature field of data exchange between machines (M2M: Machine-2-Machine).

Ensuring the Autonomy of Solutions

Modern devices generate huge amounts of data. As a result, in order to be able to function autonomously in the real environment, they must be able to take effective actions without contact with the central system (e.g. a server available in the "cloud").

This generates a further requirement for newly designed products: the ability to run ML algorithms right away on the device, without continuous communication with the servers (so called edge computing, see Levine 2016). In special cases, this may mean:

- generating data that supply algorithms immediately in a form ready for processing by machine learning algorithms (referred to as ML),
- ensuring high-energy efficiency of processors thanks to, e.g. architecture dedicated to ML calculations. This is especially desirable in the case of devices that have to function for a long time in a state without charging batteries, e.g. mobile solutions).

The Maximum Use of New Service Capabilities and After-Sales Service

One of the key results of the conducted research is the visible impact of AI class systems on the integration of various phases of the product life cycle. This is manifested particularly by changing the place, time and methods of testing, updating and servicing products (which will be presented in more detail below). The result is a reduction and change in the cost structure of these processes, and a prerequisite for achieving these benefits to design the product so that it uses the potential of new methods of service and repair. For this reason, the methods of their updating and after-sales service should be taken into consideration already at the stage of the product design.

Concentration on Systems, Not Discrete Products

Porter and Heppelmann (2014) point to another important requirement for new products as a consequence of the dissemination of "smart, connected products": a necessity to focus on systems, not discrete products.

When designing a product, it is necessary to consider the ecosystem in which it will function. John Deere tractors, for example, will probably work within the wider ecosystem of the smart farm, which will force the exchange of data not only with John Deere solutions but also with other companies' systems (e.g. responsible for hydration or other areas). As a result, they should be able to communicate with other components of the ecosystem and this means there is a need for appropriate communication protocols (downloading and sending data) and planning ways of using this data in the future (e.g. for product development, forecasting, updating price lists or even changes in a business model).

Hoang and Rothaermel (2016) illustrated the idea of generating competitive advantages due to alliances based on data exchange with the example of cooperation between BMW, Daimler and Volkswagen in the development of the HERE company. Organizations, which compete with each other, decided to jointly develop a real-time platform showing road conditions (traffic jams, weather, expected route time, etc.) based on data obtained from sensors installed in cars manufactured by partners—brakes, wipers, lights, geolocation systems or cameras. In addition to offers for customers, the platform aims to promote business cooperation with individual clients, insurance companies or local authorities. None of these companies would be able to provide sufficient data on their own to create a reliable system—but together it was possible.

It is worth remembering that in addition to quality and functionality of systems for customers, the product's ability to function in the ecosystem of already existing solutions is becoming more and more important. It raises many new strategic challenges and questions such as: "*Do you create your own standard or do you use an existing one? Do you want to create your own ecosystem? Do you want to engage in an existing, commercial standard, or support open standards? Do you want to concentrate on creating a platform that will facilitate the operation of other entities?*" These and many similar questions point to the need to focus not only on the features and functionalities of discreet products but rather on their place in the entire ecosystem of solutions.

Support for New Business Models

A simple consequence of the previous paragraph is the issue concerning a product support for new business models. It can be implemented in at least two ways:

1. Creating a platform connecting various entities.
2. Transition from the transaction model to the "product as a service" model.

An example of the first approach is Uber. It is the most often identified with the competition for local taxi carriers, yet in fact, it is a company investing large funds in artificial intelligence and creating a platform that makes it possible to earn money for other entities on the basis of the logistics system based on the drivers cooperating with Uber. For example, see http://developer.uber.com; other companies can use Uber drivers to create fast parcel delivery services, restaurants provide food to their clients, and hotels encourage travelers to take advantage of their own offers.

The product model as a service is yet another very strong trend that began to grow dynamically due to the dissemination of the Internet of Things and in-depth analysis of data from sensors. Nowadays, most companies (but also more and more often individual customers) prefer solutions that minimize investment costs with the full acceptance of the higher variable costs associated with it. To put it simply: a customer would rather have access to the service offered by the device than to be its owner.

The simplest examples are city bike systems. Instead of buying and moving your own bike, it is more convenient to rent a bicycle from one position and set it aside at the destination. This makes it easier to transport the bike itself, but also does not enforce its purchase. In the case of companies, the sharing of printers and copying machines in the model of a monthly payment for the number of printed or copied pages, fleets of cars made available in the form of leasing and even making tools available in the Pay-Per-Use model are all increasingly common—see, for example, Hilti's offer *Tools on demand*. From the producer's perspective, solutions of this type are a high risk factor and a challenge that can be minimized due to the in-depth analysis of data generated by systems and devices during their use by end users. Crossing this barrier, however, becomes, in the case of success, a source of a strong competitive advantage.

Implementation and Monitoring of "Ethical" Criteria

The last requirement, which may seem exotic at first glance, yet which is becoming more and more often treated seriously by experts, is the need to implement and monitor ethical criteria of AI systems. Artificial intelligence, CC systems or robotics will undoubtedly have a huge impact on humanity. Apart from the obvious benefits, they can, however, generate threats with often-unpredictable consequences.

For this reason, works on the creation of ethical standards for AI systems is underway (see e.g. https://futureoflife.org/ai-principles/). It can be expected that the design of products in accordance with these guidelines, and later, monitoring the functioning of such systems, will soon become not only an ethical but also legal obligation (the need to comply with the standards set by regulators).

3.3.1.2 New Design Methods

AI class systems can not only improve the quality or the functionality of products but also significantly affect the design process itself. Below, the way in which the solutions analyzed during the tests change the methods of value creation for the client, improve the design processes and generate the need to change the methodologies and rules of these processes is indicated.

The Use of Data to Increase the Value for the End User

In very competitive markets, more and more often companies have to compete not only with the quality or price of products but also with other values important to users. For example, the best practices of using the product by other users can be such a value.[1] Traditional companies have been building their own best practice bases for years; however, nothing prevents us from using appropriately processed data generated by products in the process of their exploitation by end users. For this reason, new products should be designed in such a way that the maximum use of data on their exploitation is a value in itself for the end user.

An example of using the best practices of the product exploitation to increase its value is Asana: a popular system supporting project management. In addition to its rich functionality, it offers many usage scenarios in various industries and situations. This increases the quality for those who decide to choose a system of this type: they receive not only a tool, but above all, proven methods of its use.

In the case of designing new products and services using AI solutions, it is possible to conceive a business model in which the product itself is sold at a relatively low price, while the producer earns on the sale of methods of its use. The detailed data on the manner of use, context and effects of actions after processing by analytical systems enable identification of behavioral patterns and the best practices. As a result, at the very beginning of using the product, the new client will receive recommendations of the best possible methods of its use, which will significantly increase their satisfaction. In the extreme cases, you can imagine a model in which the user receives a product for free, and pays for personalized recommendations for its use in a given situation.

Using AI Class Systems to Improve Solution Design Processes

Out of more than 323 analyzed solutions, almost 30% supported, to a smaller or greater degree, the processes of designing new products. It can, therefore, be assumed that the design stage is currently one of the key areas in which AI solutions are used.

The first group of solutions supporting design are advanced, industrial expert systems such as Predix, C3IoT, Maana or SightMachine. By integrating data from many different devices and entire factories, they help formulate and verify various hypotheses that may later be the basis for implementing new solutions or optimizing current processes.

Artificial intelligence is also successfully used in the medical and pharmaceutical industry, especially in drug design processes (e.g. Atomwise, Numerate, Recursion Pharmaceuticals, DeepGenomics or

TwoXar). In this case, the advanced modeling methods drastically shorten the time of designing new particles that are the candidates for the so-called active substances in innovative medicines.

Solutions from the area of the Internet of Things and advanced data mining are also used in an interesting way in agriculture (e.g. SkyCatch, Kindred, BlueRiver, Mavrx, Tule, Trace Genomics, TerraVion, Trimble or Udio). In this industry, the spectrum of applications of new technologies is very wide: from monitoring the state of hydration, through modeling the optimal structure of crops to monitoring their health. It is worth emphasizing that there are many advanced solutions dedicated to the agricultural industry, which makes the development of the smart farming real.

Automotive is another industry where AI can significantly support design activities. Among the analyzed cases, solutions of such companies as Drive.ai, AdasWorks, Mobileye, nuTonomy and Auro Robotics should be underlined. They offer components that extend the capabilities of cars (with the focus put on autonomous transport) as well as support the processes of designing traditional vehicles.

Due to the large number of generated data and the high dynamics of the markets, the industry to which many AI class solutions are dedicated is the financial industry. Systems such as the Sentient, Quandl, Ayasdi, DataRobot, Yseop, Paxata, Trifacta and Yhat analyze large amounts of data, often in near-real time, and on the basis of the conclusions of these analyses they design investments as well as new financial products.

New Methodologies for Solution Design, Modularization

Among the analyzed 323 cases (see Appendix 3 of Chap. 5), nearly 50% of solutions are offered in the Software as a Service (SaaS) model, while nearly 15% provide an application programming interface (API). Such a formula for providing advanced services has large consequences, both for the design process and the economics of using these solutions.

The provision of services in the SaaS formula or through the API means that you can quickly incorporate them into your own solutions with relatively low costs. As a result, the creation of even very advanced AI class systems can be compared to the assembly of a larger whole of independent blocks: the API interfaces, in this case, function as "connectors" between the blocks.

This has huge consequences for the process of solutions design as well as for further use of them. Virtually every designer has to make decisions as to what to create in-house, what to commission to produce outside, and which components to buy as ready-made products. These decisions depend particularly on the already possessed resources (especially, competence and technology), the investment budget, the planned launch date, industry specifics and legal regulations.

In a very large approximation, the creation of solutions from those available on the market is fast, cheap, guarantees development in the future and as a result carries little risk. On the other hand, almost all knowledge on the details of the solution's operation is on the part of the supplier, and in the case of digital products (the value of which is based on data), additionally, a set of data on user behavior goes to the component supplier. As a result, the creators of solutions using AI class systems face a big dilemma: create a solution quickly and cheaply, but ultimately become dependent on the supplier, or invest in their own competencies and technologies (which is expensive and takes a lot of time), but thanks to this, build a lasting competitive advantage.

It can be expected that these challenges will provoke project teams to develop new organizational methods. They can be reduced to a strong integration of the customer's R&D teams and the external service provider. For the purposes of this study, and perhaps also future research, we propose this method to be called Dev-ExP: Development and external Provider team). The teams of suppliers better know the current possibilities and limitations of the solutions used in the design process, and in the future they will be responsible for the maintenance and development of products. Both of these factors point to the need for close cooperation between customer and supplier teams, and in a sense broaden the concept of organization.

New Rules for Managing Project Teams

Porter and Heppelmann (2014) point to the increase in the interdisciplinarity of design processes. In the past, industrial devices contained mainly mechanical components; nowadays, widely understood electronics and digital solutions are an integral part of practically every device. What is more, their software not only operates locally (on the device) but it must also communicate with other devices in close proximity (e.g. on a smart farm) or with central servers in the cloud (this communication must also be usually bilateral).

For this and many other reasons, new products should be designed according to new rules. They should enable standardization of devices by updating software, personalization or remote monitoring and service. Designing should also take into account the full potential of digital solutions, particularly those resulting from the possibility of monitoring the use of solutions by end users.

Therefore, project teams should be interdisciplinary (and particularly engage specialists in the areas of data analysis and IT), while the processes of designing, maintaining and developing products should be integrated with each other (which is actually implemented, e.g. within the Dev-Ops (development and operations) concept, in which the software development and operation teams are unified). The high dynamics of technology changes indicates the need to develop and implement flexible project management methodologies.

3.3.1.3 New Methods for Testing Products

As can be seen, AI class systems significantly affect the requirements for new products and the design processes themselves. It turns out that the methods for testing prototypes and ready-made solutions are also changing.

According to Porter and Heppelmann (2014), today, we are dealing with continuous quality management processes. In the past, designed devices were tested in laboratories, but today continuous real-time access to detailed data from devices allows for continuous testing and refinement. As a result, the concepts of "testing" and "laboratory" are considerably extended, both in time and space.

Additionally, due to the Internet of Things, it is possible to transfer the testing process directly to the customer. This process is the simplest in the case of web or mobile applications: advanced reporting systems in near-real time provide insight into how to use programs, and the combination of user profiles with their online behavior gives an incredibly complete picture of the value offered to customers. The supplements of this are the systems supporting the search of target groups (e.g. Deep 6 AI analytics for drug testing) and solutions using machine learning to test digital solutions (e.g. Rainforest system).

Not only is the place of testing changing, but also its moment. In the past, the products were tested before making them available to the customer. Today, prototypes are more and more often checked in the process of use. Users of modern mobile phones or computers in particular experience this.

As a result, testers also change; once, they were employees of dedicated quality control teams, today, more and more often these are advanced users who agreed to it (participation in the so-called beta testing programs). They are usually friendly to the company, fond of novelties and understanding customers, which is why feedback from such tests is particularly useful.

The last change in product testing processes concerns the methods of collecting information about test results. It used to be observations and surveys, today, these are more and more often data sets automatically generated by various types of sensors. This naturally changes the methods of data interpretation and inference about test results.

3.3.1.4 New Methods of Modifying and Updating Products

The last area of design, which can be significantly influenced by AI class systems, are the methods of product modification and update. One of the most interesting examples is the Tesla car, which is compared to a big smartphone by some customers: its software is updated regularly, affecting not only minor functionalities (e.g. changes to the computer interface) but also more advanced ones related to, for example, engine operation.

Porter and Heppelmann (2014) draw attention to the fact that it was once produced in discrete generations (a given generation, e.g. a car, had a strictly closed range of functionality, design, etc.), while the possibilities of modern digital systems allow for a departure from this model towards a virtually continuous update process. In other words, the mechanical component of the product will remain reasonably stable, while the main carrier of the new value will be the software. This trend is particularly visible in personal computers: the same computer can be used for many years, and its value for the user lies primarily in software that can by dynamically updated.

The upgrade costs are also constantly decreasing. Once, in traditional products, modernization required changes of physical parts, which generated not only material costs but also human costs (service). The update of "smart" products is often a remote software update, which is not only fast, but also cheap. A quite exotic but interesting example are professional sound systems for musicians: once the opportunity to achieve different sounds required access to various amplifiers, today, there is a large offer of companies that offer software professionally simulating the sound of even exotic, real solutions.

Finally, it is worth mentioning that digital products greatly simplify the adaptation of products to local markets (i.e. a broadly defined location), and thus reduces the costs of foreign expansion.

3.3.1.5 New Planning Methods

Material Requirements Planning (MRP), demand for company's own products and services, or phenomena in the environment that may affect them (e.g. demographic changes, natural disasters or epidemics of illnesses) are an important elements of planning processes and, in a sense, "designing" of further processes of producing and delivering goods and services.

McKinsey's experts, in their report on the potential of artificial intelligence in business (Bughin et al. 2017) put "planning and forecasting" in the first of four separated groups of company's activities: Project, Product, Promote and Provide. This somewhat simplified, but also clear classification allows for the capture of the interesting phenomenon resulting from the digitization of business processes: continuous feedback from markets and systems of product use analysis by customers necessitates their (products) frequent updates and as a result reduce production series and place forecasting and planning in the group of project activities.

In the manufacturing industry, the predictive potential of artificial intelligence systems is used for forecasting a company's own demand for materials and components and the assessment of suppliers' and partners' reliability (Bughin et al. 2017). As a result, companies can automate and optimize negotiation processes with suppliers and business partners, which directly translates into shortening the time of these processes and reducing transaction costs (the reduction of employment while servicing negotiation processes).

The commercial industry uses artificial intelligence systems in a similar way. The German giant of e-commerce sales Otto.de, is able to predict the demand for its assortment of products for 30 days in advance with 90% precision. It enables automatization of product ordering from suppliers before receiving individual customers' orders, leading to a decrease in transaction costs, significant shortening of delivery time, improvement in customer satisfaction, with a resulting competitive advantage.

In the healthcare industry, AI algorithms support epidemic forecasting and classification of patients due to the risk of disease. This improves the effectiveness of preventive measures and reduces the total cost of treatment.

In **education**, AI systems are used for identification of factors determining the development of individual students and forecasting the demand for specialists with specific competencies. It improves educational processes (support in discovering company's own strengths, personalization) and planning the educational programs.

3.3.1.6 Challenges

As can be seen, AI class systems can provide many new values at the product design stage. Along with opportunities, however, challenges also appear. Below, the most important problems that managers may encounter at various levels of management are presented:

1. Strategic decision related to the choice of place in the industry ecosystem. How could the existing ecosystem fit in? Or maybe we should create our own? Or design and implement a platform that allows other entities to share their own services?
2. Designing products so that their further development could be possible without significant interference in the hardware part. It will increase their lifespan, facilitate future updates and remote service, reduce costs and change their structure.
3. Designing new models of financial and operational controlling considering the various architectures of AI class solutions. Especially:
   (a) calculation of future variable costs in the case of using smart components from external suppliers and making them available by suppliers in the Pay-Per-Use model;
   (b) the use of data generated by products to assess the effectiveness of new business models, e.g. the offer of proprietary solutions in the Pay-Per-Use model.

3.3.1.7 New Competencies

In order to fully release the potential of AI class systems at the design stage of products for those responsible for these processes, we recommend mastering the following competencies:

1. The knowledge of methods and techniques that enable equipping products and services with "intelligence."
2. The ability to design systems in particular that would use the acquired experience for continuous self-improvement; for example, using the mechanisms of reinforcement learning.
3. The ability to design products so that they meet the company's strategic assumptions in the area of creating their own ecosystems or adapting to the existing ones.

4. The ability to use data generated by products to create a new value for the customer.
5. The awareness of the possibility of using CC class solutions to support design processes.
6. The awareness of the need to develop new methods for designing solutions.

3.3.2 Production and Logistics

The previous chapter indicated the manner in which AI class systems could affect changes in the processes of designing new products and services. One of the possible consequences is the blurring of the boundary between the processes of designing, servicing and the development of products. This presents further arguments for the need to revise the design—production—service cycle as a sequence of operation groups, each of which adds value to the value chain.

The first part presents various solutions which increase the autonomy of the components of production systems. The second and third parts show how modern systems enabling the management of data generated by sensors can affect the place of production processes in the value chain. The third part indicates the challenges for future production systems; in particular, the impact of AI class systems on changes in the production process, the need to redefine the term "factory" and possible changes in the role of people in these areas of the organization.

3.3.2.1 Autonomous Systems on the Production Line and in Logistics

Autonomous systems on the production line and in logistics through automation lead to shortened production and delivery times, fewer errors, increased production, reduced costs, (mainly human work) and improved safety. No wonder then that the adaptation of robots (both autonomous and cooperating with people) is very popular among many companies and is the source of new economic phenomena (e.g.

transferring production from Asia to Europe—see the Adidas autonomous production line) and is treated as one of the pillars of Industry 4.0.

Among the analyzed systems supporting production, special attention is paid to the delivery solutions provided by the autonomous robots. In addition to solutions that fully automatize the production line (e.g. ABB systems), machines cooperating with people (co-bots) are becoming increasingly popular, offered, for example, by Rethink Robotics. Their most important distinguishing feature is the ability to recognize images and continuous learning. As a result, they can support people in simple assembly work, quality control, moving things, and so on, while generating significantly lower costs. Robots of this class can use their own software or IT systems of companies specializing in creating programs that increase the efficiency of autonomous robots, such as Osaro.

Autonomous transport systems on the production line constitute a separate category, for example, Jaybridge, Fetch Robotics, Clearpath Robotics or OTTO Motors. These companies offer both ready-to-run solutions and systems for creating their own autonomous transport robots.

Autonomous transport in warehouses is another technology that optimizes logistics processes. Ocado, a British Internet supermarket, practically fully automated its warehouses: autonomous robots collect products ordered by customers, pack and pass to drivers for delivery. In the next step, the dedicated AI system recommends optimal delivery routes. The benefits include reduced labor costs, acceleration and optimization of processes as well as the improvement in stock turnover, increased effective warehouse space (no need to create paths for staff) and improved safety.

The group of solutions that has probably the greatest impact on increasing the efficiency of logistics activities is route optimization systems, for example, Routific, Uptake or ClearMetal. A considerable value is also added by the solutions facilitating anomaly detection and forecasting vehicle technical inspections, for example, Acerta or Pitstop. The autonomous air transport solutions are also worth mentioning, such as Skydio or Osaro.

Industry solutions are also interesting. It turns out that the market of robots dedicated to agriculture is very mature. Systems of companies such as Harvest Automation, Tule and Blue River support not only transport but also autonomous irrigation of farms and, for example, Mavrx, DroneDeploy or Skycatch remote field monitoring (images from aircraft, satellites or drones) and crop optimization.

3.3.2.2 Predictive Systems in Production and Logistics

Predictive systems form a separate category of AI applications in production and logistics prediction systems. They enable forecasting failures, demand for components and potential thefts (e.g. of electricity or gas).

They enable service inspections of devices not on the basis of time or mileage, but on the actual risk of failure (predictive maintenance). This reduces costs in a natural way (the review is carried out only when it is necessary) with simultaneous risk minimization (the sensors placed in the machines are able to give an early indication of the risk of failure).

The benefits of implementing such solutions include reducing the risk of breakdowns, reducing repair costs and, as a result, reducing total operating costs.

In this category of solutions it is worth distinguishing anomaly detection systems. They allow identification of abnormal states, which may signal a failure (e.g. on the production line), the risk of quality deterioration, or attack (e.g. in IT security systems). Increasing the number of data of various types coming from industrial systems (Big Data) and resulting from the automation of drastic acceleration of processes in practice enforce the "transfer" of monitoring and control activities to machines: the human is no longer able to independently analyze and interpret such large and varied data flowing in a very short time.

It is worth stressing that failure forecasting systems integrate many different methods and technologies. For example, in the energy sector reviews of energy transmission lines involve:

1. Autonomous drones with implemented image recognition systems, which, flying along power lines, observe their condition and inform operators about registered suspicious places.

2. Anomaly identification system and the Internet of Things sensors (so-called smart grids) that transmit signals of failure to operators.
3. Forecasting systems using machine-learning algorithms to predict types of failure, its place and moment.

3.3.2.3 Knowledge Management and the Internet of Things

Production systems generate huge amounts of data. To release their potential, they need to be aggregated, integrated with external systems and the necessary information and knowledge should be extracted from them.

The solutions by companies such as Splunk, Sentenai, Konux or Logz.io. enable aggregation of data from the Internet of Things. By using highly advanced information technologies, they are a key infrastructure component that ensures not only aggregation but also adapting the pace of this process to the speed and volume of generated data, their "cleaning" and protection.

Data from given devices often gain value only after the integration with external information systems. Very interesting examples of this solution are the following:

- Orbital Insight and Planet.os providing satellite images and climatic data, respectively;
- aiWARE, DroneDeploy and Skycatch that use drones to share data for the industry;
- Mavrx and Prospera for field monitoring (agriculture) from the air;
- TerrAvion supporting genetic analyses of crops.

The data collected and integrated with external data must be sorted out and properly interpreted. The conducted research indicated the following subcategories of IT systems in this area:

- Preparation of data for analysis, e.g. Datalogue;
- Data interpretation and pattern identification, e.g. Preferred Networks; Splunk, Paxata and Kensho;

- Predictive analytics, e.g. Imubit and Konux;
- Discovering knowledge, e.g. Maana, SparkCognition, Cycorp, Uptake, Alluvium or Sight Machine.

The systems supporting discovering knowledge are particularly complex. Very different forms, large volume, generation speed and significance for various aspects of the production process force the creation of new forms of presenting and organizing knowledge. An interesting example is the Maana Knowledge Graph, which points to the interesting trend of production management as areas shaping the field of knowledge management.

3.3.2.4 Information Systems Based on Data from Sensors

The infrastructure outlined above (systems enabling the generation, aggregation, integration and interpretation of data) is the basis of a new generation of business information systems (hereinafter BIS) based on the Internet of Things.

BIS has evolved from systems supporting the management of material requirements needs management (MRP: Material Requirements Planning), through production management systems (MRP II: Manufacturing Resource Planning) to IT systems that integrate not only the entire organization (ERP: Enterprise Resource Planning), but also customers (CRM: Customer Relationship Management) and supply chain management (SCM: Supply Chain Management). In most cases, the data source were transactional databases, largely logistic, production and financial.

The Internet of Things makes it possible to create a separate class of business information systems based on sensor data. Very good examples are the solutions of Predix, which belongs to General Electric (GE), and C3IoT.

Predix implements the GE digital strategy. It provides clients with solutions enabling a creation of advanced analytical and industrial applications using data generated by devices (mainly machinery) provided by GE. The goal, apart from the obvious value for the end customer, is to create an ecosystem that integrates users of GE solutions: both customers and partners (hardware, IT and implementation). Due to the new quality of this class of solutions and their potentially large impact on the industry, the details of the Predix systems are presented below.

Predix (see www.predix.io) divides its solutions into two categories: operational services and analytical services. Operational services include solutions enabling

- remote starting and monitoring of devices;
- communication: M2M (Machine-to-Machine), M2C (Machine-to-Cloud) and M2H (Machine-to-Human);
- digital simulation of machines (digital twins);
- analytical systems;
- anomaly detection;
- access and security management;
- management of the smart background, e.g. traffic management, intelligent traffic light systems, intelligent parking lots, monitoring and planning of pedestrian traffic, analysis of indoor users' movement (entry/exit time, location, direction of traffic, etc.), the analysis of environmental conditions (lighting, temperature, the number of people, etc.);
- geolocation services (location and movement analysis, intelligent mapping);
- environments for application developers;
- operational management (service management, event management, log system reporting, automation of logistics and production processes).

In turn, analytical systems enable:

- anomaly detection,
- exploration and data preparation,
- text analysis and text drilling,
- analysis of time series,
- data attribute management,
- machine learning,
- network analysis,

- predictive modeling,
- quality control,
- signal processing.

The modular structure of the system allows Predix/GE customers a relatively simple configuration of their own solutions from previously prepared modules and creating proprietary, advanced programs. The modules are delivered by Predix as well as by a growing group of partner companies. Clearly, GE's strive to create an ecosystem based on its own infrastructure, co-created by clients and business partners, is clearly visible.

C3IoT offers similar solutions. In addition to the integration platform, the environment enabling the collection of all data in one place (data lake) and the environment for creators, C3IoT offers applications oriented on the implementation of strictly defined industry needs, in particular,

- predictive maintenance,
- capital asset planning,
- energy management,
- fraud detection,
- supply network risk,
- sensor health monitoring,
- monitoring of the state of the machine parks
- vehicle fleet, smart grid and energy customer analytics.

As mentioned earlier, an important complement to this category of systems are solutions that enable the building of knowledge structures based on sensor data, offered by companies such as Cycorp or Maana.

Industrial information systems based on the Internet of Things such as the Predix or C3IoT solutions presented above have a different architecture than ERP systems: other data sources, communication protocols, development methods, and so on. For their implementation, it is necessary to develop dedicated methodologies and access to human competencies other than in the case of ERP class systems. The aforementioned factors and decentralized mechanisms of software development (giving large autonomy to the client and business partners) may ultimately lay the foundation for a new category of IT solutions. In a natural way, this is a source of opportunities, but also some challenges, which will be described later.

3.3.2.5 The Factory Expansion Concept

An interesting reflection on changes in the production process in the area of personalization can be found in Porter and Heppelmann (2014). In the past, tailoring the final product to individual needs took place in the factory after receiving a specification from a client (see e.g. configuration of Dell computers via the Internet). Today, more and more often, personalization takes place directly at the clients and is carried out directly by them during, for instance, the first launch of the product (see e.g. Apple smartphones, which delivered to customers all around the world virtually in the same form and immediately after launch, provided them with a simple configurator allowing e.g. the choice of language or an interface). In this case, the production line function is slowly taken over by the cloud computing infrastructure: the transmission of information about the use, product updates and, increasingly, the remote service are based on the communication of the device with the central server.

In connection with the above, Porter proposes an extension of the factory concept: this is not a single place, strictly defined in space, but the space in which the user uses the product and/or the business partner performs its service and updating. The whole is integrated due to digital communication in device-server, device-other device and user-device channels.

This trend materializes not only in the concept of autonomous networks, intelligent factories (trend *Industrie 4.0*, named from German under the influence of the advanced technologies development strategy adopted by the German government in 2013) but also in the model of GE Brilliant Factories, in which the data generated by the machines are gathered in one place (data lake), analyzed and used to optimize production processes.

Porter's proposal provokes further fundamental questions:

1. In the context of the development of AI class solutions: **What does it mean that something has been produced?** Since the users get solutions in the testing phase, followed by their continuous personalization, update and service directly at the client's, then the product's life cycle changes significantly.
2. Similarly, the question arises: **What is a physical product today?** It used to be a value in itself, mostly usable, bringing pleasure or enhancing prestige. Today, it is becoming more and more often a vehicle for delivering value. An example of this is smartphones: they are a natural source of income for their producers, but for example, for Apple, a significant part of profits comes from applications purchased in the app store (Apple App Store). As a result, you can imagine a business model in which Apple would sell its phones at a low price in order to make money on the intermediation of trade in applications (sold by partner companies and bought by smartphone users).
3. Another important question is: **Who is the owner of the product after purchasing it?** Since intelligent components of solutions can be created by the device manufacturer through integration with external AI class systems through programming interfaces (API) in the pay-per-use model, then the source of the value offered to the clients is actually not only the device they bought but also the external company's service provider. It raises problems not only as for the ownership but also in the area of financial controlling.

As a result one can expect the variable cost go down the value chain towards the client and the necessity to include this phenomenon within the process of calculating the product selling price. Imagine a smartphone that recognizes the user after the pupil of the eye, in which the module responsible for this function was purchased by the manufacturer from an external company in the pay-per-use model. As a result, the producer bears the cost already after the device is purchased by the customer and, therefore, it must be included in the price of the device. The two extreme possibilities are: (1) high selling price with no variable costs after purchase (risk at the producer's side), or (2) low purchase price of the device combined with a subscription fee transferred to the user, depending on the intensity of using this function. There are, of course, indirect variants, but this example indicates, however, the need to modify models of financial and operational controlling related to the implementation of AI class solutions.

3.3.2.6 Challenges

The new solutions in the area of production, as outlined above, are the source of both opportunities and challenges identified in the research process.

Undoubtedly, the challenge will be the development of methods for generating knowledge from data coming from sensors. The cognitive abilities of a human being establish the limits: the speed of response, the ability to analyze a large amount of information, the identification and interpretation of patterns in large data, and so on. This can be solved by creating models relating to knowledge structures that can be interpreted by a human being (as it is done, for example, by Maana as part of the Knowledge Graph model), or by delegating larger ranges of competencies to machines, for instance in the area of reaction to threat signals (e.g. in power engineering or IT security).

Another challenge is the development of new methods of implementation and development of information systems based on the Internet of Things (IoT). These methodologies should take into account the specificity of information and informative architecture of IoT as well as the methods of system modules development, its integration with already existing ERP class systems and interdisciplinary character of implementation teams and new ways of creating business cases for such implementations (which further strongly affects, for example, schedule and acceptance criteria of such projects). As can be seen, there are many new areas to be dealt with, which in the end is quite a challenge for both researchers and practitioners.

Previously signaled enormous amounts of data, the new quality and the speed of data generation exceed the possibilities of human analysis, interpretation and reaction. As a result, one can expect a progressive broadening of the spectrum of competencies (in the sense of entitlements) given to the machines. They may concern security areas (internal, e.g. failure; external, e.g. digital attacks), quality management, control (e.g. in the area of typing of energy consumers suspected of fraud) or making decisions, for instance, about granting loans. In each of these cases, we are dealing with the reallocation of decision centers from people to systems and a direct consequence of this phenomenon, a redefinition of the role of the human in the organization, probably in the direction of determining the function of the machine target and monitoring the degree of its implementation. There the questions arise: Who really makes decisions? On what basis and in what way? And who is responsible for them? As a result, one can expect an increase in the interest in research on the scope and dynamics of these changes in various industries.

The extension of factory concept generates another challenges:

1. Working out effective methods of scattered structures management.
2. Designing new models of financial and operational control by taking account of the effect of variable cost transfer down the value chain and the necessity of including this phenomenon in the calculation process of the product selling price.
3. The problem of propriety in the systems saturated with AI: who is the owner of a product, whose majority of components is delivered by various suppliers such as SaaS?

The simplest, direct consequence of the implementation of autonomous systems in industry is the high, justified concern of the risk of replacing people by machines. Recent reports (see e.g. "The future lies in automation," 2017) indicate a strong trend of supporting people by robots on the production line (co-bots) or their complete replacement (Koelblin 2017). There, the questions typical of technological breakthroughs appear, and they concern the limits of using economic arguments in the development and implementation of technology (the cost of the robot's working hours is estimated at 5 EUR, while the cost of a man-made production is around 50 EUR in Germany and 10 EUR in China). Some proposals also pop up; for example, taxation of robots, and the transfer of income from this tax to education and retraining of workers (interestingly, the author of this proposal is Bill Gates…). Exotic initiatives include the aforementioned ethical rules for the creation of intelligent systems, or the first proposals for the creation of working robots' rights related to the awareness studies in AI systems.

Another consequence is the risk of people losing the ability to monitor and control key business processes. AI systems collect huge amounts of increasingly diversified data and information, and use them to control key processes. As a result, thanks to optimization, the time of events and processes is reduced, sometimes by hundreds of times. It is more and more often beyond the reaction (time) and analytical (quantity and diversity of data) possibilities of a human being. As a result, it is necessary to assign monitoring and control functions to AI systems, which creates the risk of losing control over them by people.

To sum up, the implementation of artificial intelligence systems in production systems generates the following challenges:

1. Development of methods for generating knowledge from data coming from sensors.
2. Development of new methods of implementation and development of information systems based on the Internet of Things.
3. Developing effective methods of managing distributed structures.
4. Increasingly shorter time (events, processes, production cycles) combined with a growing number of very different information and the associated risk of losing control over systems (the need to assign these activities to machines).
5. Development of new models of financial and operational controlling, taking into account the effect of transferring the variable cost down the value chain, and the need to include this phenomenon in the process of calculating the product sale price.
6. The problem of ownership in AI saturated systems: who is the owner of the product, whose most of the components are supplied from different suppliers e.g. in the SaaS model?
7. Competence management (in the sense of entitlements) given to machines and management of reallocation of decision centers (who really makes the decision? on what basis and in what way? who is responsible for it? and so on).
8. What will be the role of human in the factories of the future?

3.3.2.7 New Competencies

Due to the many opportunities and challenges that AI class systems generate in the production area, new needs arise in the area of managerial competencies. As a result of the conducted analyses, the development of the following features of middle and upper management is proposed:

1. The awareness of the possible added value of AI class systems at various stages of production.
2. The knowledge of AI class architectures in industry, particularly, of systems enabling data collection, integration with external data and generation of knowledge.
3. The knowledge of trends in the development of information systems using the Internet of Things, especially their possible business cases, architectures and implementation methodologies.
4. Skills for assessing the impact of different architectures of smart systems on the structure of product revenues and costs, especially in the cases of possible transfer of variable costs up the value chain.
5. The awareness of expanding the "factory" and its processes in time and space.

3.3.3 Sales and Marketing

The previous analyses were focused on the impact of the Internet of Things and artificial intelligence on the integration of design and production processes. In this part, the third component of the value chain will be described: the area of marketing and sales and the related processes of using the product by the customer. The data sources and types of information that can be obtained from them will be presented, along with the new types of relations and communication with clients, the impact of AI class systems on the design and implementation of marketing and sales activities and solutions supporting campaign effectiveness assessment, customer behavior forecasting and risk management. At the end, new challenges for managers will be presented and the useful competencies that will help to meet these challenges will be recommended.

3.3.3.1 Data and Information in Marketing and Sales

The systems of artificial intelligence use data to optimize algorithms, due to which they can effectively support people or autonomously optimize business processes. For example, in marketing and sales, the appropriate technologies based on the age, sex, place of residence, salary, education and behavior data of a client enable designing a personalized offer, price list or discounts. Good quality of data is crucial in this process; therefore, the analysis of the impact of AI class systems on sales marketing should be preceded by a short presentation of sources and the type of data on user behavior available through modern IT systems.

Sources and Types of Data

Sources of data about user behavior can be classified in a number of different dimensions, particularly on the basis of:

1. Relation to the producer:
   (a) data generated by own products and systems,
   (b) data generated by business partner systems,
   (c) data from external sources.
2. Technology/access channel:
   (a) website Based Applications,
   (b) mobile app,
   (c) sensors,
   (d) etc.
3. User's level of awareness in the scope of data sharing:
   (a) data shared intentionally,
   (b) data shared unconsciously.

The awareness of systems architecture, thanks to which the organization can obtain data on user's behavior, is crucial for the design of business cases for AI class projects. The growing complexity of systems and the dynamic development of industries based on digital technologies create not only new opportunities but also are a source of challenges related to, for example, the issues of identifying and assessing the value of data sources on customer behavior. This issue is significantly beyond the scope of this study; therefore, for illustrative purposes only, an example of a digital product, an application that users can use via web and mobile channels, will be outlined.

Imagine a system that users can access through the website (via a browser) and a mobile application. The basic source of information will be reports from the web server (so-called system logs), which can be accessed either directly (which is a relatively rare practice), or through the intermediary of more or less advanced analytical tools (e.g. free Google Analytics system). Many analysts just stay with this source, taking advantage of the very small range of analytical capabilities of the solution. More advanced users, like Google Analytics users, take advantage of the functions that enable, for example, conversion tracking, retention and even grouping of users in the cohorts, which after correct interpretation may already be a source of competitive advantage.

These data are increasingly combined with data registering the use of mobile applications by clients (e.g. in the Google Analytics version for mobile applications), although according to the author of this study, the awareness of the existence and capabilities of this tool is just beginning to be created. Even smaller is the awareness of more advanced, also free, analytical tools such as, for example, Google Tag Manager.

Very few customers are aware of the possibility of combining data about the behavior of the users with their behavior on other websites. They offer third-party data providers, and the Polish company Cloud Technologies is a good example of such a solution. These providers offer the opportunity to optimize marketing campaigns based on behavioral profiles of people who use the company's applications. The data, based on which they build the characteristics of the Internet users, are acquired from partner networks, most often advertising ones, and then after processing they are sold in the form of services.

The key concept in the analysis of data sources is digital trace. This term is defined as a set of traces left by users in widely understood information systems. Digital traces are divided into active and passive. In the case of active traces, the users are aware that they leave them; this is the case with online communication (e.g. in social media or on discussion forums), or when filling out registration forms or surveys. Passive traces are data left by users unknowingly (although the law imposing on the company the obligation to inform about the tracking of so-called cookies is a step towards making the public aware of the fact of registering data about behavior). An example is not only the behavior on websites or in mobile applications but also a huge amount of the contextual data, for instance, current geographical location (which can be combined, for example, with the weather or landscape), type and detailed technical specification of the device we use, and even current information about the state of our body (e.g. when using devices monitoring its condition, like smart watches or heart-rate monitors).

Information on User Behavior

The potential of the technologies described above is huge. After the proper analysis, these data enable the identification of behavioral patterns and, as a result, the creation of behavioral profiles and automatic segmentation of clients, not only based on location or demographic data, but also behavior and psychological profiles resulting from it. Companies have the ability to identify the functions most often used by specific groups of clients (and the functions they do not use), which can be the basis for personalizing solutions, creating new product lines or identifying new trends. It is also possible to identify the emotions evoked by the product (through face analysis, see e.g. the solution by Affectiva) or data from body condition monitoring systems.

For example, a company using the services of an external data provider is able to define the profile of its client's interests at first encounter with the application (e.g. on the web channel), immediately adjusting its appearance and content to the user's expectations. In turn, the Apple patent ("United States Patent Application: 0140025620," 2014) on advertising based on mood opens up the possibility of addressing ads not only based on the profile of user behavior but also on the current state of their emotions.

On the other hand, practically perfect facial recognition systems enable the creation of a full human profile based on the analysis of its behavior in the real and virtual world. Algorithms of companies such as Baidu, VKontakte or Facebook recognize faces better than people (see e.g. Kemelmacher-Shlizerman et al. 2015), which opens the possibility of tracking customer activity in the physical world. For example, cameras in stores offering cosmetics after connecting to such services will be able to identify customers entering the store, combine their identity with their social media accounts, and then accurately track their behavior at the shelves to determine in real time their interest in buying a specific product. Furthermore, it will be able to supplement their behavioral profile created on the basis of the online behavior of customers' physical activity, as well as to broadcast an advertisement encouraging the purchase of a product they wanted to buy (but did not buy) in the traditional world.

Another practical application of image recognition systems is the AmazonGo store in the USA. It enables shopping without cash registers through advanced tracking of user behavior in the store. From the customer's perspective, the system is very simple: after entering the store, you should launch the appropriate Amazon application, and then simply put the goods in the basket. When leaving the store, the application shows a shopping list and asks you to accept the amount that is later charged to your credit card. A complete analysis of the shopping basket is on the part of advanced image recognition and machine learning algorithms implemented in devices (mainly cameras installed in the store).

Advanced analytical systems allow the analysis of the behavior of not only individual users but also entire social groups. There is a wide range of solutions in the area of sentiment analysis, which are able to determine the mood of social groups or their attitude to the brand (or, for example, a political party) in near-real time. No wonder that nowadays organizations aware of the possibilities of such solutions may not only monitor the state of moods of groups that are important to them but also, what is on the borderline of ethics, test the impact of various actions and messages on the emotions of entire communities.

As can be seen, AI class systems create great opportunities not only to analyze user behavior in order to personalize relations in real and virtual worlds but also they can significantly simplify traditional shopping. This is not only a source of comfort for the end user, but it can also cause a revolution in the labor market by eliminating some types of professions, such as a seller. An in-depth analysis of the social consequences of this class of solutions goes beyond the scope of this study, but for the avid readers the book by Nick Bostrom, *Superintelligence*, is highly recommended (Bostrom 2014).

3.3.3.2 Relations and Communication with Clients

Client Engagement

Nowadays, attention is one of the most valuable values. The largest companies engage teams of the best world experts to create attractive content and forms of their messages so that their recipients spend more and more time on their "consumption." This is well illustrated by the statement of Netflix's president Reed Hastings, who treats sleep as the biggest competitor of his company (Hern 2017).

No wonder that attracting attention is one of the biggest challenges today. Big competition forces the client to engage in conversation and then to maintain it and enrich it in the best possible way, with minimal effort on their own (especially in the case of mass global products). Thanks to the advanced systems of personalization of interaction, it is possible for particularly intelligent conversational machines (bots) to provide clients with important advice as well as maintain a dialogue and extract valuable information from them.

Companies are devoting more and more resources to this issue by moving the communication strategy to the early stages of solution design. In the past, the product was designed by one team, produced by another and put on the market by yet another one, these processes were only partially dependent on each other. Today, strategies and techniques of communication with clients are increasingly modeled at the very beginning of designing the solution, thus being another factor modifying the company's value chain. Below, the influence of the latest technologies on changes in personalization of communication with the end user is presented.

New Forms of Communication

Today, as never before, there is a strong coupling between technologies and methods of communication between people. Many years ago, people communicated mainly via speech or writing (manual or printed). The development of technology has enabled remote communication (e.g. light or telegraph), requiring the use of dedicated languages (e.g. Morse code), which naturally restricted its widespread use.

Popularization of mobile telephony and SMS communication services (Short Message Service) caused one of the most interesting changes in people's communication habits: the transition from longer, synchronous voice communication to short (a significant reduction in the possible number of characters in communication), asynchronous text communication. It turned out that the above restrictions (number of characters, text, asynchrony) positively influenced the popularization of SMSs.

The first explosion of new forms of communication took place along with the development of the Internet: prototypes of communicators like Internet Relay Chat (IRC), email or discussion forums. Over time, audio and video channels were added to enable remote conferencing.

The next stage in the development of interpersonal communication was related to the popularization of social media and their availability on mobile devices (smartphones). The implementation of instant messaging—applications enabling real-time text communication within social groups—significantly influenced the communication habits of people, especially young people: in mid-2015 there were more people using only messengers in social media rather than using the portals of this type (see "Messaging apps are now bigger than social networks," 2016). As a result, modern communication methods such as email have been superseded by social media (e.g. Facebook) or instant messengers (e.g. Facebook Messenger).

New technologies and communication channels have a strong impact on language and communication styles. For example, SMSs forcing short text messages cause, especially among young people, stylistic and grammatical abbreviations that are often unacceptable to people with traditional habits, which can often be perceived as a sign of disrespect or the lack of manners. They also naturally limit the depth of the message, reducing it to a purely informational function, more and more often also incomprehensible to the recipient accustomed to traditional communication. As a result, it can be said that new languages are being created, characteristic of social groups and communication media that they use.

This phenomenon may be deepened due to the development of further communication technologies. The first examples were emoticons: pictograms (pictures) symbolizing different emotions or situations, used in communicators (online and mobile) and as a complement to SMS communication. The high popularity of the initially modest sets of these graphics provoked the developers of the application to expand their libraries, which further increased their popularity as a means of expression (characters) in communication. This resulted in conversations mostly based on pictograms, using symbols that could be read often only by closed social groups, and as a result they were incomprehensible to "external" recipients – in this sense, one can speak about the formation of new languages.

If we add to this the growing popularity of smart watches that allow the reception of animated pictograms and combined with various vibrations, the picture becomes even more complicated. Users of such media freely create their own communication patterns, are hermetic for specific groups, and lose their ability to communicate with people using other methods.

As it can be seen, the development of new forms of interpersonal communication is currently stimulated by the development of digital technologies. AI class systems play a dual role here: on the one hand, they help create new conversational interfaces, on the other hand, they support companies in establishing and maintaining conversations with these channels (most often as business agents—bots).

Conversational interface technologies enable end users to communicate with devices in a natural language, both in voice and text. They use natural-language processing (NLP) methods and natural language generation (NLG). In the analyzed cases, the creators of components that enable creating their own interfaces (e.g. MindMeld, Octane.ai, Automat.ai, Cognicor or Snips) and companies building their own service ecosystems around these interfaces were identified (e.g. Amazon

Echo, Google Assistant or Apple Siri). What is also worth emphasizing is the development of methods and tools from the areas of natural speech understanding (e.g. kitt.ai) or based on the conversational artificial intelligence (e.g. Semantic Machines).

Business agents are systems that enable automation of communication with the end user at various stages of marketing, sales and after-sales service. Most often, they enable text-image communication using dedicated messengers. An interesting example is mode.ai, enabling fashion industry companies to establish an interactive dialogue with a potential client, with photo presentation functions or appearance simulations (the dialogue on behalf of the company is, obviously, carried out by an appropriately prepared algorithm). Similar solutions also function for the financial industry or other services, there are also systems enabling an independent creation of such agents (e.g. msg.ai).

Contemporary clients use many different digital services (portals, applications, social media, etc.) via many devices (smartphones, tablets, portable or stationary computers). In a natural way, therefore, the need to manage the omni-channel communication appears. Due to its complexity, this communication must be supported by advanced IT systems that increasingly use AI components. Among the solutions integrating and analyzing data about user behavior on various channels, the following can be distinguished: DataXU, ActionIQ, DataSift, Clarabridge, Appier and Nexidia. Companies using them have the opportunity to get a full picture of the behavior of their clients as well as to customize (personalize) communication on different channels.

Personalization of an Offer and Interaction

The data from systems registering user behavior enables the creation of profiles of their behaviors and interests, while omni-channel communication systems reach customers with a dedicated message. However, how to create the best possible message (offer) for a given user at the moment?

These processes support systems that use the recommendation systems. The algorithms underlying them have been using statistical modeling methods (especially cluster and basket analyses) or, more recently, neural networks. Among the advanced solutions of this class analyzed in the research process, the following are worth distinguishing:

- Arimo and Layer6.ai: supporting customization of products to the individual needs of clients;
- Persado: personalizing the calls to action that increase client engagement in interacting with the product based on the constantly updated user's cognitive profile;
- CareSkore: a system supporting personalization of interaction with patients in the health sector;
- KNewton: a solution enabling providers of training systems to gain advanced personalization of the didactic process as a function of the learner's behavior and progress.

Recommendation systems can successfully operate in traditional trade. For example, in supermarkets, AI systems based on the analysis of images from cameras in shopping carts and the history of purchases of other customers (basket analysis) may recommend purchasing other products, after acceptance, automatically indicate not only places in the store where the products are available, but also the optimal shopping route.

A separate category consists of solutions enabling personalization of price offers and dynamic pricing. More and more systems in e-commerce differentiate prices depending on the demographic characteristics of the client (age, sex, education, occupation, estimated earnings, place of residence, etc.), but also identify more unusual variables determining the maximum price that a client is willing to pay at a given moment. An example is the dependence of the price on the operating system (computer or mobile device) used by the user; already in 2012, the Orbitz hotel chain discovered that users of Apple devices (more specifically Mac computers) are willing to pay a 30% higher price per night, which was successfully used (WSJ 2012).

Other interesting solutions allow optimization of the retail space, particularly the placement of products in the store and on shelves, and experiments with various types of music with different intensity of sound based on the analysis of customer behavior (e.g. thanks to the analysis of AITV camera recordings). Such geospatial modeling not only increases sales but also stimulates customers to buy (for example, loud and dynamic music and aggressive colors increase the so-called cognitive overload and weaken control processes, which promotes compulsive shopping—but only in specific social and age groups).

As a result, the advanced personalization of interaction with the end user, which uses the latest artificial intelligence methods, allows the following:

1. Very good, "automatic" (without direct human involvement) adaptation of the offer to the individual needs of the user, which translates into the increased sales efficiency, increased customer satisfaction and loyalty.
2. Automatic and effective creation of offers (prices, function ranges, service options, etc.) addressed to specific market segments.
3. Creating more sophisticated price lists, taking into account the needs of specific clients.
4. Optimization and personalization of User eXperience (UX), particularly the shape of a product or application interface as well as trade space (space, sound, color).

As can be seen, AI class systems can effectively support the currently strong trend of mass customization. The access to such solutions in the SaaS model (Software as a Service) or through the API (programming interfaces) often in the Pay-Per-Use model means that small companies can personalize not only communication but also their offer on a very large scale, which has been only the domain of the largest companies so far.

3.3.3.3 Design and Implementation of Marketing and Sales Activities

Data on users' behavior and information obtained from it about users' current preferences constitute a good basis for designing and implementing marketing and sales activities. It turns out that the marketing industry, which has been based on human creativity for years, is also very vulnerable to the impact of AI class systems.

Marketing campaign planning is most often carried out according to the following scheme:

1. A company interested in advertising its product determines:
   (a) campaign goals: product, target group, desired customer behavior, etc.,
   (b) budget,
   (c) time frame,
   (d) other parameters, specific for the campaign or industry
2. The company establishes cooperation with a company specializing in the design, implementation and monitoring of campaigns (usually the media house) and together with it creates the mediaplan—the strategy of campaign implementation specifying advertising techniques and forms, advertising space, partial budgets, measures of effectiveness and implementation schedule.
3. The campaign is started and monitored on a current basis. The teams of the client and the marketing company make mutual decisions and possible changes in the advertising forms or media.

In this process, key tasks are carried out by people: campaign strategy, creations (graphics, texts, marketing messages, etc.), the interpretation of implementation reports, campaign optimization, and so on. IT systems perform a supportive function, providing primarily data and reports on the results of the promotion.

The marketing industry is saturated with data. This applies primarily to digital marketing, where (in contrast to outdoor, press, radio or even television advertising) you can register not only the place and time of broadcasting a given advertising form but also information about the interaction of recipients with ads combined with their full context (see e.g. the digital traces described above). These data alone create a huge field for interpretation; on the one hand, you can track the attractiveness of various advertising forms for not only entire customer segments, but even at the individual customer level.

The possibility of advanced reporting of the results of digital campaigns underlies the new methods of online advertising. Advertising exchanges were created (e.g. Google Ad Exchange) to connect people/

organizations owning advertising spaces with companies interested in advertising. Over time, the "trade" processes on these exchanges were automated, for example by introducing auction mechanisms, which created a new market for Real-Time Bidding (RTB).

The development of highly efficient algorithms used in these processes has enabled the development of the Programmatic Marketing, practically fully automating the processes of designing, implementing and optimizing digital campaigns. This group of solutions shows the greatest impact of AI class systems.

Solutions in the field of Programmatic Marketing (e.g. companies such as DataX or Motiva) enable practically complete automation of design and implementation of the campaign. The creator of the advertisement determines the initial expectations of its effects (e.g. target group, product, examples of messages or creations, expected measures of effectiveness, etc.), provides the budget and launches the campaign. The system, most often using the media available on the ad exchanges, creates different versions of the advertisement itself (e.g. combinations of texts and graphics), broadcasts them in various media, to various recipients and on different devices, then in near-real time optimizes the campaign. The effects are often much better than the effects of the work of even very experienced teams of marketing specialists, and AI class mechanisms make the algorithms underlying these solutions constantly improve.

Predictive marketing and sales systems constitute an important class of solutions that use AI technologies in marketing. They use advanced data analysis to predict individual customer behavior or are used to assess the sales potential of business customers. Among the solutions of this class, the products of Lattice, Mintigo or Radius (predictive marketing) as well as InsideSales and Clari (predictive sales) stand out.

Additionally, the AI systems enable classification of business clients groups as far as their potential is concerned (see e.g. Bughin et al. 2017). Due to that manufacturing companies can have their sellers focused on clients with the highest potential and in this way increase the effectiveness of sales departments.

Technological development and the consequent flood of information affect not only the language of interpersonal communication but also the ways of media consumption. The information overload favors a cursory analysis of the content and prefers a visual message from the text (requiring increased attention, which, as has already been underlined, is a scarce resource). As a result, digital media users are more and more often viewing content in a passive way, preferring images and omitting the text. This creates a new type of challenge: How can the current interest of the customer be identified, if they are not interested in the text? Companies such as Netra, which enable behavioral profiling of clients based on the analysis of their interaction time with images that are previously classified using machine-learning algorithms, provide the help. As a result, the information about the time spent in a given graphic form is enough to identify the user's interests— the rest of the analyses will be carried out by the IT system.

The risk associated with the loss of a client's trust should be underlined here. The vast majority of AI systems intensively uses data on clients' behavior: not only about their activities on the Internet sites, in social media or on the use of mobile appliances but also on the way of using various "things" and even identifying their emotions or intentions as well as influencing their purchase decisions. A company should not only focus on the clients' comfort (e.g. by informing them how the data is processed, stored or shared with external subjects or making it available to be seen and edited) but also on the compliance with the legal regulations.

As it can be seen, digital traces, both passive and active, left by clients in the digital sphere can be the basis for the design and implementation of various marketing activities. These functions are increasingly taken over by AI class systems, replacing, for example, the creative departments previously responsible for marketing and sales. In the further part of the study, the impact of intelligent solutions on systems of analysis, forecasting and risk management related to customer interactions will be presented.

3.3.3.4 Analysis of Effectiveness, Forecasting and Risk Management

The last group of AI solutions in the field of marketing and sales identified in the research are analytical tools supporting analyses of the effectiveness of marketing campaigns, customer potential, forecasting their future behavior and risk management in relations with clients.

Rating the impact of marketing activities on sales is a real challenge. The solutions, exemplified by BrightFunnel, use data from many channels of interaction with clients to determine the impact of various sales activities as accurately as possible.

In turn, the systems of companies such as Arimo or Mintigo enable analysis of sales potential to a specific client, taking into account their behavioral profile and using advanced methods of forecasting their behavior. Anticipating future customers' reactions is the basis of risk management in relations with them.

Due to the AI systems, manufacturing companies can also forecast the level of their own servicing and repair support, mainly thanks to the analyses of sensors enabling the evaluation of a product use intensity by given groups of clients and the failure frequency resulting from these analyses. Therefore, it is possible to plan service resources more accurately (e.g. partner networks) or future incomes from this type of service (which is particularly significant in the automotive industry).

3.3.3.5 Challenges

The above-mentioned impact of AI class systems on marketing and sales is both a source of opportunities and challenges.

As indicated by Porter and Heppelmann (2015), the data on the use of products by customers

1. gives insight into how products deliver value to customers, and as a result, helps to position the product better and communicate value in the marketing message;
2. improves the quality of customer/market segmentation and allows products to be matched to maximize value for customers in individual segments. As a result, you can price products higher and generate higher margins.

This is supported by faster and cheaper product changes, which is possible in the case of software updates, and more difficult for changes in physical components.

The next consequence will be the change in the role of the product: utility value will become a value delivery vehicle. The producer will have continuous contact with the client through the device, which will not only provide them with the possibility of giving the client various messages or values but also the possibility of gathering valuable data about the user's behavior or condition in near real-time. After proper processing, these data can be a commercial value (such as data from the body monitors).

Porter and Heppelmann (2015) indicate the following challenges in the role of sales department resulting from the above trends:

1. Constant value design for the client: identification of trends, values and needs based on data generated by products.
2. Constant value provision. In the past, after the purchase, the service department would then take care of the customer. In the near future, the moment of the transaction will be just the beginning of the sales department dialogue with the client, and the product will be a vehicle for delivering the newly discovered value for the client.

To carry out the above tasks effectively, sales staff should skillfully use AI class solutions: identify clients, assess their potential, and classify or identify the best possible channels and communication styles.

More and more often, it turns out that products are the transfer vehicles of values from clients to companies. They are offered practically for free and the value for company comes from the clients' behavior data use. This results in the risk of accustoming users to free products and services and the loss of their trust in the case of "discovering" the real business model.

3.3.3.6 New Competencies

The AI class system offers many possibilities. In order to fully use their potential, the spectrum of managerial competencies should include:

1. The awareness of the diversity of digital data left by users (digital fingerprint).

2. The ability to draw conclusions based on information generated by advanced analytical systems supporting marketing and sales processes.
3. Understanding the impact of technology on the habits and styles of communication of digital media users.
4. The awareness and the ability to assess the business potential of different methods of behavioral profiling and personalization of customer relations.
5. Understanding the mechanisms of modern electronic marketing methods such as real-time bids or programmatic marketing.

3.3.4 Personalization, Service and After-Sales Service

The AI class systems introduce a new quality to the design, production, marketing and sales processes. Their ability to learn constantly, solve problems independently and communicate in natural languages is beginning to have a significant impact on the service and after-sales service processes. In addition, augmented reality technologies enable new methods of repairing and updating products.

3.3.4.1 Personalization

Personalization is the adaptation of a product or service to individual customer needs. AI systems support the personalization of marketing communication as well as the product itself and the method of its delivery.

Artificial intelligence systems find more and more applications in the area of personalized medicine. Mindmaze enables customized rehabilitation, while Ginger.io recommends the optimal time to take medicine based on the metabolism of a given patient. On the other hand, Turbine.ai share personalized therapies in cancer diseases. The effect is the decrease in the number of therapy side effects, lower costs of treatment, shorter treatment time and longer life of patients.

In the area of personalized education Knewton enables providers of electronic training to adjust the scope and pace of the training process to the individual needs, abilities and progress of the learner. Similar mechanisms in the area of teaching mathematics are offered by DreamBox Learning: the effects are, for example, increasing the pass rate of tests and exams and reducing the number of students not receiving promotion to the next class.

Both of the above-mentioned application areas relate to the provision of services. In the area of transporting physical products, delivery drones have become a very dynamically developing industry. Deliveries using autonomous drones are a big challenge, mainly due to the security and still limited range of deliveries. Despite this, Flirtey has recently received the right to transport small packages with its drones, which opens the way to completely new services and generates many benefits. For example, one of the most important applications is the rapid provision of first aid medical supplies for hard-to-reach places such as the places of accidents, natural disasters, and so on.

3.3.4.2 Automation of After-Sales Service

The previous chapters show how modern technologies influence the quality of interpersonal communication. Manufacturers can contact customers through websites, mobile applications, social media, instant messaging, and even via their own products. In combination with close-to-perfection speech recognition, speech generation systems and learning abilities, AI allows almost full automation of after-sales service processes.

Conversational Interfaces

Conversational interfaces play an important role in modern customer service. Systems such as Amazon Echo, Microsoft Cortana, Google Assistant and Apple Siri enable two-way communication in natural language. For example, a person using the Amazon Echo interface (a small device of the size of a glass, equipped with a microphone and a loudspeaker and permanently connected via the Internet with the Amazon Alexa artificial intelligence system) may:

1. **Ask to play a favorite melody**. The system will recognize the voice of the person, check which music service they use, which melodies they like the most at any given time of the day, and after that, it will connect with the website and play the appropriate songs.
2. **Ask about the current weather in the place a person is just going to**. The system will check the preferred weather service and describe it in natural language.
3. **Ask about the next events on the calendar**. The system will identify the application used to run the calendar, check the upcoming events in it and briefly present the agenda of the day.

Amazon Echo (combined with Amazon Alexa) offers many similar opportunities, but they are constantly developed and improved not only by Amazon, but also by the growing network of its partners. As a result, a rich ecosystem of applications, whose heart is the Amazon solution, is created. The possible impact of such ecosystems on the value chain at the level of markets will be presented later in this chapter, here it only needs to be emphasized that companies such as Microsoft, Google, Apple, Facebook or Uber make every effort to become a monopolist of the end-user interface.

Conversational interfaces are not limited to the audio channel. The bots market, namely, systems enabling text dialog, is developing dynamically. An interesting example is the Kik company, offering other companies not only the opportunity to create their own conversational machines but also to launch them as a part of their own social platform, with nearly 300 million users (mainly teenagers) registered there. As a result, stores like H&M have the opportunity to initiate and conduct an interactive dialogue with potential, young customers. Interestingly, not many young people are aware that they are conducting discourses with automatons…

Optimization of Interaction

Despite the growing popularity of the modern communication channels described above, "traditional" communication, for example, via a telephone is still very popular. It turns out that AI systems are also playing an increasingly important role here.

Solutions of companies such as Qurious, Gridspace, Talkiq or Clover enable real-time analysis of telephone conversations conducted by customer service employees (or sales assistants). An example scenario of such usage is as follows:

1. A customer or company employee initiates a conversation.
2. The system monitors its course in real time. Using natural language processing algorithms (NLP) it:
   (a) analyzes the content;
   (b) classifies the stages of the conversation (e.g. greeting, presenting the offer, question about the product, question, raising doubts, referring to the competition, price information, purchase decision, etc.);
   (c) monitors the emotions of the interlocutors;
   (d) intervenes in the event of crisis situations;
   (e) records the effect of a conversation (e.g. a decision to buy or resign);
   (f) writes a full transcript along with its analysis in the database.
3. Based on the analysis of thousands of monitored conversations, the best and worst practices are identified, on the basis of which talk-patterns are created (playbooks).

As it can be seen, speech recognition and analysis systems can be used to improve the efficiency of customer service and sales teams, create bases of best practices, and the results of their actions constitute the basis of training processes. The development of NLG (Natural Language Generation) systems in combination with the already-perfect systems of text-to-speech conversions (see e.g. Text-To-Speech, by Wang et al. 2017) may soon lead to the replacement of employees of the customer service department with automatic systems.

Intelligent Customer Service

Artificial intelligence systems enable significant improvement of customer service processes. A very good example of solutions skillfully combining human knowledge with AI class systems is the Digital Genius system. It analyzes customer inquiries, based on the information contained in the knowledge base, identifies possible responses, assesses their level of confidence, and then if the answer is very likely correct, it passes it on to the client; if highly probable, it recommends a customer service representative who verifies and personalizes it. This is an interesting example of cooperation between people and machines, this time in the area of after-sales service, which can be a very strong trend in the future.

Similar solutions are offered by Cognicor, Wise.io or one of the leaders in the segment of systems supporting customer relationship management, Salesforce (within the Einstein system).

The benefits from the virtual agents implementation are, for example:

1. The increase of reactivity by the shortening the time of accepting a prompt.
2. Shortening of orders realization time and client service.
3. Atomization of service process.
4. The increase of availability (24/7 service).
5. Improvement in client satisfaction.

3.3.4.3 Change of Time, Place and Methods of Repair

Porter and Heppelmann (2015) show the impact that smart, connected products can have on changing the time, place and methods of repair and product updates. These factors will be briefly presented below, and supplemented by observations resulting from the research conducted by the author.

Changing the Moment of Repair

Once—and in the vast majority of cases, now—service was typically reactive or subjected to a predetermined regime; either temporary or relating to some simple measure of exploitation like, for instance, mileage.

AI class systems using predictive algorithms enable a significant increase in the flexibility of the time of service. As a result of the conducted research, the following categories of systems of forecasting the occurrence of various risky situations, predisposing "subject" to "service" or other "repair action" were identified[2]:

1. **Systems supporting forecasting check-ups and maintenance services**, such as Presenso (for production lines), Preteckt and Pitstop (for cars) or Trace Genomics (plant diagnostics in agriculture).
2. **Anomaly detection systems**, e.g. Anodot or dedicated Predix or C3IoT modules.
3. **Diagnostic and predictive systems in medicine** (CareSkore, Grail), **medical imaging** (Enlitic, Arterys, Imagia, Zebra) and **genetics** (Color Genomics).
4. **Predictive systems in logistics**, e.g. ClearMetal.
5. **Building monitoring systems**, e.g. Verdigris.
6. **Systems that help detect fraud**, e.g. Sift Science and dedicated SAS solutions modules.

As can be seen, the maturity of solutions that allow forecasting of broadly understood risks enables the increase of flexibility of check-ups, which can significantly reduce the costs of using, for example, a machine park (too-frequent check-ups are unjustified cost, and on the other hand, too rare can lead to failure). By forecasting the moment of failure, AI class systems affect the schedule of remedial actions not only generating large savings, but also modifying processes in the area of service and maintenance.

Changing the Place of Repair

The remote monitoring and control systems based on the Internet of Things infrastructure enable changing the place of repair. As Porter describes it, once mechanics teams with a set of necessary information, parts and tools had to go to the place of repair. Today:

1. Data and information about the device status can be downloaded remotely (thanks to communication with sensor systems).
2. Often there is no need to send specialists to the place of repair; thanks to teleconferencing systems you can instruct a local employee how to do it.

3. Advanced machine management systems (e.g. ABB solutions) enable the creation of digital copies of machine software security, their remote updating and restoration in the event of a failure.

As a result, people repairing the device are more and more often in a location other than the machine.

Change of Repair Methods

In the area of changing the repair methods, it is worth pointing to two trends related to AI class systems.

The first of these are digital twins. They can be imagined as very accurate, digital models of specific industrial devices, which, thanks to communication with sensors, represent their current state in real time. They enable accurate diagnosis of failures and simulation of optimal repair methods. They are used in cases of difficult accessibility, for instance, drilling platforms or aircraft engines. Systems of this class are developed, for example, by General Electric.

The second technology that can significantly affect the repair methods of devices is augmented reality. Solutions of this class impose on a real image a digital layer (information and instructions necessary in a given context), greatly improving the service process and its security. One of the most mature systems in this class is Microsoft's HoloLens solution.

3.3.4.4 Improving Knowledge Transfer Processes

Knowledge is currently one of the key values: on the one hand as a component of the offered solution (e.g. the best practices database), on the other hand, as a condition for the correct use of products. No wonder that companies are looking for new solutions in the area of training and knowledge transfer to the client and service partners—artificial intelligence is increasingly used here.

E-learning systems supported by artificial intelligence make it possible to classify and organize content from knowledge databases and make them available to clients in the right context, place and time. The above-mentioned technologies are also useful in augmented reality: by imposing a real digital layer on the image with appropriate training content, they significantly reduce cognitive overload (the user does not have to shift the eyes from e.g. a book to the real image and "decode" the information given in symbolic form to the image from the background) (Porter and Heppelmann 2017). If we add to this the trend of sharing dedicated analytical tools (both in the energy and banking sectors) to individual and business clients, we will see that the area of knowledge transfer to and from the user or business partner is a very important area in which advanced, intelligent systems can provide value.

3.3.4.5 Challenges

The possibilities described above will have a significant impact on the management processes in the areas of service and maintenance. The following can be expected:

1. The structure of service and maintenance costs will change (fewer breakdowns, other times and schedules of repairs, lower share of human costs).
2. Predictive analyses will change the moment of repair and reduce their costs.
3. Modern service systems will affect the requirements for products at the design stage (products should take into account the full possibilities of their subsequent repair and updating).
4. The roles of people in the customer service and repair department will change, from direct solutions to problems in the assessment of credibility of recommendations generated by AI systems.
5. This will change the competencies required of people working in these departments: technical knowledge will be less important, and the key will be the ability to fully use the capabilities of intelligent systems.

3.3.4.6 New Competencies

The changes described above indicate the following new managerial competencies:

1. The awareness and ability to assess the business potential of the new capabilities of after-sales and service systems.
2. The ability to manage the product design process to take full advantage of the potential of these solutions when the product is launched on the market.
3. The ability to model after-sales service processes and service using AI class systems.
4. The related ability to determine the cost structure of after-sales service.
5. The ability to use data and information generated during value design service for the customer and to increase competitive advantage.

3.3.5 Human Resources Management

AI systems affect not only the core areas of the value chain, but also a group of support activities. The analysis of changes in this category of organizational activity will begin with the analysis of human resource management.

3.3.5.1 Recruitment

The modern world is full of paradoxes. On the one hand, the development of the Internet and modern methods supporting education facilitated the access to very modern knowledge, which was impossible in the past. Yet, the development of technology and constant changes in the economic reality force the necessity of constant updating of the competencies. As a result, companies find it increasingly difficult to acquire qualified employees.

One of the areas of human resource management supported by AI class systems is recruitment. The first, relatively simple but very streamlining solution is the Textio product. On the basis of the analysis of content and effects of millions of job advertisements, it recommends to HR department employees the optimal content of the announcement so as to maximize the chance of attracting the right employees. To do this it uses machine-learning algorithms, particularly from the natural language processing group.

The SpringRole company's solution goes one step further. A human resource employee enters a job advertisement into the system. Machine-learning algorithms analyze them and identify the most important, desired competencies. Then, they compare them with the skills acquired from a similar analysis of profiles of jobseekers (or active on social networks like LinkedIn) and indicate people with the best matching ratio. In this way, they save hours of tedious work devoted to analyzing profiles of candidates for a given position.

The system offered by Unitive complements the Textio and SpringRole solutions with the recommendation of the structure of the interview and the criteria for assessing its results, optimal for a given job position. Entelo, on the other hand, extends the recruitment space, supporting the processes of external as well as internal recruitment.

Another company, HireVue, provides solutions supporting recruitment and coaching processes using teleconferences (audio and video). The solution uses advanced algorithms of voice and image analysis to examine the candidate's psychological profile and predictive algorithms to determine its potential at the selected workplace. As a result, it is an example of how in the near future the experience and intuition of the recruiter can be supplemented, and perhaps even replaced, by machine knowledge.

Finally, Wade & Wendy's solution is worth mentioning, which is a very interesting, and in a sense extreme, way of using the latest capabilities of AI class systems in the area of recruitment. The company offers support for job seekers as well as employers looking for employees, by providing personal agents in the form of bots. Specifically, a jobseeker has the option of creating a bot[3] who knows their competencies, experience, preferences regarding the workplace, responsibilities, time load, and so on. Knowing the profile of its "client," this agent initiates text conversations with people who are likely to represent employers, present their offer and initiate negotiations of employment conditions. Similarly, Wendy is an agent (bot) for a company seeking employees; knowing the staffing needs, competencies and experience required in these positions as well as the characteristics of the job offer, it looks for potential employees and encourages them to cooperate. It may turn out that Wade will be negotiating with Wendy, which is a very interesting signal for the analysis of the labor market future.

3.3.5.2 Talent Management

The development and maintenance of valuable employees is a huge challenge, even more than their acquisition. No wonder that the creators of the largest talent management systems (e.g. SAP Success Factors, Oracle Taleo or Saba) use the latest technologies to support motivational and development processes. Solutions of companies such as HiQ use machine-learning algorithms to assess the risk of departures of the most valuable employees and automate the creation of desirable competency maps at workplaces. As a result, development plans are optimized and the risk of losing the best staff is minimized.

3.3.5.3 Productivity and Teamwork

Another area that AI class systems are entering is personal productivity and group work.

Work efficiency strongly depends on the environment in which it is performed. Portable computers and mobile devices are an everyday work tool for most white-collar workers. They improve work in a natural way, yet on the other hand, they can significantly reduce efficiency (e.g. by providing a lot of unnecessary information, disturbing concentration and increasing information overload). The answer to these challenges is intelligent IT solutions supporting personal productivity and group work, often using advanced machine-learning algorithms.

An example of an advanced system supporting personal productivity is Sapho. The application analyses various internal and external information systems of the company, identifying the tasks and decisions that an employee should take, then groups them and presents them in the form of a friendly "workflow" on a mobile device or computer. In this way, it minimizes the effort involved in connecting to various subsystems, analyzing information provided in various formats and the associated information overload. The user is also supported by the system's ability to prioritize tasks and provide specific information in a context appropriate to them.

In the area of group work support, Slack is a very interesting solution that uses the latest communication methods. By combining functionalities supporting project management with the communicator, it skillfully creates an application ecosystem that uses advanced capabilities of AI class systems. An example of an intelligent application in the ecosystem is Howdy.ai: an environment enabling the creation of bot integrated with Slack, allowing project managers to virtually ask colleagues about the status of tasks. Another interesting solution is Talla: knowledge management system, supporting employees in their daily work, allowing reporting problems and providing answers to frequently asked questions.

Systems supporting personal productivity and group work are complemented by performance monitoring solutions, e.g. the previously described Gridspace, TalkIQ or Chorus systems.

3.3.5.4 Challenges

The solutions described in this chapter indicate many new competencies necessary to fully use the potential of AI class solutions in an organization. These competencies concern not only individual employees but also entire interdisciplinary teams and their skillful management, especially in the context of fast-changing technologies and business environments, requires new meta-competencies: talent management skills, heterogeneous teams, and so on.

The construction, implementation and development of AI class systems in organizations will also require more fundamental changes, perhaps even at the level of organizational culture. These systems are very interdisciplinary: they involve engineers, programmers, marketing specialists, sales and customer service specialists, often scientists or artists. It can be expected that the need to reconcile people with such different professions, styles of work and characters as result-oriented ventures will require not only the development of a dedicated project management method, but also new motivational systems.

3.3.5.5 New Competencies

On the basis of the above analysis, the following desired managerial competencies allowing full exploitation of the potential of AI class solutions in human capital management are recommended:

1. The awareness of the possibilities of information systems in the area of automatic modeling of competencies desirable at work positions.
2. The ability to use IT systems in the processes of job and employee valuation as well as risk assessment and the consequences of losing the most valuable employees.
3. The ability to assess the costs and benefits of implementing various advanced systems supporting personal productivity and group work. In particular, the ability to assess the impact of these solutions on both the efficiency of business processes and the satisfaction of employees.
4. The ability to manage interdisciplinary teams that connect people with different work styles, characters and motivations. Willingness to experiment with different project management methodologies for AI class systems implementation combined with the ability to reflect and learn from mistakes.

3.3.6 Information and Knowledge Management

In the previous chapters, a lot of space was devoted to new data, information and knowledge possible to obtain thanks to the AI class systems. The impact of these solutions on value chain processes related to Business Intelligence analysis and knowledge management is presented below.

3.3.6.1 Acquisition and Integration of Data

Most experienced specialists or managers working for years in their industry are well aware of various sources of information from a given area. The problem is often not to obtain these data (they can be purchased or free sources can be used), but their skillful integration and processing into valuable information. In response to this challenge, a group of solutions was created ordering and integrating data from many different sources.

An interesting example of this class of systems is Bottlenose. The platform aggregates information from over 2 million different digital and traditional sources in real time, and uses the advanced algorithms of machine learning, data mining and predictive analysis to provide its users with the most important conclusions and observations. As a result, the company's clients do not lose energy and time for tedious data processing, and they can devote more time to their interpretation and inference.

Other interesting examples of similar systems are Quandl (financial sector) and Premise (trends and global indicators). In near-real time, Quandl integrates financial data from many digital sources, not only transactional ones (e.g. stock exchanges), but also presenting expert statements. As a result, the solution user has access to processed information, which significantly simplifies the reasoning and decision-making process.

A similar solution, this time for the medical industry, is offered by CloudMedx. It uses artificial intelligence to support clinical analysis processes. The system, addressed to hospitals and research centers, facilitates the inference based on large amounts of raw data (e.g. from electronic patient cards), processed later using the latest algorithms of natural language processing and machine learning. The system is also used by the public sector, particularly in the case of predicting the dissemination of epidemic information, or to analyze the effectiveness of various medicines for groups of patients.

An interesting example of the use of satellite data in macroeconomic analyses is Orbital Insight. By analyzing images from satellites, it allows:

- estimation of sales trends in the US based on the analysis (in real time) of the parking load of the main retail chains,
- assessment of oil turnover by analyzing the degree of immersion of tankers carrying it (thanks to the analysis of the shadow cast by freighters),
- determination of the dynamics of economic development of the selected region (e.g. in China) based on the number of cars and newly constructed buildings.

In turn, Cape Analytics allows using satellite images to support the process of real estate risk valuation. After entering the precise location of the object, the image recognition system evaluates, for example, the material from which the roof was made, the condition of the building, the house surface and the ambient features that may affect the insurance risk. The agent using the solution receives a report that can significantly accelerate the process of risk assessment and preparation of the insurance offer.

As a result, system users have access in near-real time to information that has been offered so far by global consulting companies or statistical bodies of selected countries with a delay of several months. Orbital Insight and Cape Analytics are examples of how advanced data aggregation systems can accelerate, increase credibility and improve access to macroeconomic information.

3.3.6.2 Generation and Presentation of Knowledge

High availability of data in various forms, better methods of their processing and growing expectations of companies in relation to their business potential generate the need to develop new methods of generating and presenting knowledge.

An interesting example of this trend is the Quid system. It enables the visualization of knowledge in the form of graphs of often very complex relations between various aspects of the functioning of related companies, thus facilitating their interpretation. Ayasdi, on the other hand, uses artificial intelligence to visualize the relations between data in the form of three-dimensional models (data shapes).

Spatial modeling of data is one of many possible ways to get valuable information and knowledge from raw data. Companies such as Narrative Science or Yseop use the latest methods of Natural Language Generation (NLG).

For example, Quill, a Narrative Science product based on reports with information about various aspects of the company's operations available in the form of a spreadsheet creates a report in natural language, presenting in particular the basic descriptive analysis of data, strengths and weaknesses, and recommendations for future actions along with their justification. As a result, it performs the work of a business analyst, but without human burdens (e.g. emotions or sentiments) and mistakes (e.g. incorrect use of statistical methods). Yseop offers a similar solution: it draws conclusions from data, summarizes them and justifies them.

3.3.6.3 Combination of AI Algorithms with Human Expertise

From the analyses presented above, a somewhat pessimistic picture of a situation in which super-intelligent algorithms can replace people in virtually every area may emerge. In practice, however, it turns out that even the most mature solutions using AI class systems require active cooperation with field experts—the proof of this is the class of solutions presented below, whose full potential is released thanks to the combination of human knowledge and skills with high technologies.

IBM, the creator of the AI class system model (Watson), in many ways emphasizes the key role of the human in the implementation of the application. For example, the process of preparing Watson to work in a hospital as an independent doctor requires:

1. **Creating the body of knowledge containing reliable information in a given field (e.g. oncology)**. The indication of **reliable** sources of data is the crucial for this stage: it turns out that many scientific publications in the field of medicine should be approached with caution, sometimes complementing them with more reliable data from internal hospital databases.
2. **Watson support in assessing the quality of his diagnoses and hypotheses**. The expert system in the first phase of its operation can be compared to a novice employee: despite all efforts, due to lack of experience, they can make mistakes. For this reason, at the very beginning of the implementation, it is crucial to have the continuous cooperation of the system with an experienced physician, who, on one hand, indicates the correct diagnosis, and on the other hand, draws attention to the mistakes and pays attention to their possible causes.

3. **Supervision in the medical care process recommended by Watson.** Even the well-prepared, "experienced" Watson can make mistakes—for this reason, human supervision is also necessary at this stage.

As can be seen, there are many indications that the full autonomy of AI class solutions in critical applications (such as health care) is still far away, and the best results can be achieved only through optimal cooperation of machines with people.

CognitiveScale, another provider of mature AI class solutions, in the methodology of implementing its solutions also puts emphasis on close cooperation between human teams and high technologies. This finds expression in specifying the software as augmented intelligence software. The symbolic division of works assumes the involvement of people in memorizing, perception, anticipation, problem-solving and decision-making; while machines are involved in recognizing natural language and images, conversations, data analysis and machine learning.

In turn, Collectiv[i] enables the use of AI and modern work techniques in the group to release the potential of knowledge and experience of sales staff. For this purpose, not only the latest machine learning algorithms are used but also the knowledge of external experts with extensive sales experience.

Other platforms combining human knowledge with the capabilities of AI class systems are CrowdFlower, Logz.io and DataIQ. In each of these cases, IT systems complement the capabilities of people who are necessary for the entire solution to function.

3.3.6.4 New Architectures and Services

The systems described above facilitate the use of ready-made AI class systems (in the software model as SaaS or API programming interfaces) or creating custom solutions. However, not all companies are interested in developing competencies in the area of advanced use or creating smart applications, at the same time wanting to use their business potential.

This need has created a place for new services "in the cloud." The classical division of Cloud Computing systems is distinguished by the following services:

1. **Infrastructure as a Service: IaaS**, e.g. virtual servers, computing power or disk surfaces.
2. **Platform as a Service: PaaS**, enabling the creation of applications made available "in the cloud."
3. **Software as a Service: SaaS**, i.e. online applications supporting various areas of the organization's activity.

The awareness of the potential of data and simultaneous fears of high costs of investment in technologies has enabled the development of new layers of remote services. Some of them stand out:

1. **Insight as a Service**, under which the user provides the service contractor with raw data, and receives deeper analysis often with recommendations and their justification (IBM).
2. **Conversation as a Service**, in this case, the service provider's systems comprehensively support the conversation with the client, using the knowledge bases provided by the user and modern methods from the areas of processing and generating natural language (NLP and NLG). This type of services is promoted by, for example, Microsoft.

Of course, the solutions of this class have many advantages (such as, for example, minimization of investment and service costs or drastic shortening of the service introduction to the market), but they also bring many challenges, which are described in more detail below.

At the end of the considerations devoted to new methods of creating new knowledge from data, the intensive development of systems whose aim is to create General Artificial Intelligence (GAI) is worth emphasizing. In this area, companies such as DeepMind, Maluuba, Cogitai, Kimera, Nnaisense and Numenta are leading the way. Interestingly, they are already slowly emerging from the basic research stage: some of the solutions developed there (e.g. the intelligent energy management system consumed by Google servers developed under DeepMind) are already being used in practice. A closer analysis of the projects carried out by these organizations indicates that the superintelligence described, for example, by the Bostrom (2014) study may already be in the range of technologies developed there.

3.3.6.5 Challenges

As can be seen, the automation of data aggregation processes and the increasingly perfect methods of their processing definitely broaden the possibilities of their analysis. Of course, this creates many new opportunities, but it is also a source of many challenges.

The first one is the change of decision-making processes and reallocation of decision centers. Systems that supervise energy systems have long replaced humans in situations requiring rapid response to failures. The example of the Narrative Science Quill system indicates how a business analyst can someday be replaced by an intelligent machine. In the financial industry, neural networks "support" making many decisions, for example about granting credit. There are many examples like that.

These changes are the source of many challenges. Obviously, there is a fear of the role of a human in the functioning of the organization: if they are no longer able to make decisions better than the machine, what function should they have? Perhaps, they can create goal functions for it and then monitor its implementation? If not, then what?

It is possible that even a greater challenge will be the lack of understanding of machine decision-making mechanisms. While it is possible to reconstruct and understand the mechanism of decision-making by an algorithm that uses statistical procedures, understanding the decisions taken by neural networks is inherently impossible.[4] Interestingly, due to their high efficiency, neural networks are becoming more and more commonly used for example, in recognition of text, image, but also classification of diseases or making investment decisions. As a result, we rely on the recommendations of such structures, having no insight into the basis on which they were generated. This problem was addressed in one of the projects of the US DARPA government research agenda, whose aim was to create the so-called self-explanatory artificial intelligence (Gunning 2017).

Another challenge is the risk of losing knowledge crucial for the functioning of the organization. As has been emphasized many times, a large part of the AI class systems is made available via programming interfaces (APIs) or made available as software (SaaS). On the one hand, it is very beneficial (low investment or service costs, virtually only variable costs, very fast implementation, etc.); on the other hand, it can be very dangerous in the long term. The model in which we send data to an external entity, which on the basis of its analysis sends back recommendations, generates the following risks:

1. The risk of **the lack of control over decision-making mechanisms**. Recommendations are generated by systems to which we do not have access and whose operating principles we do not understand. And, we have no control over them whatsoever.
2. The risk of **the loss of knowledge about the key areas of the company, including customer behavior**. Providing data for analysis by an external entity is convenient, but it can be compared to continuous use of advisory services: a company that does so, loses its key competencies, which significantly increases the risk of failure, e.g. in a situation of being cut off from regular advisors.
3. The risk of **the market takeover by the company to which we provide data**. Of course, it can be controlled, for example, by legal agreements, but it should be taken into account that:
    (a) Many other companies in our industry use our partner's services.
    (b) Nowadays, even anonymized data, after proper processing, can have tremendous value. As a result, there is a risk that the service provider will create a competitive business: having extensive knowledge of customer behavior, they can create a product/service better suited for the needs of the market than our solutions.

These and many other threats emphasize the need to take into account not only the opportunities that these solutions create but also the risks associated with them when planning to implement AI class systems.

3.3.6.6 New Competencies

Managers who want to make full use of the class systems in decision-support processes should develop the following competencies:

1. The ability to identify different data sources and solutions that enable their integration.
2. The ability to interpret data and information generated by AI systems, in particular, using new methods of their visualization (graphs, shapes, etc.).
3. The awareness of the challenges that can arise from various AI class architectures and the ability to design implementations so as to maximize the potential of these systems while minimizing the risks associated with them.

3.4 AI Influence on Competitiveness and Markets

From the perspective of the organization's goals, the main goal of primary and support activities in the value chain is to generate a competitive advantage by providing the best possible value for the customer at the lowest possible cost. Artificial intelligence systems support companies in implementing competition strategies, proposed by Porter (cost and distinction) as well as the value configuration added later by Stabell and Fjeldstad. The aim of this part of the chapter is to show the ways in which AI systems can influence the generation of value by companies and, as a result, the rules of competing in the markets.

In today's complex chains and value networks, a given entity is very often a supplier, producer and customer at the same time. For this reason, the division of AI systems presented below should be treated as symbolic; it refers to a more selected role of a given organization in the value structure than a group of enterprises.

At the beginning, the analysis of the impact of AI on the value generated by producers will be described. Their consequences for the products and processes of companies will be summarized, and different categories of benefits, costs and threats resulting therefrom will be indicated.

Next, the impact of AI on customers: their needs, values and, similarly as in the case of producers, potential threats on the part of artificial intelligence will be shown.

Further analysis of the impact of AI on suppliers, competitors and new players will bring us closer to analyzing new developments in the markets, identifying new sources of competitive advantages and entry barriers. The proposal will end with the criteria for assessing the business potential of new AI projects.

3.4.1 Manufacturers

The previous chapter described in detail the impact of AI systems on primary and support activities in the company's value chain. Below, the most interesting observations, crucial from the perspective of generating value and gaining competitive advantages will be presented.

In the design area, modularization of AI solutions is quite popular; companies interested in using advanced services in their own business can run them, through APIs or services available in the SaaS model, practically without their own investments and relatively quickly. What's more, thanks to the increasingly better data exchange standards, effective switching between the services of different suppliers or their configuration into new services (mechanism for building blocks construction) is possible.

Less weight of declarative reporting of needs for new functionalities or features of solutions is also interesting. Intelligent systems analyzing user behavior and ways of using products or services enable (semi-) automatic identification of system imperfections or (unverified) needs. As a result, differences within the organization are blurred, both at the level of processes and organizational units; the design, production, marketing and customer service departments must be integrated as never before (see the Dev-Ops system described above).

The amount of data generated and their increasing diversity causes the necessity of development of new methods of analysis and inference as well as new forms of knowledge representation. As a result, it is increasingly difficult to understand the mechanisms of AI systems—vide the problem of "the black box" and the trend of self-clarifying artificial intelligence.

Products made by people are more and more autonomous. The autonomous transport systems are becoming more and more common, intelligent robots enable the practical implementation of Industry 4.0, and increasingly more digitized devices like cars, which update themselves and optimize their operation. Soon, it may turn out that it is realistic to create Self-Driving Enterprise—the first inspiration can be an Amazon standalone store: Amazon Go.

Therefore, understandings and concerns about the role of human in such an ecosystem are understandable. What will be the role of designers? Who will define and manage the device objective functions? What will happen if the area of autonomy is extended to the objective functions (vide Ng and Russell 2017)?

Advanced IT systems, including artificial intelligence and the Internet of Things, expand the spectrum of value-added services that carry physical products (see e.g. Porter and Heppelmann 2014). Digital product components are starting to deliver more value than their "physical" components. It can lead to replacing physical parts with digital ones (which is already happening e.g. in the case of displays in cars). As a result, the share in the production costs of "physical" parts will decrease (and the role of their suppliers will start to decrease); however, there will be a demand for suppliers of components necessary for the operation of the "digital" part of products (sensors, communication infrastructure, preinstalled operating systems, data storage systems, analytical systems, etc.).

The ever-greater product encryption, the ever-better systems of data standardization and their communication force the cooperation of companies competing to create market standards enabling the merging of products into entire systems (Porter and Heppelmann 2014). As a result, the end customer recovers value not so much from a specific product as from the entire ecosystem (see e.g. the Apple ecosystem or systems supporting smart farms), and the differences between companies supplying products are blurred (see, for example, the service system constructed around intelligent Amazon Alexa's assistant or smart home systems).

3.4.1.1 Benefits: Positive Impact of AI Systems on Value Generation

What benefits can the company expect from the implementation of intelligent systems, particularly artificial intelligence? Below, the benefits identified in the analysis process of nearly 400 companies offering similar solutions and using them in practice are presented (see Appendix 3 of Chap. 5 for a complete list of companies and projects investigated).

Companies using AI solutions can do more. They have more information (about customers, partners, products, etc.); they can produce and sell more.

They can operate and sell cheaper. It is possible thanks to optimization (the use of resources and processes) and automation. The effect is increased productivity (people, machines, processes).

They also work faster. Automation and optimization of design, production and delivery cycles shorten process times and increases reactivity.

AI systems are also improving quality. Optimized processes are easier; companies more accurately assess the market potential or ideas for new products and operate more safely (fewer failures, less catastrophic effects, greater resistance to attacks or a risk of fraud).

Companies can offer new products and produce them differently. AI systems enable creation of new, better relations with clients and partners, and make it easier to generate new ideas and entering in new forms of interaction thanks to new communication channels.

Due to the above-mentioned factors companies are more profitable; by cheaper production, they provide more value to their clients.

3.4.1.2 Costs and Threats: Negative Impact of AI Systems on Value Generation

In a natural way, the implementation of AI systems requires investment and costs.

There are many uncertainty factors that can prevent new companies from starting such ventures.

Investments, mainly in infrastructure and experts, are subject to high risk. Its sources lie mainly in the lack of the ability to create business cases, assessing the potential of ideas and high risk of AI projects.

The implementation of AI also requires development of new competencies not just the entire organization (organizational culture, project management methodologies) and employees (competencies directly related to the creation of AI and the ability to cooperate with such systems), but also partners (new forms and models of cooperation) and customers (new product opportunities). The effort put into learning is undoubtedly a considerable cost.

AI systems change and shorten business processes. As a result, a change in the existing approach is needed, and we should learn to react in completely new, shorter time scales (for example, computer attacks on computer networks require reaction in near-real time). These changes are also a source of costs, both financial and organizational.

In addition to costs, AI systems also generate threats. Below, the factors that may have the strongest (negative) impact on the recovery of value from AI systems are presented.

Concerning the area of primary and support activities of the organization and generally understood management, and bearing in mind the considerations presented in the previous part of the work, it is worth emphasizing:

1. In the design area:
   (a) The development of product ecosystems requiring high technological competence from partners, high flexibility and responsiveness, and openness to cooperation with competitors (coopetition). The decision to enter the ecosystem made too late or ineffective (from the perspective of the client and other system members) functioning in it may result in the elimination from the market and/or isolation (see the example of the company BlackBerry Ltd., manufacturer of BlackBerry devices).
   (b) The shift of variable costs down the value chain and associated with it the risks to revenue models. The errors made at the design stage of controlling systems can result in a significant loss of profit, e.g. from services (in the situation of self-updating products or high autonomy of customers) or due to underestimation of variable costs related to the use of intelligent services provided by external entities in the formula "Pay-Per-Use."
2. In production and logistics:
   (a) Increasingly shorter time (events, processes, production cycles) combined with a growing number of very different information

and the associated risk of losing control over systems (the need to assign these activities to machines).
   (b) And more generally: the threat of the human role in production and logistics processes (e.g. as a result of autonomous line or transport implementations).

3. In marketing and sales:

   (a) The increasing customer expectations, e.g. in the area of personalization and related costs and risks.
   (b) The need to manage relations between promises made in offers and production capabilities (own and partners).
   (c) The growing role of the product as a vehicle for transferring value from customers to the company (e.g. products virtually for free and benefits from the sale of customer behavior data). The risk of users getting accustomed to free products and services and losing their confidence in the "discovery" of a real business model.

4. In after-sales and service:

   (a) The risk of lower revenues from maintenance services (better and better self-improving products).

5. Company management:

   (a) The lack of understanding of the mechanisms of AI in key areas of the company (e.g. risk assessment or recommendations).
   (b) The risk of a too early implementation of immature solutions, and related costs (service, error repair, etc.).
   (c) Uncontrolled reallocation of decision centers: Who really makes the decision? On what basis and in what way? Who is responsible for it?
   (d) Impairment of key organizational skills related to transfer of appropriate activities to AI systems.
   (e) The threat of jobs and, more generally, the role of people in the ecosystem.
   (f) The threat to the ownership model: Who is the owner of the product, whose components are provided by various suppliers, e.g. in the Pay-Per-Use formula?

The market risks should be added to the above-mentioned "internal" factors.

A new threat, not yet described, may be the need to race against competitors:

1. **Competition has very similar possibilities** and if it uses them, it can significantly jeopardize competitive position.
2. It stimulates companies to **a race that can be a source of unjustified costs** (see e.g. "race on functionality" described in Porter and Heppelmann 2014).
3. There may also be a threat in **transferring key knowledge about products and clients to AI solution providers**. Having such information, they may threaten the position of the company over time (e.g. Knewton in education, Third Data Providers in e-marketing, the suppliers of recommendation engines supporting B2B and B2C sales).
4. Another possible consequence of using third-party solutions may be **the dependence on their services** in a key area for the company.

Porter and Heppelmann (2014) also point out the threat of entering new players so far operating into other industries (e.g. FitBit wristbands in the sports heart rate monitor industry or Apple watches in the life monitor in medical industry).

Product ownership model (ibid.) may also be at risk. PaaS services (Product as a Service) are slowly replacing owned products (e.g. online music services, e.g. Spotify, replace CDs or MP3 files), similarly sharing economy models (e.g. ZipCar for sharing cars or city bike systems).

The last threat can be regulations. An example is the unregulated cryptocurrency market—companies that want to create financial products based on blockchain technology must take into account that over time, regulators will also limit this technological area.

3.4.2 Customers

Nowadays, customers, to a large extent due to the possibilities offered by advanced technologies, are connected (flow of information, opinion and trust—thanks to blockchain), more demanding, less loyal and more autonomous. How can AI systems help suppliers to meet the needs of such customers, and what can it mean to them?

3.4.2.1 Benefits

As described above, manufacturers can provide products to customers via AI systems in a cheaper and faster way. These key values for many do not, however, exhaust the full spectrum of AI capabilities.

Thanks to artificial intelligence, products and services can be better. Safer, more accessible (place, time, simplicity of use, technology platform, communication channels), durable and attractive.

They can also in a better way meet the individual needs: provide values exactly as they are needed in a given context (place, time, situation)—neither less nor more.

Products and services can also generate new needs: new functionalities of electronic devices stimulate the emergence of new micro-industries, such as currently wireless charging systems. New markets, in turn, are interested in stimulating the demand for their own products.

Finally, AI systems can increase the autonomy of customers—thanks to them, it will be easier to change the supplier (modular product architecture can lead to modular value structures and markets), which will increase the customer advantage in the market.

3.4.2.2 Threats

To provide the values described above, manufacturers have to collect many, often sensitive, data on users' behavior. Such collected and processed data is often made available to other entities, which carries a lot of different threats.

What's more, advanced AI systems create advanced behavioral and psychological profiles of clients and, as a result, they may be more able to recognize their current and future needs from the clients themselves. The knowledge of these characteristics can also be the basis of various manipulations, for example:

1. **Generating new needs.**
2. Attempting to **make customers addicted to the product,** for example, watching movies or using social media, see e.g. the Hook model used in application design.
3. **Closing the user in the so-called "recommendation bubble"** through better and narrower recommendation of products, activities or people who are likely to like them.

3.4.3 Suppliers

The AI class systems and, more generally, advanced IT technologies, will generate an increase in the market of digital products (sensors, communication infrastructure, preinstalled operating systems, data storage systems, etc.) (Porter and Heppelmann 2014). Therefore, the role of suppliers of such components and the decline in the importance of suppliers of physical components (ibid.) can be expected.

The growing autonomy of customers may force the transformation of business models of producers and suppliers to market coordinators. A very interesting example of this phenomenon in the energy industry is presented by the Bloomberg report (*Digitalization of Energy Systems* 2017). The authors of the report expect that intelligent IT systems in the power industry will strengthen the role of small energy producers (e.g. from renewable sources) so that the current large producers will have to consider changing their models from production and transmission to coordination. Coordination in this case means automatic control of energy flows in local networks so as to maintain the stability of electricity supply from very unpredictable sources (such as wind farms).

AI systems can significantly reduce the role of intermediaries: manufacturers using systems installed in their products will not only gain direct access to data on customer behavior but also the chance to become independent of intermediaries (see Porter and Heppelmann 2014).

On the other hand, intelligent solutions can generate new intermediaries with a stronger position than current suppliers. An example is the "interface owners" described below, like Amazon with its Alexa system or Flipboard in the digital publishing industry.

3.4.4 New Players

AI systems generate new opportunities not only for existing markets, but also create new markets and new players. On the one hand, it is a natural response to the needs (and an opportunity for many customers), and on the other hand, a threat to entities already operating in many industries.

The first trend that draws attention is the entering of large IT companies into mature, "non-IT" industries. For example, IBM implements its Cognitive Computing system in hospitals. General Electric enters the markets of information systems for industry, while Google enters the automotive industry.

The creators of ecosystems, particularly "interface owners", are beginning to play an increasingly important role. A very interesting example is the Amazon company, which offers personal assistant Alexa (via the Amazon Echo Conversation Device), also offers the services of many other providers. You can expect that after some time, the users of the Alexa system will feel more of Amazon customers than specific service providers, which will significantly strengthen the role of this "owner of the interface."

Special types of intermediaries are platform coordinators connecting different players with each other. The examples are: Uber (connecting drivers with passengers, but also offering environmental companies interested in running their own ventures), Pitstop (connecting car users, manufacturers and services), Zephyr Health (associating life science companies with doctors and clinical centers), Algorithmia (connecting developers of algorithms with clients who need them) or Kaggle (associating talented people who deal with the broadly understood field of Data Science with companies seeking experts and interested in solving their own problems).

The development of AI systems also promotes formation of new business models. More and more companies offer their solutions in the Product as a Service model, e.g. city bikes, tools or "powers" on demand; a lot of them offer Insight as a Service or even such exotic solutions as "Conversational Understanding as a Service." On the one hand, this is due to the increasing specialization of intelligent services (and, consequently, the growing costs of independent creation of competitive solutions); on the other hand, this results from modularization of IT systems (popularity of cloud services, better infrastructure supporting them such as telecommunications, billing systems, etc., and standardization data exchange interfaces).

3.4.5 Markets

The phenomena described above have a natural influence on the dynamics of the markets.

Porter and Heppelmann (2014) analyze the impact of smart, connected things on the dynamics of markets using the model of five market forces. The analyses of the impact of modern technologies on the forces of buyers, manufacturers, suppliers, new players and the threat of substitutes demonstrate that at present the concept of the industry is expanding; products evolve from autonomous solutions to the complex ecosystems of cooperating products and services provided by various suppliers. In effect, the basis of competition shifts from the functionality of a discrete product to the efficiency of the entire system that this product is a part of.

As a result, a very important feature of the product is its ability to cooperate with other products/services of the ecosystem, while the key competence of the organization is its ability to cooperate with other companies in the industry, even if they are its direct competitors. New market rules enforce common standards setting, data exchange, value design, and so on (Porter and Heppelmann 2014).

According to Porter (ibid.), the consolidation of industries can be expected, while its pioneers will have a big advantage, and this phenomenon will be the strongest in the industries that are currently developing most dynamically.

3.4.6 Sources of Competitive Advantage

The analyses of sources of competitive advantages and barriers to entry into specific markets are important for the companies themselves as well as for their owners and investors.

In order to create value, a company should build high entry barriers for both competitors and increasingly independent customers. The higher the barriers, the higher the prices accepted by the market and the higher the profitability. In turn, these profits can be reinvested in the development of further values and strengthening of competitive advantage.

In his fundamental research, Porter recommends two strategies of competing: cost and differentiation. Stabell and Fjeldstad (1998) propose an additional competition strategy based on their research on shops and value networks value configuration.

Detailed analysis of the impact of artificial intelligence systems on the strategies of generating value will be presented in Chap. 4; in the present chapter only the most important methods of companies competing using advanced AI solutions in their operations will be pointed out.

3.4.6.1 Traditional Sources of Competitive Advantages

One of the key "traditional" barriers to entry in technology-saturated industries is high fixed costs related to entering the market. This includes the costs of ICT investments, "digitizing" products (e.g. product equipment with sensors) or adapting production lines to their manufacturing. The costs of a complicated technological process are a special position, often fortified by a complex system of licensing rights and patents, requiring the acquisition of eminent experts and appropriate patent policy.

Another category of barriers is the high cost of supplier changing. As described above, AI systems use data about user behavior for personalization and almost a continuous process of improving products and services. With time, a satisfied user closes in the supplier's ecosystem (e.g. mobile devices, mobile and stationary computers with integrated services, as in the case of Apple), which makes it difficult not only to change the platform but also habits (interface ergonomics, habits, aspect aesthetic, etc.). And the lower the customer's willingness to change supplier, the greater the difficulty for the competition of obtaining a given user.

Companies that already have digital solutions can compete (and build entry barriers) using the economies of scale. According to this, along with the increase in the scale of operations, the operational costs (e.g. server infrastructure) are reduced and, thanks to lower costs, it is possible to lower prices and expand the market. An example of business models that use the effect of scale are cloud-based solutions like Software as a Service (SaaS).

Another source of competitive advantage are skillfully designed and managed network effects. They occur in situations where the value of a given ecosystem or solution grows for the customer, along with the number of users and interactions. These mechanisms are used, for example, by the creators of social networks, auction platforms or telecommunications networks. The strategy usually boils down to acquiring a sufficiently large number of users, implementing well thought-out mechanisms that encourage customers to establish and maintain contacts with each other and develop commercial services based on these relations. The examples of these include Facebook.com, applications such as Slack or WhatsApp, or even operating systems: iOS, Android or Windows.

Interesting examples of the mixture of economies of scale and network effects are Apple application ecosystems (Apple Store), Google (Google Play) and Amazon computing services (Amazon Web Services). In each of these cases, the more application providers, the greater the attractiveness for end customers (network effect), which allows the reduction of operating costs and the increase in the scale of operations (economies of scale).

The last competitive advantage worth mentioning in the context of intelligent systems is loyalty, that is, customer attachment to the brand. The advanced AI systems support manufacturers in developing advanced marketing and sales campaigns and designing habit-shaping products (see, for example, www.hookmodel.com), using more and more recent psychology achievements (mainly cognitive and consumer) and the knowledge about a given user acquired from analytical systems. On the other hand, customers are becoming more and more autonomous and less loyal, which can shake up companies that build their advantage on reputation and brand awareness.

3.4.6.2 New Sources of Competitive Advantages

In industries saturated with intelligent systems, the ability to analyze a huge amount of information (often publicly available) about the behavior of potential customers in near-real time is becoming the source of competitive advantage. Companies should be able to aggregate, process, analyze, apply and make decisions based on information from such systems.

Another key ability is described earlier—the ability to construct business cases (see e.g. Bughin et al. 2017). Teams designing their solutions so that they are immediately focused on business value are able not only to gain the trust of sponsors/investors and the funding related to it but also manage their projects more effectively.

An interesting new source of competitive advantage may be designing systems so that they learn constantly on the experience gained in order to optimize their operation, for example by using reinforcement learning mechanisms. It can generate some interesting effects for high business potential:

1. **Economics of learning**: the more cases analyzed, the better the quality of the algorithms and the efficiency of the system.
2. **Negative amortization**: as the system is used, its value increases (not decreases).
3. **The strength of the control point** occupied by the provider in the network structure depends on:
    (a) **the number of supported events** (for example, recommendations or identified anomalies),
    (b) **quality of data sent by customers**,
    (c) **quality of the methods of experience-based learning system**,
    (d) **number of customers** (but to a lesser extent than in the case of a network effect).

To be able to take full advantage of the learning economics effect, companies should focus on:

1. Acquiring customers with a possibly good quality of their own data and the most frequent service requests (that is, those who can provide the best interaction for learning the system).
2. Improving the quality of systems supporting self-improvement (e.g. reinforcement learning).
3. Improving the mechanisms of joining, particularly simplification and automation of

(a) integration processes with customer systems;
(b) preparation of customer data for processing by algorithms (preferably so that it takes place on the supplier's side, but as soon as possible and at a minimum cost);
(c) user interfaces, both programming and analytical;
(d) integration processes with solutions of complementary service providers or improving the quality of own solutions.

According to Chen (2017) another source of competitive advantages may be the so-called intelligence systems: domain solutions (dedicated to specific industries or companies), addressing strategic problems, particularly enabling the automation of key business processes or creation of new ones possibly fully exploiting the possibilities of advanced technologies, and implementing these solutions in complex organizations. Providers of such solutions will be able to base their competitive advantage on:

1. **Narrow, specialist domain knowledge**: access to experts is a traditional, often difficult to overcome entry barrier.
2. **The synergy effects of expert knowledge with the capabilities of AI systems**: this combination of human skills and advanced technologies gives an advantage over purely technological companies.
3. **Complexity of systems** addressed to complex organizations. This source of advantage is also indicated by the authors of the McKinsey report (Bughin et al. 2017).

Another, though controversial, source of competitive advantage is the access to good quality data. The data is critically important for the efficiency of AI systems, while the process of enrichment and quality assessment is still quite expensive. This indicates access to data as a fairly solid basis for competition and a barrier to entry. On the other hand, however, (1) the data is very "transferable" (it is easy to copy and share it), and (2) regulations regarding data rights are so complex that relying solely on data as a source of advantage can be very risky.

Other sources of competitive advantage often explored among technology companies are:

1. **Sharing your services in the "cloud,"** e.g. in the form of Software as a Service (SaaS);
2. Use of **advanced artificial intelligence algorithms**;
3. Very well designed full **user experience** (User eXperience: UX), particularly the application interface.

According to Chen (2017), the three aforementioned features of solutions should no longer be treated as sources of competitive advantages; they are already so easy to achieve that they do not constitute a significant barrier to entry. They are still important, but they will not ensure a permanent market position.

3.4.6.3 Recommendations for AI Solution Providers

To sum up the above considerations, it is worth recalling the recommendations of McKinsey's experts addressed to AI solution providers (Bughin et al. 2017):

1. Use technologies to solve real business problems.
2. Develop knowledge in the area of a given industry to understand its key problems and needs and to design the best possible solutions for it.
3. Recognize closely the value chains of your customers and their data ecosystems.
4. Improve interfaces between machines and people, focus on comfort and user experience.

3.5 The Influence of Artificial Intelligence on the Role and Competencies of Employees

The influence of artificial intelligence on the place and role of a man is so important that it is worth sacrificing a separate section. Partly indicated in the sections devoted to the influence of AI on the management of human resources and barriers in the adoption of such solutions, this issue will be described in more detail in this part of the study.

The research shows that currently most of the artificial intelligence systems support, rather than replace humans (see Ross 2017; Vargo and Lusch 2004). The tasks of employees and the way they work are changing. Over time, you can expect an increase in the demand for employees with specialist skills; particularly those able to cooperate with advanced machines and evaluate their recommendations at the expense of the demand for employees performing non-specialist activities (easy to automate). For example (Ross 2017):

1. Anomalies detection systems:
    (a) shorten the time and reduce the effort required to detect anomalies, such as theft;
    (b) require additional activities such as, for example, the decision on what to do with the identified cases?
2. Financial analysis systems:
    (a) shorten the time of identifying key facts in a large amount of data; but
    (b) only add real value if we put in more time and effort to assess the consequences of these facts and make the right decisions following the question "What should be done?"
3. Intelligent systems supporting customer service:
    (a) allow you to shorten the service time (thanks to automation); but
    (b) they provide value only if we put more effort into understanding the reasons why the client has such and no other problems with the product.

As a result, the implementation of AI systems will require both the development of new ones and the adaptation of already existing competencies. With a high degree of probability, these systems cannot replace all professions, but certainly employees using the capabilities of AI will start replacing those who do not use them (Ransbotham et al. 2017). This is confirmed by the observations of the authors of the AI Index report (Shoham et al. 2017), according to which in the United States the share of professions requiring AI knowledge increased in the period from 2013 to 2016 by 4.5 times.

3.5.1 New Competencies

As already mentioned, the implementation of AI class systems requires the development of many new competencies (their summary will be found in Appendix 1 of Chap. 5). According to MIT researchers Sloan and BCG (Ransbotham et al. 2017), the key is the intuition of the AI's capabilities among the management, especially understanding of the impact of this class of solutions on the company and its environment and understanding the role of data, algorithms and teaching processes. In addition to this, the following points are important: (1) the intuition of AI's capabilities among the management, especially understanding the impact of this class of solutions on the company and its environment and understanding the role of data, algorithms and teaching processes. In addition, AI skills and Data Science are significant; that is, the knowledge of AI methods and algorithms and the ability to design, test and implement production of such systems, and **technical skills**, particularly the programming of such solutions and the management of appropriate infrastructure.

A very interesting set of new, "soft" competencies necessary for a more complete use of the potential of AI solutions is proposed by Ross (2017). According to the author, the most important of them is action-oriented "consumption" of intelligence, particularly requiring the ability to

1. interpret and inference based on data from AI;
2. make decisions based on predictions and statistical assessments;
3. asking questions:
   (a) What are the prediction possibilities?
   (b) What can/should be recognized, provided?
   (c) How should the AI agent learn to constantly improve its predictive capabilities?

In turn, according to Agrawal, the ability to assess the consequences of actions recommended by AI systems is crucial (Agrawal et al. 2017). As the predictive algorithms improve, the human role will be shifted towards the assessment of the consequences of the AI recommendation (*What happens if I take this action?*), but also aesthetic and ethical evaluation (making responsible decisions), creativity (based on the capabilities of AI, see e.g. Generative Adversarial Networks: GAN technologies), emotional intelligence and defining good tasks for AI systems. According to the author, in the near future, the machines will make better decisions than humans—then people will have to be able to formulate optimal target functions for AI systems.

In conclusion, people interested in the effective use of the potential of AI solutions should develop the following competencies:

1. Understanding the impact of AI solutions on the company and its environment:
   (a) The assessment of the business potential of AI solutions;
   (b) The assessment of the impact of AI on workplaces;
   (c) Evaluation of the impact of AI on the industry.
2. Understanding the role of data, algorithms and processes of their "training."
3. Understanding the mechanisms of AI systems (translators).
4. Interpretation and inference based on AI system recommendations.
5. Making decisions based on predictions and recommendations of AI systems:
   (a) The ability to assess the consequences of actions recommended by AI;
   (b) Ethical evaluation of these activities;
   (c) Their aesthetic evaluation;
   (d) The ability to ask good AI questions.
6. Ability to ask questions about the possibilities and limitations of AI recommendations:
   (a) What are their options?
   (b) What can/should be recognized, provided?
   (c) How should the AI agent learn to constantly improve its predictive capabilities?
7. Ability to specify and manage AI system objective functions.

3.5.2 New Roles in Organizations

A very inspiring vision of new roles and occupations of the future closely related to the implementation of AI systems is presented by Wilson et al. (2017). According to the authors, for the optimal use of the potential of artificial intelligence in organizations, three roles will be crucial: coaching, explaining, and maintaining.

Coaches they will deal with the broadly understood teaching of AI systems. The examples of their tasks are

1. **improvement of natural language processing algorithms**, particularly language translation systems by correcting machine translations;
2. **improvement of customer service systems** through teaching the understanding of the nuances of human communication, e.g. sarcasm detection. For example, Yahoo has developed an algorithm with 80% accuracy that recognizes sarcasm in social media, not only in the text (see https://finance.yahoo.com/news/watch-tone-machine-learning-algorithm-203819664.html), but also in communication using emoticons (see https://finance.yahoo.com/news/smiley-face-emojis-teach-mit-174046929.html);
3. **teaching algorithms of emotional sensation and empathic conversation**, which is very important for solutions such as Apple Siri or Amazon Alexa;
4. showing the global context and consequences of decisions.

As a result, among these "trainers" one can expect to shape, for example, the following "specialties" (Wilson et al. 2017):

1. **Coaching of the client's speech tone and understanding of meaning**, teaching a more complete understanding of the meaning of the message, e.g. by identifying sarcasm.
2. **Coaching of intelligent employee imitation,** teaching the machine an effective and intelligent imitation of employees, e.g. accounting activities in the process of classification of invoices.
3. **Coaching of a wider view,** preparing machines to identify a wider context of undertaken actions, e.g. the meaning of the concept of being "fair."

The next category will be created by the so-called explainers. They will be intermediaries between the world of technology and business. In particular, they will explain: Why the algorithm issued such and no other decision? Such an "autopsy," i.e. a step-by-step analysis of the principles of the algorithm, will be particularly important in critical situations.

1. **why did it recommend it, not something else?** This will be particularly important in the context of the "right to clarify" contained in European regulations on the protection of personal data (GDPR);
2. They will also **assess the usefulness of AI in a given situation**: When is it worth using? And when is it better to use proven principles/procedures/methods?

The LIME method (Local Interpretable Model-Agnostic Explanations) is worth pointing out as a very interesting, already available method supporting the work of the "explainers": https://www.oreilly.com/learning/introduction-to-local-interpretable-model-agnostic-explanations-lime. It examines the way the algorithms work by slightly changing the input data and observing changes in results. This trend in research is very promising, both from a technical and applicational perspective.

The last role indicated by Wilson et el. are sustainers. Their role will be to maintain AI systems, in particular to

1. **ensure that AI algorithms work as they should,** and their unpredictable/risky behavior is quickly identified and addressed;
2. **ensure ethical correctness** recommendation of algorithms, e.g. objectivity and non-discrimination;
3. **identify human value systems** (see e.g. Ng and Russell 2017).

3.6 Summary

As can be seen, the growing adoption of AI systems will significantly affect the structure of competencies desired on the market. One can expect the elimination of jobs that are easy to automate, which does not necessarily mean a reduction in employment. There will be a growing demand for people who will be able to cooperate with machines and use their potential, and to teach, understand and develop them.

Notes

1. Producers identify the most interesting product use case scenarios and provide them to new consumers. This way, "the best practices of using the product by other users" becomes a real value added.
2. Quotation marks are used due to the fact that in the case of medical solutions, an "object" can be a human being, and a "repair" an appropriate therapy.
3. A machine that can establish and maintain a text conversation using messengers within social media.
4. Let's remind ourselves that the learned neural network is actually a collection of layers of virtual "neurons" connected with each other with links of different strength (weight). Looking into this network only shows its topology and the strength of connection weights.

References

Agrawal, A. K., Gans, J. S., & Tetlock, P. E. (2017). What to Expect From Artificial Intelligence. *MIT Sloan Management Review*, Spring.

Bostrom, N. (2014). *Superintelligence*. Oxford: Oxford University Press.

Bughin, J., Hazan, E., Ramaswamy, S., Chui, M., Allas, T., Dahlstrom, P., et al. (2017). *Artificial Intelligence*. McKinsey Global Institute. Retrieved from https://www.mckinsey.com/~/media/McKinsey/Industries/Advanced%20Electronics/Our%20Insights/How%20artificial%20intelligence%20can%20deliver%20real%20value%20to%20companies/MGI-Artificial-Intelligence-Discussion-paper.ashx

Chen, J. (2017, April 24). The New Moats – Greylock Perspectives. Retrieved January 2, 2018, from https://news.greylock.com/the-new-moats-53f61aeac2d9

Digitalization of Energy Systems. (2017). Bloomberg Finance LP, pp. 1–61. Retrieved from https://www.siemens.com/global/en/home/company/topic-areas/sustainable-energy/digitalization-of-energysystems.html

Five Management Strategies for Getting the Most from AI. (2017, September 19). *MIT Sloan Management Review*, pp. 1–6. Retrieved from https://sloanreview.mit.edu/article/five-management-strategies-for-getting-the-most-from-ai/

For Robots to Work with People, They Must Understand People. (2017, August). For Robots to Work with People, They Must Understand People. *The Economist*. Retrieved from https://www.economist.com/science-andtechnology/2017/08/17/for-robots-to-work-with-people-they-must-understand-people

Grudzewski, W. M., Hejduk, I. K., Sankowska, A., & Wańtuchowicz, M. (2008). Cultural Determinants of Creating Modern Organisations – The Role of Trust. In *Pervasive Collaborative Networks* (Vol. 283, pp. 323–332). Boston: Springer. https://doi.org/10.1007/978-0-387-84837-2_33.

Gunning, D. (2017). Explainable Artificial Intelligence (XAI). Retrieved June 13, 2018, from https://www.darpa.mil/program/explainable-artificial-intelligence

Hoang, H., & Rothaermel, F. T. (2016). How to Manage Alliances Strategically. *MIT Sloan Management Review, 58*(1), 69–76.

Hern, A. (2017, April 18). Netflix's Biggest Competitor? *Sleep*. Retrieved January 31, 2018, from http://www.theguardian.com/technology/2017/apr/18/netflix-competitor-sleep-uber-facebook

Kemelmacher-Shlizerman, I., Seitz, S. M., Miller, D., & Brossard, E. (2015). The MegaFace Benchmark – 1 Million Faces for Recognition at Scale. *2016 IEEE Conference on Computer Vision and Pattern Recognition (CVPR)*. Retrieved from http://arxiv.org/pdf/1512.00596. For more details: https://www.researchgate.net/publication/311609513_The_MegaFace_Benchmark_1_Million_Faces_for_Recognition_at_Scale

Koelblin, S. (2017, April 3). *Robots Take Over – The Apparel Production*. Retrieved January 31, 2018, from https://www.linkedin.com/pulse/robots-take-over-apparel-production-susanna-koelblin

Kolodner, J. L. (1992). An Introduction to Case-Based Reasoning. *Artificial Intelligence Review, 6*(1), 3–34. https://doi.org/10.1007/BF00155578.

Levine, P. (2016, December 16). *The End of Cloud Computing*. Retrieved January 30, 2018, from https://a16z.com/2016/12/16/the-end-of-cloud-computing/

Lohr, S. (2014, August 17). For Big-Data Scientists, "Janitor Work" Is Key Hurdle to Insights. Retrieved December 31, 2017, from https://www.nytimes.com/2014/08/18/technology/for-big-data-scientists-hurdleto-insights-is-janitor-work.html

Messaging Apps Are Now Bigger Than Social Networks. (2016). *Business Insider*. Retrieved from http://www.businessinsider.com/the-messaging-app-report-2015-11

Ng, A. Y., & Russell, S. (2017, August 17). *Algorithms for Inverse Reinforcement Learning*. Retrieved December 27, 2017, from http://bair.berkeley.edu/blog/2017/08/17/cooperatively-learning-human-values/

On Orbitz, Mac Users Steered to Pricier Hotels. (2012, August 23). On Orbitz, Mac Users Steered to Pricier Hotels. Retrieved December 29, 2017, from https://www.wsj.com/articles/SB10001424052702304458604577488822667325882

Porter, M. E., & Heppelmann, J. E. (2014). How Smart, Connected Products Are Transforming Competition. *Harvard Business Review, 92*, 64–88.

Porter, M. E., & Heppelmann, J. E. (2015). How Smart, Connected Products Are Transforming Companies. *Harvard Business Review, 93*(10), 96–114.

Porter, M. E., & Heppelmann, J. E. (2017). A Manager's Guide to Augmented Reality. *Harvard Business Review*, 11–12.

Ransbotham, S. (2017). AI and the Need for Speed. *MIT Sloan Management Review*, 1–4.

Ransbotham, S., Kiron, D., Gerbert, P., & Reeves, M. (2017). Reshaping Business with Artificial Intelligence. *MIT Sloan Management Review*. Retrieved from http://sloanreview.mit.edu/projects/reshaping-business-with-artificial-intelligence/

Ross, J. (2017). The Fundamental Flaw in AI Implementation. *MITSloan Review*, Winter 2017, 1–5. Retrieved from https://sloanreview.mit.edu/article/the-fundamental-flaw-in-ai-implementation/

Shoham, Y., Perrault, R., Brynjolfsson, E., Clark, J., & LeGassick, C. (2017). *Artificial Intelligence Index* (pp. 1–101). Retrieved from https://aiindex.org/#report

Stabell, C. B., & Fjeldstad, Ø. D. (1998). Configuring Value for Competitive Advantage: On Chains, Shops, and Networks. *Strategic Management Journal, 19*(5), 413–437. http://doi.org/10.1002/(SICI)1097-0266(199805)19:5<413::AID-SMJ946>3.3.CO;2-3.

The Future Lies in Automation. (2017 April 8). *The Economist*. Retrieved from https://www.economist.com/special-report/2017/04/08/the-future-lies-in-automation

Vargo, S. L., & Lusch, R. F. (2004). Evolving to a New Dominant Logic for Marketing. *Journal of Marketing, 68*(1), 1–17. https://doi.org/10.1509/jmkg.68.1.1.24036.

Wang, Y., Skerry-Ryan, R. J., Stanton, D., Wu, Y., Weiss, R. J., Jaitly, N., et al. (2017, March 29). *Tacotron: Towards End-to-End Speech Synthesis*. https://arxiv.org/abs/1703.10135

Wilson, H. J., Daugherty, P. R., & Morini-Bianzino, N. (2017). The Jobs That Artificial Intelligence Will Create. *MIT Sloan Management Review*, Summer.

Zawiła-Niedźwiecki, J., & Byczkowski, M. (2009). Information Security Aspect of Operational Risk Management. *Foundations of Management, 1*(2), 162. https://doi.org/10.2478/v10238-012-0010-2.

4

Model for Value Generation in Companies and Cognitive Networks

Artificial intelligence systems not only change the way the organization operates but also enable the creation of new business models and ecosystems. Below is a model proposal that can describe new value creation logics, which result in the spread of intelligent systems.

First, the classification of AI technology was proposed from the perspective of value creation models. As a starting point, classical models of knowledge value chains and models of data transformation processes in information systems were used. They were used to organize AI systems according to (1) a place in the knowledge value chain (in this approach, AI enables data transformation into information and knowledge), and (2) cognitive functions (for the purposes of the cognitive networks concept introduced later).

The above classifications were further used to develop a value generation model at the organization level and network structures. The first can be used, for example, by managers or investors interested in assessing the business potential of ventures. The second, concerning the concept of cognitive networks, is a proposal of a new model of relations and ways of generating value in network structures in which key services rely on enrichment of information by the use of AI systems.

A. Wodecki, *Artificial Intelligence in Value Creation*,
https://doi.org/10.1007/978-3-319-91596-8_4

4.1 Classification of AI Technology in the Context of Value Generation

4.1.1 Knowledge Value Chains and Data Transformation Processes in Information Systems

In Chap. 1, devoted to classical models of value generation, two concepts of the knowledge value chains were presented.

Wang and Ahmed (2013) proposed the following primary activities in the knowledge value chain:

1. Creating
2. Application
3. Enrichment
4. Distribution
5. Accumulation
6. Codification
7. Obtaining
8. Identification

These activities are supported by the following support activities:

1. Knowledge system
2. Culture of knowledge
3. Organizational memory
4. Sharing
5. Benchmarking

A slightly different model was proposed by Ermine (2013). In his view, the purpose of supplementary activities is to enrich knowledge resources. In other words, instead of primary activities (in analogy to Porter's value chain), the author introduced resources at various levels of "enrichment":

1. Data
2. Information

3. Knowledge:
   (a) Implicit
   (b) Explicit
4. Wisdom:
   (a) Competencies
   (b) Applications

Complementary activities are used to "enrich" knowledge resources—their transformation from data to wisdom:

1. **Data management**, whose aim is to achieve memorizing.
2. **Information management**, whose goal is to achieve understanding.
3. **Management of knowledge**, whose goal is to achieve learning.
4. **Competence management**, whose goal is to achieve intelligence.
5. **Capability management**, whose goal is to achieve maturity.

For the purpose of developing a value generation model in solutions using AI, it is worth referring the above proposals to models of data transformation processes in information systems.

There are many approaches and publications devoted to this issue (see e.g. Kimball et al. 2008). Below, the most important of them are presented: ETL/ELT processes, closed data processing model and the CRISP-DM model, which is probably the most popular standard in Business Intelligence methodologies.

One of the oldest concepts of data transformation is the so-called ETL (Extract—Transform—Load) (see Kimball and Caserta 2004 or https://en.wikipedia.org/wiki/Extract,_transform,_load). In this process:

1. **Extraction of data** is to obtain data from homogeneous or heterogeneous data sources.
2. **Transformation** boils down to processing (unifying, formatting and structuring) data for the purpose of further analysis.
3. **Loading** is the process of transferring data transformed in this way to the place of storage (database or data warehouse).

An alternative to the ETL process is ELT (Extract—Load—Transform), most often used in the implementation of the data lakes, increasingly popular in industrial projects like Big Data, IoT or AI. In this approach, data is entered into the storage system (e.g. a data lake) without prior processing, and the transformation process is carried out "on demand" as a function of the user's needs. It definitely speeds up the process of obtaining data; however, it requires advanced tools and methods that enable processing and serving analytical services in near-real time. In ETL it is also not necessary to define "a priori" data patterns, which not only speeds up the loading, but also does not restrict the possibilities of future analyses.

ETL/ELT are "engineering" processes, used by IT specialists mainly in data management processes in information systems (e.g. at the interface of ERP—Enterprise Resource Planning—integrated systems) and data warehouses/lakes. However, data transformation is not only the domain of IT specialists, but also analysts whose task is to solve business problems based on data and information. For this reason, alternative transformation models have been developed, the two of which are presented below.

Lin and Xiao (2017) in their study on the implementation of intelligent data platforms propose a transparent cycle of transformation activities, which consists of four stages, each divided into two groups of activities:

1. Acquisition:
   (a) Harvest
   (b) Ingestion
2. Organization:
   (a) Preparation
   (b) Enrichment
3. Analysis:
   (a) Insight
   (b) Decision
4. Operation:
   (a) Deployment
   (b) Assessment

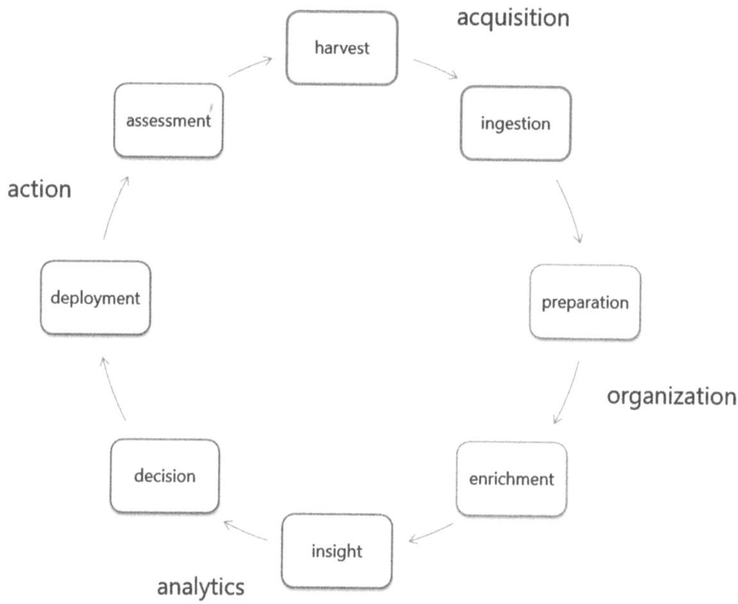

Fig. 4.1 Data processing loop according to Lin and Xiao. (Source: Own elaboration based on Lin and Xiao 2017)

At the **acquisition** stage the authors distinguish two processes (Fig. 4.1):

1. **Harvesting**, in which external sources generate data and transmit it to "a recipient". It can be done continuously without time limits (e.g. video stream from cameras, internet activity on websites or data from sensors) or in the form of discrete batches—on a periodic basis at specific intervals (e.g. blog entries or video clips).
2. **Ingestion** is the submission of data in the "recipient" systems. This process is divided into three groups of activities:

   (a) **Discovery**, based on searching and identifying data sources in corporate systems.
   (b) **Connecting**, as a result of which the target database is connected via appropriate database interfaces to data sources.
   (c) **Synchronization,** involving the transfer of data from the source to the "recipient" database.

The aim of data organization is to prepare it for further analysis. Lin and Xiao (2017) divide the process into two stages:

1. **Preparation** during which the quality of the data is improved (e.g. their integrity, accuracy and chronology). Typical activities carried out at this stage are data completion and updating, directory building, data cleaning (e.g. removing duplicated or empty records), **validation** (context, meaning) and implementation of security mechanisms (e.g. in the area of sensitive or personal data protection).
2. **Enrichment** is processing of data at the context level. Typical activities at this stage are describing data (labeling) and their modeling for later analyses (e.g. transformation into a graph form).

The analysis phase, which involves first " values recovering" from the data processing, according to Lin and Xiao (2017) can be divided into two stages:

1. **Insight** into data involves its understanding thanks to analytical processes, which may take place depending on the type and mechanisms of obtaining data in real time, interactively or at discrete time stages.
2. **Making decisions**, resulting in recommendations of actions based on the results of the conducted analyses.

The last phase is implementation and evaluation of activities, which are the result of the analytical phase. It is most often divided into deployment and assessment phases:

1. **Deployment** involves starting activities. In simple cases, it can be reduced to taking action by people responsible for a given area based on analytical reports. Increasingly, however, due to the complexity of IT systems, this phase requires the transfer of models and algorithms developed in the analytical phase to production environments—so that they are implemented in an efficient and safe way (which is a major engineering and technical challenge, and requires the implementation of systems other than those used in the "laboratory").

2. **Assessment** is based on observation and evaluation of the results of the actions, and as a result, the basis for the optimization of cycles.

Currently the most popular standard—according to the KDNuggets.com research, see "What main methodology are you using for your analytics, data mining, or data science projects? Poll" (n.d.)—used by data analysts is CRISP-DM—Cross-Industry Standard Process for Data Mining developed in 1997 by SPSS, Teradata, Daimler AG, NCR Corporation and OHRA cross-industry standard of data mining processes. It consists of the following phases (see e.g. Chapman et al. 2004):

1. **Understanding business conditions**.
2. **Understanding the data** (including data collecting and assessing its suitability).
3. **Data preparation**: transformations, cleaning, removing extreme values.
4. **Modeling** data for the purpose of developing the model.
5. **Evaluating** the model and a decision whether it is ready for a production implementation.
6. **Implementation** of the model in a production environment to be used in practice.

The diagram of the CRISP-DM process is shown in the figure below (Fig. 4.2):

4.1.2 Classification of AI Systems According to a Place in the Knowledge Value Chain

Thousands of companies are currently operating in the field of artificial intelligence systems (for example, the analytical company Index.co (www.index.co) in January 2018 indicated 2039 different projects in the category of Artificial Intelligence). These projects can be classified in various ways; see e.g. Zilis and Cham (2016) and Chap. 3 of this book. However, the development of a value generation model due to AI systems requires a separate classification.

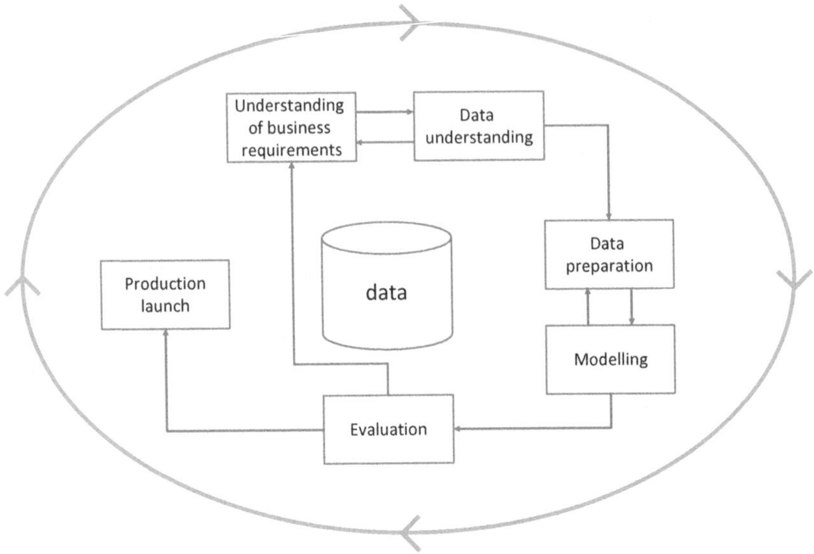

Fig. 4.2 CRISP-DM process scheme. (Source: Own elaboration based on Chapman et al. 2004)

The following proposal is based on a simple observation: IT tools enable taking actions that improve the quality of data. Below, this idea is presented in more detail.

1. Data in a given area of the company's activity may have different "degree of enrichment." While using the terminology of the concept of knowledge value chains and data transformation processes, these may be, for example:
   (a) Raw data.
   (b) Data prepared for modeling purposes (cleared, enriched, ordered).
   (c) Models: in the testing process, evaluated and implemented.
   (d) Analyzed data (e.g. in the form of reports and their interpretations).
   (e) Recommendations (forecasts, recommended decisions, consequence forecasts).
   (f) The effects of the actions and their assessment.

2. IT systems enable data transformation processes: they help the company transform these data into increasingly higher levels.
3. In effect, the source of the value of technology is its ability to increase the value of information.

Therefore, the classification of AI class systems including transformation activities (ordered according to the growing value of data in data areas, information and knowledge) and results of these activities is recommended.

The diagram of the proposed classification is shown in the table below (Table 4.1):

Below, the characteristics of individual system groups are presented.

Table 4.1 The proposition of AI systems classification in the context of knowledge transformation

support systems	research centers, incubators								
	sources of data and knowledge								
	systems supporting monitoring, data governance and data protection								
activity	registration	communication	storage	transport	analysis	modelling	recommending	autonomous activities	higher functions
result	raw data	data transferred to storage systems	registered data	data prepared for analyses	Observations, interpretations, predictions, inferences	models	activity recommendations	autonomous systems	higher systems
scope	data				information			knowledge	

4.1.2.1 Data

The data area contains a large spectrum of systems transforming raw data into data well prepared for analyses. Below, the key categories ordered in the stages of data transformation are presented.

Registration

Systems enabling data registration, for instance, sensors in robots or the Internet of Things, sensors in mobile devices, cameras, microphones or solutions for monitoring users' activity on the Internet. They are most often delivered with software with different levels of information enrichment: from the simplest interfaces enabling the transmission of raw data to built-in systems enabling the identification of objects (e.g. distinguishing a person from an object).

The effect of these systems is data registration and preparing it for sending to subsequent systems (e.g. storage or direct analysis).

Communication

Systems enabling effective communication of the recorded data to storage systems. Among them, we can distinguish:

1. **Communication systems (wired and wireless)**, e.g. network infrastructure (routers, etc.), GSM or Bluetooth.
2. Effective systems supporting the **management of large data streams**, particularly providing data (e.g. communication interfaces) and coordinating its flow.

The effect of these systems is the transmission of raw (or to some extent processed) data to other systems.

Storage

Systems enabling the storage of data that can be divided into:

1. **Infrastructural solutions**, e.g. disk arrays, scattered archaizers, etc. These systems can be made available in various models: ownership (the user buys them for their own needs), leasing and services available on demand (e.g. in the IaaS formula—Infrastructure as a Service), see e.g. Amazon Web Services).
2. **Software**, which includes various database solutions, particularly the following databases:

   (a) Relational (SQL)
   (b) NoSQL (Not Only SQL)
   (c) NewSQL
   (d) Graph
   (e) Massive Parallel Processing
   (f) Cloud Enterprise Data Warehouses

The effect of these systems is to place the information obtained in structures that enable their subsequent processing and analysis.

Processing

Systems enabling the preparation of data for future analyses, particularly its ordering, clearing and enrichment.

This group of solutions is particularly extensive:

1. Solutions are available under open-source as well as commercial licenses.
2. It is possible for them to be installed locally, on your own servers, as well as available via "cloud," e.g. in the PaaS formula (Platform as a Service) or SaaS (Software as a Service).
3. There are environments and libraries for creators (e.g. programmers) and easy applicable Data Science platforms (e.g. Dataiku or Rapidminer).
4. Solutions are dedicated to small amounts of data, as well as being highly scalable (e.g. Apache Spark or Hadoop).

The effect of these systems is ordered data, prepared for further analysis.

4.1.2.2 Information

The above-mentioned IT systems are used to register and prepare data so that it can be effectively analyzed. It is worth emphasizing that the processes in this group can consume from 60% to 80% of the entire Data Science project—but they are necessary to ensure its high quality.

Another group of solutions supports the stage of data transformation to the form of useful information and recommendations. In this group, there are solutions supporting data analysis (understanding), models creation and recommendations (inference).

Analysis

Systems supporting data analysis is another wide group of solutions creating the AI ecosystem. Among them, we can distinguish:

1. **Libraries and systems** enabling statistical calculations, machine learning and visualization support.
2. **Analytical solutions** enabling the analysis of system logs, social media, customer behavior (traditional and e-commerce) and industry analysis.
3. Data Science and Business Intelligence **platforms**, supporting the work of individual analysts and the entire Data Science teams.
4. **Specialized analytical services** in the areas of data handling, specialist solutions (e.g. speech recognition and analysis) or horizontal AI solutions (dedicated to specific areas of the organization's activities).

The effects of this group of systems are, for example:

1. **Detection** of signals, anomalies, patterns, etc.
2. **Recognition** of images, texts, etc.
3. **Data interpretation** from inside of the company (e.g. system logs) or from the background.
4. **Prediction** failures, illness, quotations, etc.

Modeling

Analytical systems facilitate the understanding of data and are often the basis for making simple decisions. In artificial intelligence systems, the results of analyses can also serve as the basis for creation of advanced models enabling, for instance, autonomous actions.

The differences between analysis and modeling are fluid. We introduce this class of solutions with the aim of separating machine learning systems and Deep Learning technologies, whose operation (especially the specificity of "teaching") is significantly different from typical analytical models.

The effect of these systems is most often models enabling; for example, recognition (objects on images, meanings of speech, patterns in data), prediction and recommendations.

Recommendations

Recommendation systems and, more generally, supportive decision-making are based on analytical systems and enabling the creation of models.

The results of their actions are recommendations (for people, e.g. employees, decision-makers, clients) and instructions (for information systems or machines).

4.1.2.3 Knowledge

Knowledge and wisdom in previous approaches was the domain of people. The temptation to create rational machines (agents) and current achievements in this area, however, encourage the creation of two new categories of IT systems: the ability to act autonomously and the implementation of higher cognitive functions.

The group of autonomous systems includes solutions which are able to

1. **independently communicate with the environment** (send and receive messages), e.g. with the use of conversational interfaces;

2. **move,** e.g. on roads, in the air or in confined spaces;
3. **constantly self-improve (learn)** on the basis of the gained experience.

The solutions capable of defining, modifying or revealing the functions of the goal (own or the users') independently are included in the systems of higher cognitive functions (see e.g. Ng and Russell 2017). For this class of solutions, we suggest including, for example, attempts to create AGI (Artificial General Intelligence).

4.1.2.4 Support Systems

The support systems include

1. systems supporting monitoring, data governance and data security.
2. sources of data and knowledge:
   (a) most often available via API data from such areas as health, finance and economics, spatial analyses and images (sea, earth), information about people, companies and places (location intelligence);
   (b) sources of knowledge in the form of on-line training, traditional courses, expert conferences and blogs.
3. research centers and incubators.

These solutions have a supporting function: they enable and catalyze the development of AI ecosystems.

4.1.3 Classification of AI Systems According to Cognitive Functions

For the purposes of the following concept of cognitive networks below, the alternative classification of AI class systems, according to cognitive functions are presented below.

The dynamic development of the previously described Cognitive Computing systems (hereinafter CC) is an inspiration. It should be reminded that these are the systems whose operation is inspired by the action of the human brain.

The development of CC class systems is on one hand, stimulated by the development of artificial intelligence systems, and on the other hand by cognitive neuroscience. The division presented below is inspired by the classic areas of this field (see e.g. Gazzaniga and Ivry 2013).

4.1.3.1 Nervous System

In this area are the following classes:

1. AI Infrastructure:
   (a) Data sets
   (b) Infrastructure and environments available in the "cloud":
      (i) Infrastructure as a Service
      (ii) Platform as a Service
      (iii) Software as a Service
   (c) Sensors
   (d) Solutions increasing computing power (processors, graphics cards, dedicated Application-Specific Integrated Circuits Chips: ASICs)
2. Environments for creators:
   (a) Programming environments
   (b) Machine learning libraries, statistics, etc.
   (c) Data Science platforms
   (d) Systems for designing and programming intelligent agents (e.g. chat-bots)

4.1.3.2 Basic Functions

In cognitive psychology, the term "basic functions" is usually understood as sensory reception and perception, recognition, memory, attention, action (including motor skills), communication and emotions.

On the basis of this classification, the following division of systems supporting development of AI can be proposed:

1. **Sensor and perception** systems enabling:
   (a) data ingestion (e.g. sensors),
   (b) extracting data from internal and external systems.
2. **Recognition**: systems enabling the understanding of media (text, audio, image, video).
3. Short-term memory (including working memory) and durable systems enabling:
   (a) in-memory processing,
   (b) analysis and inference from data.
4. **Attention**: the identification of patterns, anomaly detection, etc.
5. **Action** (motor skills, planning, realization): autonomous systems:
   (a) virtual agents: personal (e.g. Amazon Alexa, Apple Siri) and for business (e.g. chat-bots in customer service),
   (b) navigation systems,
   (c) preparatory works,
   (d) systems that automate paperwork (e.g. classification of invoices, money transfers, etc.).
6. **Communication** systems enabling:
   (a) understanding media: text, audio, image,
   (b) creative systems (using e.g. GAN technology):
      (i) audio and video,
      (ii) generating a natural language.
   (c) conversational interfaces: text and voice communication.
7. **Emotions**: empathic technologies (which recognize the mood and appropriately adjust their own communication).

4.1.3.3 Executive Functions

In cognitive psychology, executive functions are most often defined as thinking (analyzing, flexibility (switching), reasoning (verbal, abstract), problem solving), cognitive control (actions focused on achieving goals, planning, decision-making, monitoring of implementation, flexibility, etc.) and higher-order functions (e.g. awareness, free will, social rights, social cognition).

In this analogy, the following classification of systems supporting the creation of artificial intelligence solutions are proposed:

1. **Thinking**: recommendation systems and, more generally, systems supporting decision-making, rational agents.
2. **Cognitive control**: autonomous and predictive systems, solutions enabling personalization, recommendation systems.
3. **Higher-order functions**: general artificial intelligence, systems enabling detection and creation of objective functions.

Thus, the little exotic classification shown above will be useful in the description of the phenomena that can occur in the near future in the structure values tentatively referred to as cognitive networks that are proposed below.

4.2 Value Generation Model: Organization Level

In classical models of value generation (e.g. in Porter's value chain model), the value is generated by actions within a given structure element (e.g. a group of activities in a value chain). This can be done in the areas of mechanical processing (e.g. on the production line) and/or (in parallel) digital processing. The measure of the added value is, for example, a generated mark-up.

In the case of advanced information systems the value is generated at the stages of data enrichment in the value chain of knowledge. In order to optimize the process of generating this value, for the areas in which the intelligent system is planned to be implemented, it is necessary to assess

1. the quality of available data;
2. the current level of "enrichment";

3. the potential of their enrichment with the available methods and tools;
4. data processing costs (licenses, infrastructure, external services, the human costs, legal, organizational, social and other);
5. the benefits of a data transformation process.

Below, the specifics of such a model are proposed: it can be easily applied by managers to design the system using artificial intelligence as well as by researchers interested in examining the potential and efficiency of AI solutions implementation.

4.2.1 Value Generation Process

The model process of generating values can be described in the following way: in a given area the AI tool is used for taking actions that produce certain effects which in turn are the source of the value. Below, each of the mentioned key concepts is described on the basis of deep analyses of several hundred different projects from the artificial intelligence area (see Appendix 3 of Chap. 5).

4.2.1.1 AI Tools and Methods

A designer of AI solutions has different methods and resources necessary for their use.

Most popular methods (and/or algorithms) allow

1. **recognition** of images, texts, etc.;
2. **classification** of objects;
3. **prediction** of e.g. failures, events or behaviors;
4. **modeling**, e.g. geospatial or 3D, optimizing a given objective function (e.g. persistence or flow);
5. **generation** of images, videos, content, etc.

The implementation of AI systems also requires dedicated resources, specific for a given method or application. These resources can be divided into

1. **software**;
2. **infrastructure**;
3. **human resources**, particularly people with specific competencies;
4. **external suppliers**;
5. **financing**.

4.2.1.2 Operations

AI tools enable the implementation of certain activities. These operations can be characterized in a few dimensions:

1. level of autonomy,
2. time,
3. the dimension of analysis,
4. quality and precision.

First, a very interesting characteristic is the level of autonomy of action with the use of AI systems. Three levels can be distinguished here:

1. **Lack of autonomy**: a human acts on the basis of recommendations of AI system (and these recommendations are provided in discreet moments of time and not continuously).
2. **Partial autonomy**: a human interacts with the machine, with support:
   (a) **in operating activities**. The examples of this are the co-bots cooperating with people in the production line, virtual agents (chat-bots) supporting customer service employees and the systems supplementing text in the mobile appliances;
   (b) **in deciding** in the continuous mode, e.g. in the process of navigation, in the systems of augmented reality, classification of electronic mail (see email mechanisms from Google) or a medical diagnosis.
3. **Full autonomy**: the system is fully autonomous. Examples: autonomous transport (cars, drones), warehouses, production lines.

Another characteristic of the activities that are possible with AI is the dimension of time. This applies to the time resolution (e.g. analyzed events) as well as a delay (time that elapses from the execution of the tool to obtaining the result). Iafrate in his interesting study (Iafrate 2015) emphasizes that a delay in operation is the sum of delays in data availability, analytical processes and decision processes. The pursuit to create *a zero-latency organization* recommended by Iafrate must be preceded by a detailed analysis of the above-mentioned delays, so that appropriate steps can be taken to reduce them.

It should be stressed at this point that the response time of intelligent systems (such as image recognition processes)

1. in some applications is critical (e.g. determining a child going in to the street in autonomous vehicles or an attack the information systems);
2. depends significantly on the used algorithms as well as the IT infrastructure (and especially on the actions that process the signal);
3. is dynamically changing due to the development of AI methods and technologies;
4. strongly differentiates cost solutions: fast systems can be many times more expensive than slow systems, and as a result, the analysis of the desired response can be a very important factor in the design of the business case.

AI systems often support the analysis of the available data; therefore, the dimension of these analyses in a natural way is another important feature, you need to consider when choosing an AI technology. Our research on smart solutions indicated the following dimensions:

1. **Time**. AI systems can analyze
   (a) **events of the past**, for example, customer behavior in order to determine their behavioral profiles;
   (b) **the present**, for example, identify objects, behaviors or anomalies (e.g. in security systems or data from sensors placed on the production line);

   (c) **forecast the future**, e.g. potential failures, customer behavior, their potential, credibility or needs.

2. **Space.** This class is dedicated to spatial analysis solutions, specifically to

   (a) **geolocation**,
   (b) **distribution of objects** (e.g. commercial space modeling),
   (c) **route planning**,
   (d) **monitoring of industrial spaces** (e.g. construction sites),
   (e) and even **estimation of macroeconomic parameters** (e.g. the dynamics of oil trade based on the analysis of the frequency of courses and the depth of immersion of ships on the basis of satellite images).

3. **Needs.** AI systems can also support the analysis of users' needs, e.g. based on data from sensors or logs of www systems /mobile applications. Due to them it is possible to

   (a) explore **ergonomics and usability** solutions (User eXperience: UX);
   (b) correct their **availability**, for example to people with disabilities (visually impaired, hearing-impaired or having motor problems) or in difficult conditions (low/high temperatures, poor access to the GSM network/the Internet, etc.);
   (c) **personalize** products, which means adapting to the capabilities and needs of users, taking into account the context of application;
   (d) correct the **simplicity** of use, e.g. by reducing the cognitive load (using systems of augmented reality) or improving navigation and ergonomics (e.g. by adjusting the number and size of interface elements);
   (e) analyze **best practices** of the solutions use, for example, in order to offer the knowledge base, collected in this way, as the added value of your own system.

4. **Potential.** AI systems can be used to assess

   (a) **selling potential** of a given product group in a specific geographical area and for a given target group,

   (b) **shopping potential** of a given group of clients, for example to optimize the activities of sales teams,
   (c) **potential** of **employees**—in the context of their performance in the implementation of specific tasks and under specific conditions,
   (d) **resources potential**, e.g. current production capacity of production machines or transport.

5. **Risk.** AI systems are often used for

   (a) **failure forecasting**;
   (b) **attack risk assessment**, e.g. in cybersecurity;
   (c) customers **credibility assessment**, e.g. credit risk assessment, or business partners;
   (d) extortion **risk assessment**, e.g. the extortion of insurance or energy.

The last value worth mentioning characterizing the activities enabled by AI systems is their precision. Analyses and recommendations in the above-mentioned dimensions can be carried out with different accuracy and at a different rate. System costs can significantly increase with these requirements. For this reason, it is important for the business case (the generated value estimation) to define the quality requirements for AI systems as precisely as possible: too accurate and fast systems will be very expensive, and on the other hand their low precision and/or pace of action may not only fail to improve processes, but even worsen them (e.g. in the case of poorly "trained" and not that "smart" virtual assistants in the process of customer service).

4.2.1.3 Domain of Influence

Activities undertaken using AI systems may have an impact on various areas of the company's operations and its environment.

Most often, the subjects of impact are widely understood organization resources. It can be infrastructure (equipment, production lines, transport systems and devices, warehouses or store surfaces) or employees (support in everyday work, but also recruitment, identification and development of talents). A separate category of "resources" is data, information and knowledge: the impact of AI systems on the knowledge value chain in the organization, in particular their transformational value, is described in Chap. 3.

AI systems can also affect areas of the organization's activities, the primary ones (design, research and development, testing, updates, production, sales and marketing, and delivery and service), as well as supportive. A separate category is the so-called horizontal solutions affecting not only the areas of operation, but also business processes (e.g. customer service or B2B sales). They may also affect, directly or indirectly, organizational business models.

The object of interaction of AI systems is also often the environment of the organization: its customers (individual and institutional), partners or competitors.

4.2.1.4 Effects

Actions taken with the use of AI tools can generate different effects. What can change as a result of implementing smart solutions?

First of all, they can change ways of doing things through

1. **working methods** and, consequently, the related competence requirements;
2. **management methods**: projects and company management (even towards full autonomy—Self-Driving Enterprise, which can be observed in Amazon Go stores);
3. **decision-making processes**, where you can slowly talk about the reallocation of decision centers: from people towards smart systems (*Who makes the decision? On what grounds? Who can predict their consequences and how? Who is responsible for it?*);
4. **methods for measuring success and efficiency** of projects and activities, particularly the measurement tools and indicators.

AI systems also significantly affect time events and processes.

Due to predictive algorithms, it is possible to change the service moment from a fixed service plan (e.g. every fixed period or when a certain parameter, say, mileage is reached) to the one directly related to working conditions, consumption and the risk of failure. The concept of "failure" and "service" can be more generally understood as "intervention," which, for example, in the health service can mean diagnostics and preventive actions.

AI solutions also significantly affect the reduction of business activities and processes, particularly

1. **safety**—shortening the time of hazard identification (e.g. failure in the power industry or cyber-attack) and reacting to it;
2. **customer service**—shortening the reaction time and the time of solving the problem/execution of the order;
3. **logistic processes**—delivery time, goods turnover in a warehouse or transport;
4. **diagnostic processes** in medicine;
5. **legal processes**, e.g. by shortening the access time to necessary information and recommendations of legal actions;
6. **financial processes**, e.g. by reducing waiting time for a credit decision;
7. and many, many others.

The use of AI systems can also change place of service tests (updates, repairs), transport routes (in logistics) and product positioning (in stores and warehouse areas).

The most important effects for the generation of values are the effects of using AI systems to improve quality. Artificial intelligence can improve

1. **the quality of insight** of e.g. observations or analyses:

    (a) If this quality is defined as the relation of the number of perceived objects to the time of observation, then the AI systems allow either to increase the number of observations at a given time, or to observe the same number of events but in a shorter time. The

area in which it can generate this is the aforementioned cybersecurity, where the ability to quickly detect an attack is particularly important in a situation where the number of interactions with the environment (and thus also potential threats) is growing dynamically;
(b) The quality of insight can also be defined as the ability to see phenomena that have never been observed so far, e.g. anomalous events in production systems (which may be a signal of failure) or unobserved behaviors of consumers. In this area, unsupervised learning mechanisms play a special role (increasing the ability to identify new patterns);

2. **the quality of products**: their endurance, functionalities, usefulness, learning abilities or autonomy;
3. **the quality of communication**: by introducing new forms and channels of communication (e.g. conversational interfaces, virtual assistants, brain–computer interfaces (BCI), effectively integrate existing channels (especially the Internet with mobile channels) or personalized communication (e.g. marketing messages);
4. **the quality of opportunity and risk management** by identifying potentials (products, customers, geographical areas, etc.) or identifying/predicting risk factors;
5. **the quality of business processes**, which is a natural consequence of the above-mentioned effects;
6. **generating a qualitatively new business model** enabling new forms of trade (e.g. in the power industry, short-interval power trading, e.g. *Digitalization of Energy Systems* 2017), or creating opportunities for new generation models (e.g. micro-networks of energy producers, ibid.).

Raising the potential (of employees, customers, suppliers, resources, etc.) and level of knowledge (e.g. about the potential and needs of customers, the market, trends, etc.) can also constitute the effect of AI implementation.

Finally, the following new effects of AI implementations are worth noticing. Unobserved emergent phenomena, whose appearance should be carefully observed; adequately early identification of "weak signals" will enable optimal response, either to seize opportunities or to minimize risk.

4.2.1.5 Value

Knowing the possibilities of AI tools, their possible areas of influence and potential effects can be transferred to the performance value which they can provide to the organization that implements them. In-depth analyses of several hundred case studies enable the organization of these values into the following groups:

1. Automation
2. Optimization
3. Autonomy
4. Speed, reactivity and flexibility
5. Productivity
6. Credibility and security
7. Satisfaction
8. Profit

Automation and, in its extreme case, full autonomy of selected activities and entire processes is probably the most common, the most visible, benefit from the implementation of AI systems, which underlies further values generated by intelligent systems.

The optimization of the use of resources and key processes thanks to their appropriate planning and monitoring of activities is the result of the automation and analytical capabilities of AI systems.

Another value is the improvement of reactivity and flexibility, which is largely the result of the shortening of the time of key processes described earlier. It obviously significantly affects the effectiveness of activities and the value for the client, but it can also be a source of unusual threats.

The interesting risks associated with the drastic acceleration of business processes as a result of the implementation of AI solutions are described by Ransbotham (2017). In his opinion:

1. in normal (without applying AI solutions) business processes, time is spent to identify and react to unusual phenomena;
2. implementation of AI may shorten these processes so that people will not be able to analyze data in a non-standard situation and make the right decisions in such a short time;
3. environment (other dependent processes, but also customers and suppliers) accustomed to the increased reactivity will have low tolerance for delays due to human inefficiency in atypical situations, which may have unpredictable consequences;
4. competition, having access to similar methods and technologies, will be able to accelerate its own processes at a similar level.

Another interesting issue raised by Ransbotham is to shorten the time of algorithms "training". This is not a consequence of only accelerating the process, but rather the specificity of Big Data and AI solutions. According to the author:

1. More and more data on user behavior improves the quality of algorithms.
2. Better algorithms not only attract more customers, but also—thanks to, for example, personalization—increase the variability of their behavior: more options, greater diversity of products/services, greater incentive to test them and as a result more and more diverse behaviors.
3. The greater volatility of customer behavior, in turn, results in quicker outdated algorithms and the necessity of their more frequent and faster modifications.
4. Coaching and modification of algorithms is currently very time-consuming: this results in a threat to the time deficit necessary to maintain the pace of algorithm development at a satisfactory level.

Another value generated by AI systems is increasing productivity through automation (tasks and processes) and supporting decision-making processes in very different areas of activity (designing and creating new products/services, production or logistics processes) and, in general, coordination of various business processes.

For many organizations, the improvement of credibility and assessment by the environment: customers, suppliers, partners and competitors will also be of great value. This is possible largely thanks to the improvement of risk management and the increase of safety and stability of products/services.

Another benefit of implementing AI is the increasing value for customers and raising their satisfaction, for example, thanks to better, more personalized, accessible, more interesting and beautiful products.

Most of the above-mentioned effects and benefits translate into the increase in profits. It consists of

1. **lowering costs**, e.g. reducing variable costs, operational costs, energy, optimizing the use of resources, reducing the risk of lost profits;
2. **increasing revenues**, thanks to better products as well as effective, personalized sales campaigns, dynamic pricing and similar activities.

4.2.2 Value Generation Model

Having various AI tools and being aware of how they can affect different areas of operation and as a result which value they can generate, one can begin to design the business case for the implementation of artificial intelligence.

The model of value generation using AI systems should consist of the following stages:

1. **The choice of area** in which we want to generate a value.
2. **The choice of value** which we want to generate in this area.
3. The selection of the **effects** that are to be the source of these values.
4. The selection of **actions**, which in the best possible way can contribute to achieving these effects.
5. The selection of **tools (methods, AI technology)** optimal to accomplish the above action.
6. The AI solution **project**:

   (a) **Architecture solutions**, particularly

(i) configuration of tools and activities;
(ii) learning processes, systems;
(iii) the level of autonomy.

(b) **Experiment design**, enabling the assessment of the system's efficiency

(i) making hypotheses;
(ii) development of the method of their verification (mechanisms of value delivery, methods and tools for observing effects, etc.).

7. **Implementation and evaluation** of AI solutions (cyclical operations)

(a) implementation of the solution;
(b) implementation of experiments (effectiveness measurements, the analysis of results, verification of hypotheses);
(c) updating the experience database and suggestions for further hypotheses.

As can be seen, due to the high risk of implementing AI projects (see e.g. Bughin et al. 2017) in the proposed model, the approach used in flexible project management methodologies is recommended (e.g. Scrum): generating value through many incremental improvements focused on achieving measurable effects, carried out as far as possible in short (several weeks) "sprints."

Below, the list of factors that should be clarified in the process of constructing business cases using AI systems is presented (Table 4.2).

4.3 Cognitive Networks

Advanced information technologies, particularly artificial intelligence systems and, recently, blockchain, affect the relations between companies, their customers and partners by supporting and sometimes even enforcing changes in business models.

Bloomberg experts, analyzing the impact of information technologies on the energy industry, forecast its strong decentralization and, as a result (Bloomberg 2017):

Table 4.2 Recommended stages of the value generation process with the use of intelligent systems along with the detailed criteria

Area	Value	Effect	Operation	Tools
•Resources •infrastructure •human resource •information and knowledge •activity groups •designing •production •sales & marketing •deployment •service •business processes: •business model	•atomization •optimization •speed, reactivity and flexibility •productivity •credibility and security •satisfaction •profit •higher income •lower costs	•way of acting •way of work •way of operating •competency requirements •management methods •methods of effects measurements •time •prediction •shortening of time •place •tests and research •service •logistics •space •quality •insight •products •communication •chances and threats •processes •business models •potential •customer •supplier •resource •knowledge •needs •potential •risk	•level of autonomy •no autonomy •semi-auto •full autonomy •analysis •time •space •needs •potential •risk •desired timing •short •average •irrelevant •desired quality, precision •high •moderate •low	•methods •identifying •classifying •predicting •modelling •generating •resources •hardware •software •talents •suppliers, •cost,

Source: Author

1. **Changes energy producers' business models**: from its production to the coordination of micro networks, in which energy will be supplied by small, independent producers, largely from renewable sources.
2. **Changes the dominant topology of value structures**: from tree (pro ducer→distribution→recipient) to network (many sub-networks working together).
3. Ensures the stability, flexibility and security of a complex, decentralized energy generation system as the **main added value of technology**.
4. Enables coordination, prediction and self-improvement as the **most desirable features of technology**.

On the other hand, a growing number of business models using blockchain technologies (decentralized, distributed and encrypted using cryptographic database algorithms to record various transactions), often financed by the issue of virtual coins or intelligent contracts (smart contracts) in under the so-called ICO (Initial Coin Offerings) is a strong signal indicating the emergence of large, decentralized structures with the characteristics of markets that have a significant impact on current value structures.

Below, a proposal for new, decentralized value structures under the working name cognitive networks is presented, which in our opinion, by having strong support in traditional generation models, well illustrate the possible impact of AI technology on the rules of cooperation and competition in future markets.

At the beginning, we will show how AI systems can affect the phenomena described in the classic value generation models. The concept of cognitive networks will be described below, particularly the actors, the relations between them and the logic of creating values. Finally, we will present the key competencies of the organization necessary to develop competitive advantages in these structures and the resulting criteria for the assessment of new business ideas using AI technologies.

In the process of developing the model, a method inspired by Case-Based Reasoning (CBR) was used (see e.g. Kolodner 1992; Montani 2010). As one of the artificial intelligence techniques, the CBR method can be used to solve management problems and support decision-making processes (see e.g. Friedrich et al. 2002; Osuszek and Stanek 2015). This study uses its basic elements for retrieving “classical” value generation models (see e.g. Chap. 1) useful in modeling the value generation of systems using AI solutions, developing an approximate solution (identification of the most appropriate solutions, including strategic options and questions), adaptation of these solutions, their application, critical analysis of effects and development of a new solution (model of cognitive networks).

The effect of the “retrieving solutions” step pointed to chains, constellations, shops and value networks as “classical” models that can be useful in developing a value generation model with AI solutions.

At the stage of developing an approximate solution, the following components of the recommended models were indicated:

1. Value chain:
    (a) Costs and value for the client.
    (b) Activities in the chain.
    (c) Role of a product.
    (d) Goals and development of technology.
    (e) Marketing.
    (f) Aftersales service.
2. Constellations of values:
    (a) Roles of actors in value structures.
    (b) Goals of these actors’ actions.
    (c) Customers’ needs and sources of competitive advantages.
    (d) Characteristics of environments and products.
3. Value shops:
    (a) Logics of creating values related to design models (e.g. CRISP-DM) and the provision of intelligent services (e.g. SaaS, API or Cloud Computing).
    (b) Role of AI systems in primary activities in value shops.

   (c) Sources of competitive advantages in value shops, particularly learning, economies of scale and network, reputation and scope of involvement in the problem as the equivalent of vertical integration in value chains.

4. Value networks:

   (a) Impact of AI systems on the logic of value creation in networks.
   (b) Factors determining competitive advantage, including the role of network coordinators.
   (c) Impact of the reconfiguration of forms, time, place and possession on the offered value.
   (d) Influence of intermediaries and network complexity on value generation.

In the next steps, appropriate concepts from selected models were adapted and used to describe new phenomena resulting from the implementation of AI class systems and critical analysis was made indicating how intelligent solutions can influence the methods of generating value and the source of competitive advantages. The results of these analyses are presented below.

The proposed model, despite the fact that it results directly from the analyses presented in this book, should be treated as a hypothesis requiring verification in the subsequent studies. It should be emphasized that the described structures probably do not exist in the form as presented below (although some of their features are already clearly visible, e.g. in the Internet advertising exchange networks). For this reason, any conclusions and formulations regarding cognitive networks are given in either future time or conditional sentences.

4.3.1 Classic Constellations of Values and Value Systems Based on AI

In Chap. 1, the "classical" methods of value generation were described. The features of artificial intelligence systems described in Chaps. 2 and 3 can significantly affect the logic of creating values presented there. Below, the way of using "classical" concepts to formulate the model of generating value in reality saturated with intelligent solutions will be described.

4.3.1.1 Value Chain

Costs and Value for the Customer

In Porter's value chain model, the value for the customer is determined either by the level of cost reduction or by the efficiency increase possible due to the use of the product. Intelligent systems can affect both the cost structure and the concept of customer value.

4.3.1.2 Costs

If the solution is created within the organization, as an investment the fixed costs will prevail. If the solution is built from modules provided by suppliers in the Pay-Per-Use model, for instance, via APIs, then the variable costs will prevail. In the latter case, it will be necessary to modify the pricing models of products/services for the end customers so as to take into account the costs generated by them when using the product (moving the cost down the value chain).

4.3.1.3 Value Concept

Due to AI systems, the efficiency of using the product is not the only determinant of the value for the customer; new elements, unrelated to the efficiency and price, for example, the possibility of attracting new users (network effects) are also important.

Activities in a Value Chain

AI systems significantly influence the role of a human in the implementation of activities in the chain. The automatic systems owned by external entities are the work factor, and not the systems of a given company. As a consequence, its role is not so much the implementation of activities as the design, launching, monitoring and development of systems that later will perform the necessary tasks (see the modular nature of AI solutions).

The Role of a Product

In the value chain model, the product is a medium enabling the transfer of values from the company to the customer. Raw materials and semi-products are transported to the factory, where they are transformed to final products and transported to customers.

AI systems make the product not only a value delivery vehicle to the customer, but also serve as a mechanism for transferring values from the customer.

1. Companies provide free (or very cheap) products to collect information about behavior and/or advertising of other products.
2. Interface owners (e.g. Amazon Echo/Alexa, Apple Siri, Google Assistant) become intermediaries between users and providers of various services, significantly changing the rules of competition and market relations.
3. Solution providers with implemented self-improvement mechanisms (e.g. using reinforcement learning) increase the value of their solutions thanks to user engagement (see negative amortization).

Objectives of Technology Development

In the value chain model the purpose of technology development is either to reduce costs for the customer or to raise the price through better adaptation to the customer's purchase criteria.

The possibility of using the product as a vehicle for transferring value from the client to the company, especially in the area of media and Internet marketing, generated a new goal of technology development: attracting and managing users' attention (attention economy).

The Role of Marketing

In the value chain model, marketing supports two complementary processes:

1. Development and improvement of the chain by providing product specifications and demand forecasting.
2. Stimulation of demand for chain products in order to ensure stability of cooperation and optimal use of production capacities.

AI systems, especially mechanisms used in intelligent, connected things (see e.g. Porter and Heppelmann 2015) cause:

1. Integration of product research and development processes with user behavior analysis.
2. Integration of R&D, marketing and service areas, and as a result, significantly shortening of development cycles and increasing the personalization of solutions.

After-Sales Service

In classical value generation models, after-sales service ensures the correct use of products by the customer and, as a result, prevents failures or extends the life of the product.

The implementation of AI systems extends the functions of this area to collecting information on the use of products for their development and personalization and adds the customer profile in order to improve the effectiveness of marketing activities, better forecasting of future needs and behavior of customers and the possible sale of this information to other entities.

4.3.1.4 Value Constellations

The considerations presented above confirm the recommendation of Normann and Ramirez (1993) to extend the concept of Porter's value chain towards the value networks.

According to Porter, the value system consists of the value chains of suppliers, a given company, its distribution channels and customers. Due to the introduction of intelligent systems, we are dealing with value networks together with their coordinators (e.g. platform providers or interface owners) or without them (e.g. decentralized structures using blockchain technologies).

Porter also claims that the source of competitive advantage is the skillful management of connections in the value chain. Normann and Ramirez add that the complexity of offers increases along with the complexity of the partnerships necessary to deliver these offers. The best offers involve clients, suppliers and various business partners in various configurations. As a result, strategic activities should be oriented on the reconfiguration of roles and relations between partners in order to create new forms of value for the client. This observation is also very up-to-date in value structures in which advanced technologies play a key role:

1. reconfiguration of roles and relationships in value networks is supported by the modularization of AI systems;
2. AI systems increase the efficiency and quality of credibility assessment processes and enable the automation of negotiations with partners in the network (see e.g. transactions on the programmatic marketing market), which also increases the dynamics of the mentioned reconfiguration of roles.

According to Normann and Ramirez (1993) in a world where value is generated in complex constellations (and not linear chains) the purpose of the companies should be not so much creating value for customers, but mobilizing their independent creation of value for themselves using the possibilities ("density") offered by the network.

Modern customers actually expect autonomy, and often achieve it effectively, but the possibilities of AI solutions require companies to have one more key competence: creating environments enabling customers to create value for themselves.

As a result, organizations wishing to gain a competitive advantage in the world of AI should be able to

1. **create environments** allowing consumers to generate values for themselves:

   (a) for individual clients: Instagram, Snapchat, other creative systems;

(b) for business:

(i) environments that enable users to create their own AI solutions,
(ii) libraries of pre-learned algorithms that require improvement by the customer,
(iii) algorithms exchanges, etc.

2. **mobilize** users to create values by themselves:

(a) in systems based on blockchain technology: financial motivation for calculations securing a transaction by assigning virtual currencies or smart contracts;
(b) reputation systems, e.g. on the Kaggle.com portal.

In addition, due to the fact that the key to creating a unique value is to mobilize clients to cooperate, the main source of competitive advantage is the ability to coordinate the entire value creation system (Normann and Ramirez 1993). The current example of the changes described are the transformations of business models in the energy industrymfrom the rolc of producers and suppliers of energy to market coordinators (see e.g. Bloomberg 2017).

4.3.1.5 Value Shops

Another concept that can be used to model value structures in markets that use artificial intelligence intensively is that of value shops proposed by Stabell and Fjeldstad (Stabell and Fjeldstad 1998). According to the authors, these structures have the following logic of value generation:

1. Strong asymmetry between a company and its customer, which is often the reason why a customer chooses this particular company.
2. Value creation process adapted to solve non-standard problems;
3. Cyclic, iterative and undisturbed activities;
4. Sequentially significant and reciprocal relations between activities;
5. Many disciplines and specializations in spiral cycles of activities;
6. Problem-independent operations focused on acquiring information;

7. Relying on the expert knowledge;
8. Increasing effectivity due to the cooperation of support and primary activities;
9. Value system based on reputation and relations.

The convergence of this characteristic with the phenomena occurring between suppliers and recipients of intelligent services (e.g. AI services provided via "cloud" or API interfaces) is noteworthy. What is more, the structure of primary activities proposed by Stabell and Fjeldstad (1998):

1. defining the problem,
2. problem-solving,
3. choosing the best solution,
4. implementation of the chosen solution,
5. evaluation of the implementation,

is similar to the Data Science CRISP-DM project cycle:

1. understanding business conditions,
2. understanding, preparation and data modeling,
3. evaluation,
4. implementation.

The new value that AI solutions bring to the core activities of value shops is greater emphasis on solving a new problem based on already existing experience (other similar problems that have already been solved). It is possible thanks to:

1. **AI abilities to quickly identify similarities**, in this case in terms of the context and characteristics of the problem (see e.g. implementation of production manager support systems at Airbus).
2. **Transfer learning** of experiments (virtual environments→real) as well as specialized fragments of neural networks (at the software level).
3. **Reinforcement learning mechanisms, where** the perfection is achieved by continuous iterations of the cycle "hypothesis→action→

measurement of effects→verification of the hypothesis→knowledge→another hypothesis…".

Stabell and Fjeldstad (1998) indicate two key factors determining the competitive advantage in value shops: learning and scale effects. Artificial intelligence significantly affects both of these factors.

Learning in projects using AI, as has already been presented in this study, has a different nature than in traditional projects. It often boils down to experimenting with various parameters, algorithms or architectures of neural networks, powering these structures with exemplary solutions, and later supervising the operation of these systems in a production environment. As a result, the data sources, the processes of preparation and training of the system as well as its monitoring and maintenance are different. In advanced solutions (e.g. using reinforcement learning) the system can be refined automatically. As a consequence, the role of people in these processes also changes.

The factors determining the scale and network effects are also affected. For example, in AI systems using self-improvement mechanisms, the intensity of their use by the users is an additional factor that increases the quality of algorithms. As a result, there is synergy of economies of scale and network: the more often users use the solution, the better it becomes.

Reputation as a source of competitive advantage, as pointed out by Stabell and Fjeldstad (1998), is also very important on AI-intensive markets. This is particularly visible on platforms like Kaggle (where Data Science teams compete to solve difficult Data Science problems and thus build their reputation) and Algorithmia (AI algorithm exchange platform promoting the best algorithms).

Stabell and Fjeldstad also point to the range of involvement in the problem as the value shops equivalent of vertical integrity in the value chain and the scale effect in value networks. The scope of involvement means the degree to which the company is able to solve the problem of a given class on its own (without the support of external experts). The ability to manage this range is not only one of the methods of managing uncertainty, but also a way of improving communication between experts and the efficiency of evaluation processes for implementing solutions. In effect, it is therefore a factor determining both the reduction of costs and the generation of value.

The modular nature of AI solutions makes the strategy of specialization also the source of competitive advantage: the decision about the scope of competencies held within the organization is often difficult and may have far-reaching consequences.

4.3.1.6 Value Networks

Another interesting structure, proposed by Stabell and Fjeldstad (1998), is the value network. Below, the way in which this concept can be used to model relations in AI-intensive markets will be shown.

The Value Creation Logic

According to the authors of the concept, the value of the network is generated by organizing and supporting exchanges between its actors. Network operators act as club managers: they initiate, monitor and interrupt direct or indirect relationships. The value of services is a positive function of external factors on the side of the demand (network effect), and the value is captured from the access to services and their capacity. Mediation activities are carried out simultaneously on many different levels, and therefore the key factor affecting the quality of coordination and feedback in the network is standardization, which also supports partner matching and monitoring of their relations. The life cycles of implementations and operational activities differ from each other, and business relationships with partners in value networks come down to cooperation within parallel subnetworks.

How can AI systems affect the value creation logic outlined above? Leaving a precise definition of the cognitive network for later, the concept as a definition of a network structure that intensively uses artificial intelligence and intelligent, connected products is introduced below.

In networks that use AI solutions intensively, the nature of the transferred value changes. While social networks provide information, opinions, multimedia, and so on, a data enrichment service transfer in "smart" networks can be expected. For example, a company interested in recognizing the emotions of its client will send a photo (→information) to its service provider, and the service provider will send back the list of emotions (→information enriched). Similar intelligent services (Intelligence as a Service) could refer to recommendations, forecasts or anomaly detection based on raw data.

Just like in value networks, standardization will be very important for communication in cognitive networks at the technical level (currently it mainly takes place via API protocols) as well as data exchange standards. The organization of actors in thematic subnetworks (e.g. image recognition or NLP) and the implementation of mechanisms of self-organization and transaction security (e.g. using blockchain technology) will also be significant.

Such an organization of subnetworks could take place in potentially several dimensions according to knowledge-refining stages (classification as in the AI value chain), technology types (e.g. image recognition, NLP, prediction, recommendations, etc.), industry or vertical solutions. The communication would take place both in the client–supplier relation as well as in the supplier–supplier channels within the subnetwork (co-opetition) and between subnetworks.

There is also an open question about the place and possible role of network coordinators. The growing popularity of systems enabling safe decentralization and transaction security (e.g. blockchain) and the increasing capabilities of AI systems, particularly machine learning algorithms that support self-assembly of complex structures, indicate the possibility of creating markets without coordinators or with a role that is significantly different than at present. Examples of the first cognitive networks are, for example Kaggle.com, and Algorithmia.com, an algorithm marketplace, where the network coordinator functions as in the traditional model. But in very advanced structures such as Ad Exchange, for example Google Double Click or Facebook Audience Network, the autonomy of algorithms (representing both buyers and sellers of advertising, as well as coordinators) is already so large that one can slowly talk about decentralization and self-organization of these markets. The role of network coordinators may be reduced to the development of its architecture so as to maximize the effectiveness of mechanisms for connecting and reconfiguring actors' relations, for example, thanks to the advanced algorithms for identifying needs and recommending the best possible solutions (which is currently happening e.g. at Amazon, LinkedIn or on Facebook).

As in the Stabell and Fjeldstad value network model (Stabell and Fjeldstad 1998), there will be cognitive networks strong network effects. These effects will be strengthened by the increase of a network node potential (AI service providers) thanks to the reinforcement learning mechanisms. The dynamics of growth of this potential will depend not so much on the number of users as on the number of the supported events (the more recommendations, the better the algorithms are). As a result, positive internal factors on the supply side will play an important role, as in value networks.

Factors Determining the Competitive Advantage

According to Stabell and Fjeldstad (1998) network operators provide value to their users through network access options and the ability to use the offered services, wherein the main value offered is the relations with its participants. It can be expected that in cognitive networks, a particularly important service offered by operators (or structures performing coordination functions) will be the recommendation service of the best possible partner or supplier in a given context (intelligent service, computing power, etc.). Additionally, fast and cheap services might be crucial, enabling switching between suppliers (e.g. through efficient data exchange standards or interfaces), which will significantly affect the flexibility of network participants.

As a result, the ability of the cognitive network to generate values will be determined by

1. the **quality and effectiveness of algorithms for matching partners in the network**, especially:

(a) for customers: algorithms for identifying the best solutions,
(b) for suppliers: algorithms for identifying the best clients (those whose data will improve the algorithms in the best possible way),
(c) algorithms for dynamic pricing and optimization,
(d) algorithms for monitoring and quality control of these recommendations;

2. **quality and efficiency of standardization mechanisms for data exchange and transfer;**
3. **quality, efficiency and security of data transmission infrastructure.**

Stabell and Fjeldstad (1998) point out that the degree of utilization of network capabilities is closely related to the scale of operation; the high level of utilization of the potential on the one hand reduces costs, on the other hand, it can also lower the quality of provided services (e.g. network congestion). In cognitive networks, it can be expected that a high level of using the potential will not only reduce costs, but may also increase the quality of provided services. This will be possible thanks to the mechanisms of self-improvement of algorithms on the basis of experiences gained during the provision of intelligent services.

It can also be expected that in the cognitive networks there will also take place a process indicated by Stabell and Fjeldstad, (1) the need to synchronize many parallel activities generating many feedback relations between primary activities, and (2) stimulated learning by activities related to customer selection and service monitoring.

The Impact of the Reconfiguration of Forms, Time, Place and Possession on the Offered Value

Lusch et al. (2009) indicate that delivering improved value propositions to end customers in value networks is possible thanks to the reconfiguration of forms, time, place and possession of business processes. Below, the impact of these reconfigurations on the generation of values in networks that use artificial intelligence intensively will be shown.

Reconfiguration of forms will be possible due to the fusion of material and non-material forms in the smart infrastructure. The production efficiency of systems using AI depends on the infrastructure in which the algorithms are implemented, which is evidenced by the growing popularity of ASICs architectures and systems Application-Specific Integrated Circuits) and FPGA (Field-Programmable Gate Array). Modern algorithms are able to manage the ICT infrastructure so that it adapts to the current context, particularly to the necessary level of performance and security.

In the area of reconfiguration of time, Lusch et al. (2009) show that the use of start parts and smart parts in the Product Lifecycle Management (PLM) significantly shortens the production time while maintaining a high level of meeting the individual needs of users. It can be expected that in cognitive networks the equivalent of start parts will be dedicated industry solutions developed on the basis of customers' experiences, for example, with the use of transfer learning methods. As a result, the time of adaptation of expert services to the context (needs and specificity of operations) of industry users will be significantly shortened. For example, for predictive maintenance services, the new client will be able to use algorithms developed on the basis of the experience of other clients from the same industry, e.g. energy or transport.

In cognitive networks, the final version of the algorithm will be created at the end customer stage: in its environment, context, and its data. Therefore, there will be time as well as place reconfiguration.

The last factor mentioned by Lusch et al. is reconfiguration of ownership. According to the service-oriented logic, the value delivered to the customer does not have to be associated with the ownership of the service/product; the access to value is essential, not the ownership of resources necessary to it's delivery. Cognitive networks will be based largely on this form of reconfiguration: smart services will be provided in the SaaS formula or via API interfaces, examples of which are IBM Watson services or algorithms available on the Algorithmia platform. It can also be a source of interesting challenges and the question will be apparent: Who is the (co-owner) owner of the algorithms, and to what extent?

If they improve as suppliers use them, maybe the suppliers should also participate in future profits? This issue will become particularly important in the context of the Data Protection Directive (GDPR, General Data

Protection Regulation) in the European Union, and increasingly widespread distributed technologies, e.g. blockchain.

The Influence of Intermediaries and Network Complexity on Value Generation

According to Lusch et al. (2009), the factors linking the network of values are the competencies, relationships and information exchanged between network members: these resource categories are seen as the most valuable for the organization (Normann and Ramirez 1993; Vargo and Lush 2004; Evans and Wurster 1997), and the network actors become de facto their integrators (Vargo and Lusch 2008). The intermediaries support the processes of exchanging goods between buyers and sellers, and they achieve this by eliminating the gaps: spatial (between places of production and consumption), time (between the moment of production and consumption) and information (between sellers and buyers) (Lusch et al. 2009).

In cognitive networks, the role of intermediaries can be significantly changed.

Above all, the gap may be eliminated by them. The nature of the provided services indicate that the intermediaries will be eliminating the competence gap, strengthening the potential and independence of clients using their services. On the other hand, the users of such services should be aware of the risk resulting from possible dependence on the supplier.

The wide role of the standardization of data exchange and communication interfaces in cognitive networks in connection with the development of agent technologies, as well as decentralized and distributed databases (e.g. blockchain), may be conducive to generating new forms of relations that threaten traditional intermediaries. The following scenario is possible to imagine:

1. The smart service client programs their virtual agent to search for the best intelligent service providers (e.g. image recognition algorithms, recommendations or predictions).

2. The agent on behalf of the client connects to the chosen algorithm, uses it and improves it (in its own environment and on its own data).
3. This improved algorithm recommends other potential clients: for exchange, joint development or sale.

In effect,

1. the value will be generated not only by suppliers, but also by customers;
2. cognitive networks will favor the supplier–customer as well as the customer–customer relations via virtual agents;
3. one of the mechanisms for generating the value of the cognitive network will be to support this type of interaction, e.g. through technologies supporting the identification of optimal partners or common use and/or improvement of algorithms (e.g. transfer teaching, digital twins techniques or augmented reality).

An example of such cooperation is the previously described initiative of the usually competing with each other companies: Volksvagen, Daimler Benz and BMW as part of the HERE project.

The analysis presented above shows that the classical models of the value network can be used to a certain extent to model the structures that intensively use artificial intelligence and some interesting, qualitatively new phenomena can be expected. This is the basis for the concept of cognitive networks presented below.

4.3.2 Cognitive Network Concept

Cognitive networks are the structures intensely using technologies of artificial intelligence, in which actors combined by various relations exchange specific values.

In order to clarify the concept below, we will present a proposal of a model architecture of such a network (including actors, relations, communication methods and topologies), control and optimization mechanisms, possible services in such networks and potentials emergent phenomena.

4.3.2.1 Network Architecture

The actors of cognitive networks will be

1. **suppliers** of intelligent services (e.g. image recognition, emotions, conversational interfaces, predictions, anomaly detection or recommendations);
2. **customers** interested in using these services to improve the quality of their offer;
3. **network coordinators** performing coordination and management functions;
4. **data providers**—companies that collect, process and provide data on the behavior of network users (similarly to third-party data providers in online advertising networks);
5. **infrastructure providers** necessary for the network to function.

The dominant **relations** in cognitive networks will combine:

1. **suppliers with customers**—to sell intelligent services;
2. **customers**—for example in order to exchange experiences, joint improvement or to sell access to algorithms;
3. **virtual agents**, both customers and suppliers.

One can expect that establishing, maintaining and solving these relations will be highly automated thanks to algorithms provided by network coordinators. It may also turn out that with time cognitive networks will not require coordinators (see the growing popularity of stock exchanges based on blockchain technology).

Cognitive networks will use modern information technologies for communication. The standardization of data exchange, efficiency of communication protocols will be critically important for generating values (e.g. API) and services enabling actors to identify optimal services and quickly and cheaply switch between them. Relevant technologies will also be important, for instance, the Internet of Things technologies or those enabling the use of models of digital twins and augmented reality.

The ability of cognitive networks to generate value will positively affect the modular nature of AI solutions. It will enable the adaptation of services to the needs of clients and the potentially easy and quick change of the supplier. This will significantly affect the competitiveness and dynamics of the market.

Data exchange standards and effects of communication protocols will enable not only forming relationships between customers and suppliers, but also grouping of customers and/or suppliers in cooperating subnetworks. Within these subnetworks, not only customers, but also suppliers (even competing with each other, as in the HERE project) will be able to connect, while the logic of forming these structures can be based on the type of services, their possible usage (e.g. vertical or horizontal), stages of enriching information (e.g. from data acquisition, through analysis to recommendation and prediction) or cognitive functions (see classification of AI systems according to human cognitive functions). Communication systems will not only enable the contact between actors within the subnetwork, but also an exchange of information between these structures.

The control points, namely, places in the value network that allow control over business value, will be relevant in the concept of cognitive networks (see the concept of control points by Trossen and Fine (2005)) control points. The strength of these points will depend not only on the number of customers (demand) and the margin generated on the transaction (profitability) (as in Trossen and Fine) but also (or maybe above all) on the number of interactions. This will be influenced by the mechanisms of self-improvement of algorithms (e.g. by the use of reinforcement learning) along with subsequent services. As a result, a place in the network that guarantees the implementation of a large number of services will have a positive impact not only on revenues but also on the quality of the offer, which will significantly enhance the scale and network effects.

4.3.2.2 Control, Coordination and Optimization Mechanisms

For effective functioning of cognitive networks, control, coordination and optimization mechanisms will be crucial.

Control mechanisms will be responsible for the continuous monitoring of the structure operations, particularly the detection of anomalous situations and their rapid prevention. This will be specifically important in structures in which the speed of system operation will drastically exceed the capabilities of human reaction. The experience of the financial industry, especially in the area of stock exchange transactions using high-frequency trading technologies (HFT), show that too much confidence in algorithms may lead to tragic situations (compare, for example, a few-dollar fluctuation on December 29, 2016, described, for example, in "The HFT Algo-Computers Crash FX Markets—Bert Dohmen," (2016).

Coordinating mechanisms enable coordination of actors and/or their virtual agents in cognitive networks. This is already happening in Ad Exchange and energy exchanges. This is a strong trend and according to Bloomberg experts, it may influence the role and business models of large energy producers (see Bloomberg 2017).

Optimization mechanisms will rely on adapting services, infrastructure and network architectures to maximize the efficiency and security of the entire structure. They will be supported by learning algorithms, testing various configurations in terms of their impact on the quality of the entire system.

4.3.2.3 Services in Cognitive Networks

Services exchanged in cognitive networks will be the main determinant of their value for all actors. Below, the main categories of services that one can expect to see in such structures are presented below.

Supplier Services

The main service provided by suppliers in cognitive networks will be enrichment of data and information received from customers—as described, for example, in the concept of the knowledge value chain. Customers will, for example, provide "raw" data (e.g. images), and receive their interpretation or recommendations (e.g. identified emotions).

In addition, they will be able to access various consulting services (e.g. implementation) and IT services (e.g. computing power, data protection, etc.) or ensure the fulfillment of regulations such as the protection of personal data.

Most of the possible services are described in the previous part of the study, so below the focus will be put on equally interesting services offered by network coordinators (or the network itself, if it works autonomously).

Network Services

As mentioned above, the value of the network, for its actors, will be largely determined by the quality of mechanisms supporting the establishment of new, valuable relationships. For this reason, the first, highly desirable cognitive network service will be the ability to compare the efficiency of services: quality of algorithms, computing power, data enrichment processes, and so on.

The advanced recommendation systems will be crucial, offering actors optimal:

1. **products and services**;
2. their **parameters** (e.g. cost, speed, switching flexibility, etc.);
3. **providers** (based on dedicated scoring mechanisms);
4. or (for suppliers) **their clients** (e.g. those whose data quality and expected frequency of service will provide the best refinement of algorithms).

Recommendation systems may also serve as the basis for algorithms of dynamic optimization and pricing.

Another important source of value in cognitive networks will be systems supporting the reconfiguration of intelligent services that can be offered due to the high level of data standardization and effective interfaces between applications. The development of this area may lead to a new class of activities and systems that are called the Intelligence Chain Management.

It can also be expected that due to the complex nature of the relations between actors of cognitive networks, the trust management services will play a significant role. Among them, we can distinguish the reputation-building systems (similar to those that already exist on platforms such as Kaggle or Algorithmia) and partner credibility assessment systems (ratings).

In cognitive networks, data and information will be exchanged. For solution providers, the key factors will be not only data provided directly by their customers (e.g. in the process of using the service), but also data generated by them (clients) in other systems and "digital footprints" of these customers. For this reason, you can expect a boom in the collection and analysis services of this type of data as in currently operating Third-Party Data Providers.

As can be seen, intelligent technologies will favor the development of new services, and perhaps even markets. What should be the competencies of service providers, their clients and coordinators?

4.3.3 Key Competencies of Organizations Operating in Cognitive Networks

4.3.3.1 Supplier Competencies

Smart solution providers should naturally have the ability to design, create and deliver high-quality services to their customers. Below, the competencies that are important for effective competition in cognitive networks are presented below.

Due to the fact that the competitive position of the supplier will depend to a large extent on the number of events (see the discussion on the strength of the control points above), the relevant competence of the supplier will be the ability to attract customers who possess good quality data but also will often use the service.

Another key competence of suppliers in cognitive networks will be creating the environment and mobilizing clients to generate value for themselves. Creating environments will be possible due to self-service platform solutions, systems enabling creation and development of own AI solutions and educational systems. Customer mobilizing can be supported by reputation systems (such as Kaggle) or financial incentive systems (as in the case of "extracting" cryptocurrencies using blockchain technology).

Due to the specificity of industry solutions and the need to adapt services to the specifics of the clients' activities, the suppliers will have to work out efficient mechanisms for creating preconfigured, industry versions of their services. This will be supported by the ability to group customers into categories (e.g. by analysis of case similarity or using clustering algorithms) and identification of the service version that is optimal for a given client category.

The last noteworthy skill will be the ability to form strategic alliances with companies operating in the same market even if they are direct competitors (see the case of an alliance within the HERE project). It may turn out that such co-opetition will raise the subnetwork advantage in relation to other groups competing for the same customer.

4.3.3.2 Customer Competencies

In order to effectively recover value from cognitive networks, customers operating in these structures should have the following skills:

1. **The ability to develop and update the vision and implementation strategies of AI solutions in their operations**. Particularly, the ability to formulate a business case, develop a solution architecture, and good Data Governance.

2. **The ability to identify the best possible suppliers and partners** or the ability to use cognitive network services for this purpose.
3. **The ability to flexibly switch between services of different suppliers.**
4. **The ability to manage the scope of engagement**, as in the case of value shops, the degree of independence in solving key problems. It will largely boil down to a skillful outsourcing policy (*Which of the action areas should be given to the supplier?*) and risk management related to the transfer of key data, information and competencies to service providers.
5. **The ability to establish strategic alliances with other network actors**, particularly service customers, e.g. in the context of the possibility of jointly improving their own solutions using AI.

4.3.3.3 Coordinator ompetencies

The basic competence of cognitive network coordinators will be coordination of the entire value creation system. Particularly, it will require the ability to reconfigure the roles and relations between partners in order to create new forms of value (see e.g. the change in the role of energy producers from suppliers to the coordinators of local networks) or the role of conversational interface owners in platforms offering digital services.

In addition, network coordinators should skillfully design and implement the appropriate cognitive network services, and particularly be able to associate suppliers with recipients with the help of these services. Like suppliers, they should be able to create environments and mobilize customers to generate value for themselves.

The key skill can also turn out to be the ability to capture value from a huge amount of data generated by network actors and learning by testing the impact of various new services and configurations on the value of the structure for users.

4.4 Summary

Cognitive concept presented above constitutes a long-term research hypothesis, which needs to be verified in future studies. The analyses demonstrated above show that the first signs of the processes enclosed in the model can already be observed (see e.g. networks of online advertising exchange or algorithm exchange marketplaces), nonetheless we have not yet been able to identify the structure, which would have all of the cognitive network features.

A very interesting technology, which can become the foundation for cognitive networks, is Etherum (https://www.ethereum.org/), enabling the creation of scattered applications with the use of blockchain technology. The mechanisms implemented there, the so called smart contracts and the possibility of securing a transaction without needing to perform complex calculations (proof-of-stake) which consume too much energy, make Ethereum particularly interesting to suppliers of smart services. It can, as a result, become a technological platform for the concepts described above.

Nevertheless, due to very dynamic development of technologies, methods and business models using Big Data and AI, it is very difficult to forecast even the nearest future. We should hope that at least the grounds for building new solutions, described in this chapter, will stay intact.

References

Bughin, J., Hazan, E., Ramaswamy, S., Chui, M., Allas, T., Dahlstrom, P., et al. (2017). *Artificial Intelligence*. McKinsey Global Institute. Retrieved from https://www.mckinsey.com/~/media/McKinsey/Industries/Advanced%20Electronics/Our%20Insights/How%20artificial%20intelligence%20can%20deliver%20real%20value%20to%20companies/MGI-Artificial-Intelligence-Discussion-paper.ashx

Chapman, P., Clinton, J., Kerber, R., Khabaza, T., Reinartz, T., Shearer, C., & Wirth, R. (2004). *CRISP-DM 1.0* (pp. 1–76). SPSS. Retrieved from https://www.the-modeling-agency.com/crisp-dm.pdf

Digitalization of Energy Systems. (2017). *Digitalization of Energy Systems* (pp. 1–61). New York: Bloomberg Finance LP. Retrieved from https://www.siemens.com/global/en/home/company/topic-areas/sustainable-energy/digitalization-of-energy-systems.html
Ermine, J.-L. (2013). A Knowledge Value Chain for Knowledge Management. *Journal of Knowledge & Communication Management, 3*(2), 85–101. https://doi.org/10.5958/j.2277-7946.3.2.008.
Friedrich, R., Iglezakis, I., Klein, W., & Pregizer, S. (2002). Experience-Based Decision Support for Project Management with Case-Based Reasoning. *German Workshop on Experience Management*.
Gazzaniga, M., & Ivry, R. B. (2013). *Cognitive Neuroscience: The Biology of the Mind*. New York: W.W. Norton.
Iafrate, F. (2015). *From Big Data to Smart Data*. Hoboken: Wiley https://doi.org/10.1002/9781119116189.
Kimball, R., & Caserta, J. (2004). *The Data Warehouse ETL Toolkit*. Indianapolis: Wiley.
Kimball, R., Ross, M., Thornthwaite, W., Mundy, J., & Becker, B. (2008). *The Data Warehouse Lifecycle Toolkit* (2nd ed.). Indianapolis: Wiley.
Kolodner, J. L. (1992). An Introduction to Case-Based Reasoning. *Artificial Intelligence Review, 6*(1), 3–34. https://doi.org/10.1007/BF00155578.
Lin, Y., & Xiao, W. (2017). *Implementing a Smart Data Platform*. Beijing: O'Reilly. Retrieved from https://www.oreilly.com/data/free/implementing-a-smart-data-platform.csp
Lusch, R. F., Vargo, S. L., & Tanniru, M. (2009). Service, Value Networks and Learning. *Journal of the Academy of Marketing Science, 38*(1), 19–31. https://doi.org/10.1007/s11747-008-0131-z.
Montani, S. (2010). In S. Montani & L. C. Jain (Eds.), *Successful Case-Based Reasoning Applications* (Vol. 305). Berlin/Heidelberg: Springer Science & Business Media. https://doi.org/10.1007/978-3-642-14078-5.
Ng, A. Y., & Russell, S. (2017, August 17). *Algorithms for Inverse Reinforcement Learning*. Retrieved December 27, 2017, from http://bair.berkeley.edu/blog/2017/08/17/cooperatively-learning-human-values/
Normann, R., & Ramirez, R. (1993). From Value Chain to Value Constellation: Designing Interactive Strategy. *Harvard Business Review, 71*(4), 65–77.
Osuszek, L., & Stanek, S. (2015). Case Based Reasoning as an Improvement of Decision Making and Case Processing in Adaptive Case Management Systems. *FedCSIS Position Papers, 6*, 217–223.

Porter, M. E., & Heppelmann, J. E. (2015). How Smart, Connected Products Are Transforming Companies. *Harvard Business Review, 93*(10), 96–114.

Ransbotham, S. (2017). AI and the Need for Speed. *MIT Sloan Management Review*, 1–4. Retrieved from https://sloanreview.mit.edu/article/ai-and-the-need-for-speed/

Stabell, C. B., & Fjeldstad, Ø. D. (1998). Configuring Value for Competitive Advantage: On Chains, Shops, and Networks. *Strategic Management Journal, 19*(5), 413–437. http://doi.org/10.1002/(SICI)1097-0266(199805)19:5<413::AID-SMJ946>3.3.CO;2-3.

The HFT Algo-Computers Crash FX Markets - Bert Dohmen. (2016, December 30). *The HFT Algo-Computers Crash FX Markets – Bert Dohmen*. Retrieved January 23, 2018, from http://bertdohmen.com/hft-algo-computers-crash-fx-markets/

Trossen, D., & Fine, C. (2005). Value Chain Dynamics in the Communication Industry. MIT Communications Future Programme, MIT.

Vargo, S. L., & Lusch, R. F. (2004). Evolving to a New Dominant Logic for Marketing. *Journal of Marketing, 68*(1), 1–17. https://doi.org/10.1509/jmkg.68.1.1.24036.

Vargo, S. L., & Lusch, R. F. (2008). Service-Dominant Logic: Continuing the Evolution. *Journal of the Academy of Marketing Science, 36*(1), 1–10. https://doi.org/10.1007/s11747-007-0069-6.

Wang, C. L., & Ahmed, P. K. (2013). The Knowledge Value Chain: A Pragmatic Knowledge Implementation Network. *Handbook of Business Strategy, 6*(1), 321–326. https://doi.org/10.1108/08944310510558115.

What Main Methodology Are You Using for Your Analytics, Data Mining, or Data Science Projects? Poll. (n.d.). Retrieved January 10, 2018, from https://www.kdnuggets.com/polls/2014/analytics-data-mining-data-science-methodology.html

Zilis, S., & Cham, J. (2016, November). The Competitive Landscape for Machine Intelligence. *Harvard Business Review*. Retrieved from https://hbr.org/2016/11/the-competitive-landscape-for-machine-intelligence

5

Summary and Recommendations for Future Research

The aim of this work is to present the influence of artificial intelligence on the management, value generation competitive advantage of contemporary organizations.

Methods and techniques of artificial intelligence are developing at a dizzying pace, similarly to the supporting infrastructure (servers, graphics cards, dedicated processors, etc.). This is accompanied by the development of information technology, particularly decentralized, distributed architectures that enable not only data storage (distributed ledgers), but also tracking and securing transactions (blockchain) and running various applications (Ethereum, Hyperledger).

Such dynamic development generates practically unlimited possibilities of adding "intelligence," particularly autonomy, products and services, improvement (and sometimes thorough reconfiguration) of business processes and generation of new business models. It is a challenge not only for managers and investors, but also for researchers interested in effective modeling of such phenomena.

The research subject presented in this study is very wide: it covers not only many areas of organization operations, but also markets and various methods of artificial intelligence. Such a broad approach to the topic allows, on the one hand, for looking at the issue from a broader perspective, and

A. Wodecki, *Artificial Intelligence in Value Creation*,
https://doi.org/10.1007/978-3-319-91596-8_5

on the other hand, it hinders deep, precise analysis. For this reason, the natural direction of further research may be narrowing the research area to selected industries (e.g. energy or industry), areas of organization activities (e.g. design) or AI methods (e.g. prediction systems). The conclusions of the research presented in this study may be helpful in choosing the subject:

1. **Industries** to which the most intelligent solutions are addressed are high technologies (including telecommunications and IT), trade (including e-commerce), finances and health.
2. **Primary activities**, most strongly supported by AI systems are pre-production design and activity, while support activities constitute knowledge management (especially mapping and discovering knowledge).
3. **Methods and technologies** most commonly used in the studied projects are forecasting, solutions supporting the analysis of internal data as well as personalization and recommendation services.

In the context of new structures for generating values such as the cognitive networks proposed in this book, the technologies that enable the creation of distributed applications, both publicly available and controlled access, such as the Ethereum or Hyperledger from Linux Foundation (supported by such companies as Intel or IBM) seem particularly interesting. There are already projects such as Magnus Collective (https://0xmagnus.com) that use these technologies to create decentralized networks that support the creation of intelligent industrial robots and AI agents. The growing popularity of raising capital in the formula of the " Initial Coin Offering" (ICO) on portals such as ICOBox (icobox.io), ICOList (ico-list.com) or ICOBench (https://icobench.com/) creates completely new, decentralized exchanges generating more and more turnover, and as a result, interest and anxiety of regulators as well as high investment risk (see the Bitcoin crash in January 2018).

As a result, another interesting direction may be the research on the role of intelligent technologies in the decentralization of business processes and markets, particularly in the situation of increased information transparency and acceleration of transaction processes thanks to blockchain technology.

In further research, it is also worth addressing the possible impact of AI systems on the broadly understood decision-making and managing of the intellectual capital of an organization. The following issues seem particularly interesting:

1. **The influence of intelligent systems on decision-making**, especially the allocation of decision centers. How will the role of a human change in making decisions? How will this change affect the methods of creating value by organizations (vide recommendation systems or smart connected products), market mechanisms (Marketing-2-Machines) and, more generally, organizational management models?
2. **The influence of artificial intelligence on the management of intellectual resources of the organization**. Who will be the owner of the data and to what extent? How to effectively manage algorithms and mechanisms of their improvement? What will be the new models for sharing services and digital infrastructure and how can they affect the creation of new value by organizations?
3. **The role of AI class systems in knowledge management and organization learning**. How will the methods of discovering, generating, codifying and using the accumulated knowledge change?

As for the area of research methods, the dynamic development of Data Science methods, libraries, tools and platforms as well as the availability of large amounts of data allow us to model the phenomena that surround us. On the one hand, this is a great opportunity, but also a big challenge for researchers. Changes in research methods, methods of obtaining data or cooperation within teams require not only continuous self-improvement, but also modification of one's habits. As a result, similarly to Industry 4.0, one can expect a revolution in science (the question is only about the value of the suffix: while in industry 4.0 it has its justification, in science, the tracking of the revolution requires a special approach).

Undoubtedly, the research work on the models of generating value and achieving competitive advantages in the structures that intensively use artificial intelligence have enormous potential. They are not only an inspiring challenge, but they can also contribute to the generation of new research methods and provide measurable value to managers and investors. It is worth remembering about the "classical" models of value generation and competing: their message is extremely universal and valid even in the current, information technology-dominated world.

Appendices

Appendix 1: Summary of Desirable Competencies in Organizations Implementing AI Solutions

Below a summary of the key competencies described in the main part of the book is presented, the mastery of which can significantly improve the adoption of AI system solutions in the organization.

Domain Competencies

Design

1. The knowledge of methods and techniques that enable equipping products and services with "intelligence."
2. Particularly, the ability to design systems that would use the acquired experience for continuous self-improvement; for example, using the mechanisms of reinforcement learning.
3. The ability to design products so that they meet the company's strategic assumptions in the area of creating their own ecosystems or adapting to the existing ones.
4. The ability to use data generated by products to create a new value for the customer.
5. The awareness of the possibility of using AI solutions to support design processes.
6. The awareness of the need to develop new methods for designing solutions.

Production and Logistics

1. The awareness of the possible added value of AI systems at various stages of production.
2. Knowledge of AI architectures in industry, particularly, of systems enabling data collection, integration with external data and generation of knowledge.
3. Knowledge of trends in the development of information systems using the Internet of Things, especially their possible business cases, architectures and implementation methodologies.
4. Skills for assessing the impact of different architectures of smart systems on the structure of product revenues and costs, especially in the cases of possible transfer of variable costs up the value chain.
5. Awareness of expanding the "factory" and its processes in time and space.

Marketing and Sales

1. The awareness of the diversity of digital data left by users (digital fingerprint).
2. The ability to draw conclusions based on information generated by advanced analytical systems supporting marketing and sales processes.
3. Understanding the impact of technology on the habits and styles of communication of digital media users.
4. The awareness and the ability to assess the business potential of different methods of behavioral profiling and personalization of customer relations.
5. Understanding the mechanisms of modern electronic marketing methods such as real-time bids or programmatic marketing.

Personalization and After-Sales Service

1. The awareness and ability to assess the business potential of the new capabilities of after-sales and service systems.

2. The ability to manage the product design process to take full advantage of the potential of these solutions when the product is launched on the market.
3. Ability to model after-sales service processes and service using AI systems.
4. The related ability to determine the cost structure of after-sales service and service.
5. The ability to use data and information generated during service and the service of designing value for the customer and to increase competitive advantage.

Human Resource Management

1. The awareness of the possibilities of information systems in the area of automatic modeling of competencies desirable at work positions.
2. The ability to use IT systems in the processes of job and employee valuation as well as risk assessment and the consequences of losing the most valuable employees.
3. Ability to assess the costs and benefits of implementing various advanced systems supporting personal productivity and group work. In particular, the ability to assess the impact of these solutions on both the efficiency of business processes and the satisfaction of employees.
4. Ability to manage interdisciplinary teams that connect people with different work styles, characters and motivations. Willingness to experiment with different project management methodologies for AI systems implementation combined with the ability to reflect and learn from mistakes.

Information and Knowledge Management

1. The ability to identify different data sources and solutions that enable their integration.
2. The ability to interpret data and information generated by AI systems, in particular, using new methods of their visualization (graphs, shapes, etc.).

3. The awareness of the challenges that can arise from various AI architectures and the ability to design implementations so as to maximize the potential of these systems while minimizing the risks associated with them.

Managerial Competencies

1. Understanding the impact of AI solutions on the company and its environment:

    (a) The assessment of the business potential of AI solutions.
    (b) The assessment of the impact of AI on workplaces.
    (c) Evaluation of the impact of AI on the industry.

2. Understanding the role of data, algorithms and processes of their "training":

    (a) Interpretation and inference based on AI system recommendations.
    (b) Making decisions based on predictions and recommendations of AI systems.
    (c) The ability to assess the consequences of actions recommended by AI.
    (d) Ethical evaluation of these activities.
    (e) Their aesthetic evaluation.
    (f) The ability to ask good AI questions.

3. Ability to formulate good business cases for projects using AI.
4. Ability to ask questions about the possibilities and limitations of AI recommendations:

    (a) What are their options?
    (b) What can/should be recognized, provided?
    (c) How should the AI agent learn to constantly improve its predictive capabilities?

Constructing, Maintaining and Developing AI Systems

1. Teaching AI systems (coaches).
2. Understanding the mechanisms of AI systems (translators).
3. Ability to specify and manage AI system target functions (sustainers).

Organizational Culture

1. Ability to cooperate effectively: internal cooperation with partners and competitors.
2. Openness to changes and new ideas.
3. Analytical skills.
4. Vision and planning in the long run.
5. Business strategy matched to the technology strategy.
6. The ability to change existing products and services to maximize the value of new technologies.
7. Good and effective data governance.
8. The ability to establish strategic alliances with partners in the ecosystem, particularly with competitors.

Appendix 2: Challenges Related to the Implementation of Artificial Intelligence Systems

Challenges in Specific Areas of Activity

Below, the challenges, which are worth addressing by an organization planning to implement AI systems, are summarized.

Design

1. Strategic decision related to the choice of place in the industry ecosystem. How can the existing ecosystem fit in? Or maybe create our

own? Or design and implement a platform that allows other entities to share their own services?
2. Designing products so that their further development could be possible without significant interference in the hardware part.
3. Designing new models of financial and operational controlling considering the various architectures of AI class solutions. Especially:

    (a) Calculation of future variable costs in the case of using smart components from external suppliers and making them available by suppliers in the Pay-Per-Use model.
    (b) The use of data generated by products to assess the effectiveness of new business models, e.g. the offer of proprietary solutions in the Pay-Per-Use model.

Production and Logistics

1. Development of methods for generating knowledge from data coming from sensors.
2. Development of new methods of implementation and development of information systems based on the Internet of Things.
3. Development of effective methods of managing distributed structures.
4. Increasingly shorter time (events, processes, production cycles) combined with a growing amount of very different information and the associated risk of losing control over systems (the need to assign these activities to machines).
5. Development of new models of financial and operational controlling, taking into account the effect of transferring the variable cost down the value chain, and the need to include this phenomenon in the process of calculating the product sale price.
6. The problem of ownership in AI saturated systems: who is the owner of the product, whose most of the components are supplied from different suppliers e.g. in the SaaS model?
7. Competence management (in the sense of entitlements) given to machines and management of reallocation of decision centers (who

really makes the decision? on what basis and in what way? who is responsible for it? etc.)
8. The role of the human in the factories of the future.

Sales and Marketing

1. Constant value design for the customer: identification of trends, values and needs based on data generated by products.
2. Constant value provision.
3. In the past, after the purchase, the customer was transferred to the care of the service department. In the near future, the moment of the transaction will be just the beginning of the sales department dialogue with the client, and the product will be a vehicle for delivering the newly discovered value for the customer.
4. The growing role of the product as a vehicle for transferring value from customers to the company (e.g. offering products virtually for free and deriving benefits from the sale of customer behavior data). The risk of users getting accustomed to free products and services and losing their confidence in the "discovery" of a real business model.
5. To carry out the above tasks effectively, sales staff should skillfully use AI class solutions: identify clients, assess their potential, and classify or identify the best possible channels and communication styles.

Personalization and After-Sales Service

1. Adaptation to changing service cost structure and customer support (fewer breakdowns, other repair times and schedules, lower share of human costs).
2. Adaptation to changing moments of repairs and their lower costs (also smaller revenues from this area of activity).
3. The necessity to take into account new requirements for products at the stage of their design (products should account for the full possibilities of their subsequent repair and updating).

4. Changing the role of employees in the customer service and repair department: from direct solutions to problems in the assessment of reliability of recommendations generated by AI class systems.
5. Changing the competencies required of people working in these departments: technical knowledge will be less important, and the ability to fully use the capabilities of intelligent systems will be crucial.

Human Resource Management

1. The need to develop new competencies among employees, focused on improving the ability to cooperate with intelligent machines.
2. The necessity for the HR departments to master new competencies in the areas of talent management, heterogeneous teams, etc.
3. Developing new motivation methods.

Information and Knowledge Management

1. The risk of the lack of control over decision-making mechanisms. Recommendations are generated by systems to which we do not have access and whose operating principles we do not understand. And, we have no control over them whatsoever.
2. Risk of the loss of knowledge about the key areas of the company, including customer behavior. Providing data for analysis by an external entity is convenient, but it can be compared to continuous use of advisory services: a company that does so, loses its key competencies, which significantly increases the risk of failure, e.g. in a situation of being cut off from regular advisors.
3. The risk of the market takeover by the company to which we provide data. Obviously, they can be controlled, for example, by legal agreements, but it should be taken into account that:

    (a) Many other companies in our industry use our partner's services.

(b) Nowadays, even anonymized data, after proper processing, can have tremendous value. As a result, there is a risk that the service provider will create a competitive business: having extensive knowledge of customer behavior, they can create a product/service better suited for the needs of the market than our solutions.

Challenges and Barriers to Design and Implementation

1. Difficulties in acquiring and developing talents.
2. AI projects competing with other projects in the company.
3. Safety aspects of systems using AI.
4. Cultural barriers in the adoption of AI.
5. Limited (or lack of) technological capabilities (analytical, data management, IT, etc.).
6. Lack of leadership support for AI initiatives.
7. Unclear or lack of business cases for these types of projects.
8. The risk associated with hasty implementation of immature solutions.
9. Convincing managers that the purchased solution is ready for use (no training required) and the risk of errors in implementation associated with it.
10. The risk of impairing the key competencies of the organization as a result of assigning relevant activities to AI systems (e.g. the knowledge about customer needs, security monitoring or broadly understood reactivity and flexibility).

Appendix 3: The List of Analyzed Projects and Companies Using AI or Supporting Its Design

Remarks

1. Projects are in an alphabetical order.
2. The state of web pages is as for December 20, 2017.

6sense, https://6sense.com/
Acerta, http://acerta.ca/
ActionIQ, https://www.actioniq.com/
AdasWorks, https://adasworks.com/
Affectiva, http://www.affectiva.com/
Affirm, https://www.affirm.com/
Agolo, https://www.agolo.com/
AImotive, https://aimotive.com/
AirPR, https://www.airpr.com/
Airware, https://www.airware.com/
Alation, https://alation.com/
algocian, http://algocian.com/
Algorithmia, https://algorithmia.com/
Alluvium, http://www.alluvium.io/
AlphaSense, https://www.alpha-sense.com/
Amazon Alexa, https://developer.amazon.com/alexa
Amazon DSSTNE, https://github.com/amznlabs/amazon-dsstne
Amazon Mechanical Turk, https://www.mturk.com/mturk/welcome
Anki, https://anki.com/
AnOdot, http://www.anodot.com/
Apache Spark, http://spark.apache.org/
Appier, https://www.appier.com/
Apple Siri, http://www.apple.com/ios/siri/
AppZen, https://www.appzen.com/
Aras Innovator, http://www.aras.com/
Arimo, https://arimo.com/
Arterys, https://arterys.com/
Atomwise, https://www.atomwise.com/
AuroRobotics, http://www.auro.ai/
Automat, http://www.automat.ai/
Aviso, http://www.aviso.com/
Ayasdi, https://www.ayasdi.com/
AYLIEN, http://aylien.com/
babylon, https://www.babylonhealth.com/
Baidu, http://research.baidu.com/
Beagle AI, http://beagle.ai/

BenevolentAI, http://benevolent.ai/
Betterment, https://www.betterment.com/
BigML, https://bigml.com/
BloomReach, http://bloomreach.com/
BlueJ, http://www.bluejlegal.com/
Blue River, http://www.bluerivert.com/
Bonsai, https://bons.ai/
Boston Dynamics, https://www.bostondynamics.com
Bottlenose, http://bottlenose.com/
BrightFunnel, http://www.brightfunnel.com/
Butterfly Network, https://www.butterflynetinc.com/
C3IoT, http://c3iot.com/
Cadence, https://www.cadence.com/
Caffe, http://caffe.berkeleyvision.org/
Cape Analytics, https://capeanalytics.com/
Capio, http://www.capio.ai/
Captricity, https://captricity.com/
CareSkore, https://www.careskore.com/
CBInsights, https://www.cbinsights.com/
Cerebellum Capital, http://www.cerebellumcapital.com/
Chorus.ai, https://www.chorus.ai/
Chronocam, http://www.chronocam.com/
Cirrascale, http://www.cirrascale.com/
Citrine, https://www.citrine.io/
Clarabridge, http://www.clarabridge.com/
Claralabs, https://claralabs.com/
Clari, http://www.clari.com/
clarifai, https://www.clarifai.com/
ClearMetal, http://www.clearmetal.com/home
ClearPath, https://www.clearpathrobotics.com/
CloudMedx Inc., http://www.cloudmedxhealth.com/
Clover, https://cloverintelligence.com/
Cogitai, http://www.cogitai.com/
Cognicor, http://www.cognicor.com/
CognitiveScale, http://www.cognitivescale.com/
Collectiv[i], https://www.collectivei.com/

Color Genomics, https://www.color.com/
Cortica, http://www.cortica.com/
Cortical.io, http://cortical.io
CrowdAI, http://crowdai.com/
CrowdFlower, https://www.crowdflower.com/
Cycorp, http://www.cyc.com/
Cylance, https://www.cylance.com/
Darktrace, https://www.darktrace.com/
DataBricks, https://databricks.com/
Datacratic, http://www.datacratic.com/
DataFox, http://www.datafox.com/
Dataiku, http://www.dataiku.com/
Datalogue, https://about.datalogue.io/
Dataminr, https://www.dataminr.com/
DataRobot, https://www.datarobot.com/
DataSift, http://datasift.com/
Deep Genomics, http://www.deepgenomics.com/
Deep Genomics, https://www.deepgenomics.com/
Deep6 Analytics, https://deep6analytics.com/
Deepgram, https://www.deepgram.com/
DeepInstinct, http://www.deepinstinct.com/
DeepLearning4j, https://deeplearning4j.org/
deepomatic, https://www.deepomatic.com
deepsense.io, deepsense.io
deepvision, http://deepvisionai.com/
Demisto, https://www.demisto.com/
DescartesLabs, http://www.descarteslabs.com/
Diffbot, https://www.diffbot.com/
Digital Genius, https://digitalgenius.com/
Digital Reasoning, http://www.digitalreasoning.com/
Dispatch, http://dispatch.ai/
DJI, http://www.dji.com/
Domino Data Lab, https://www.dominodatalab.com/
Drawbridge, https://www.drawbridge.com/
DriveAI, https://www.drive.ai/
DroneDeploy, https://www.dronedeploy.com/

Earnest, https://www.earnest.com/
Eigen Innovations, http://eigeninnovations.com/
Eloquent Labs, https://www.eloquent.ai/
Enigma, http://enigma.io/
Enlitic, http://www.enlitic.com/
Entelo, https://www.entelo.com/
EverLaw, http://everlaw.com/
Explosion AI, https://explosion.ai/
Facebook M, https://www.wired.com/2015/08/facebook-launches-m-new-kind-virtual-assistant/
Fetch Robotics, http://fetchrobotics.com/
fido.ai, http://fido.ai/
Freenome, http://www.freenome.com/
Fuse Machines, https://www.fusemachines.com/
Fuzzy.ai, Fuzzy.ai.
Gigster, https://gigster.com/
Gingko Bioworks, http://www.ginkgobioworks.com/
Google Assistant, https://assistant.google.com/
Google DeepMind, https://deepmind.com/
Google Self Driving Car, https://www.google.com/selfdrivingcar/
Google TPU, http://bit.ly/2g5J1wi
GradeScope, https://gradescope.com/
Grail, http://www.grailbio.com/
Graphistry, https://www.graphistry.com/
Gridspace, https://www.gridspace.com/
H2O.ai, H2O.ai
Harvest Automation, http://www.public.harvestai.com/
HiQ, https://www.hiqlabs.com/
HireVue, https://www.hirevue.com/
Howdy, https://howdy.ai/.
Hyperopt, http://bit.ly/2g5K3sl
IBM Watson, http://www.ibm.com/watson/
IBM Watson Health, https://www.ibm.com/watson/health/
iCarbonX, https://www.icarbonx.com/en/
Imagia, http://imagia.com/
Import.io, Import.io

Imubit, http://www.imubit.com/
Index.co, http://index.co
InsideSales, https://uk.insidesales.com/
Intel (Nervana), https://www.nervanasys.com/
IntelligentLayer, http://intelligentlayer.com/
iSentium, http://isentium.com/
Isocline, http://www.isosemi.com/
JayBridge, http://www.jaybridge.com/
Kaggle, https://www.kaggle.com/
Kasisto, http://kasisto.com/
Kensho, https://www.kensho.com/#/
Keras, https://keras.io/
Kik, http://www.kik.com/
Kimera, http://kimerasystems.com/
Kindred, https://www.kindred.ai/
Kite, https://kite.com/
Kitt.ai, Kitt.ai
Knewton, knewton.com
KNUPATH, http://www.knupath.com/
Konux, https://www.konux.com/
Kyndi, http://www.kyndi.com/
Lattice, http://www.lattice-engines.com/
Layer 6 AI, http://layer6.ai/
Legal Robot, https://www.legalrobot.com/
Lendo, https://www.lenddo.com/
Lexalytics, https://www.lexalytics.com/
LightIgniter, http://www.liftigniter.com/
Lily, https://www.lily.camera/
Logz.io, http://logz.io/
Loop AI Labs, http://www.loop.ai/
Luminoso, http://www.luminoso.com/
Lunit Inc., http://www.lunit.io/
Maana, https://www.maana.io/
Maluuba, http://www.maluuba.com/
MatterMark, https://mattermark.com/
Mavrx, https://www.mavrx.co/

Microsoft CNTK, https://github.com/Microsoft/CNTK
Microsoft Cortana, https://www.microsoft.com/en-us/windows/cortana
Microsoft DMTK, https://github.com/Microsoft/DMTK
MindMeld, https://www.mindmeld.com/
minds.ai, minds.ai
Mintigo, http://www.mintigo.com/
Mirador, https://www.miradortech.com/
MLDB.ai, MLDB.ai
MLlib, http://spark.apache.org/mllib/
Mobileye, http://www.mobileye.com/
Mobwoi, http://www.chumenwenwen.com/en/site/index.html
Mode.ai, http://mode.ai/
MonkeyLearn, http://monkeylearn.com/
Motiva, http://motiva.ai/
MSFT Cortana Intelligence Suite, https://www.microsoft.com/en-us/cloud-platform/cortana-intelligence-suite
Msg ai, http://msg.ai/
MXNet, https://github.com/dmlc/mxnet
Nanit, https://www.nanit.com/
Nanotronics, http://www.nanotronics.co/.
Nara LogicsReactive, https://naralogics.com/
Narrative Science, https://www.narrativescience.com/
Nauto, http://www.nauto.com/
Nervana Neon, https://github.com/NervanaSystems/neon
Netra, http://www.netra.io/
Nexidia, http://www.nexidia.com/
Nnaisense, https://nnaisense.com/
Numenta, http://numenta.com/
Numerate Medical, http://www.numerate.com/
Nutonomy, http://nutonomy.com/
NVIDIA Deep Learning, http://www.nvidia.co.uk/object/deep-learning-uk.html
Octane.ai, https://octaneai.com/
Oncora, https://oncoramedical.com/
OpenAI Gym, https://gym.openai.com/
Orbital Insight, https://orbitalinsight.com/

Osaro, http://www.osaro.com/
PaddlePaddle, https://github.com/baidu/Paddle
Palantir, https://www.palantir.com/
Paxata, http://www.paxata.com/
Persado, https://persado.com/
"Petuum, Inc.", http://www.petuum.com/
Pilot.ai, Pilot.ai
Pitstop, https://www.pitstopconnect.com/
Planet Labs Inc., https://www.planet.com/
PlanetOS, https://planetos.com/
Pogo AI, pogo.ai
PopUpArchive, https://www.popuparchive.com/
Preact, http://www.preact.com/
Predata, http://www.predata.com/
Predix (part of GE Digital), https://www.predix.io/
Preferred Networks, https://www.preferred-networks.jp/ja/
Premise, https://www.premise.com/
Presenso, http://www.presenso.com/
Preteckt, http://www.preteckt.com/
Prospera Technologies, http://prospera.ag/
Proteus, https://www.proteus.com/
PyBrain, http://pybrain.org/
Qualcomm Tenstorrent, http://tenstorrent.com/
Quandl, https://www.quandl.com/
Quid, https://quid.com/
Qurious AI, http://www.qurious.io/
Radius, https://radius.com/
RainforestQA, https://www.rainforestqa.com/
RapidMiner, https://rapidminer.com/
RavelLaw, http://ravellaw.com/
Recursion Pharmaceuticals, http://www.recursionpharma.com/
Retention Science, https://retentionscience.com/
Rethink Robotics, http://www.rethinkrobotics.com/
Ross, http://www.rossintelligence.com/
Routific, https://routific.com/
Salesforce, https://www.salesforce.com

Sapho, https://www.sapho.com/
SAS, http://www.sas.com/
ScaleContext, https://www.contextrelevant.com/
scikit-learn, http://scikit-learn.org/
Seal, http://www.seal-software.com/
Seldon, http://www.seldon.io/
Semantic, http://www.semanticmachines.com/
SentenAI, http://sentenai.com/
Sentient, http://www.sentient.ai/
SentinelOne, https://sentinelone.com/
Sentrian, http://sentrian.com/
Shield AI, http://shield.ai/
Shift Technology, http://www.shift-technology.com/
Sift Science, https://siftscience.com/
Sight Machine, http://sightmachine.com/
SigOpt, https://sigopt.com/
SkipFlag, skipflag.com
Skycatch, https://www.skycatch.com/
Skydio, https://www.skydio.com/
Skymind, https://skymind.io/
Slack, https://slack.com
Snips, https://snips.ai/
space_know, https://spaceknow.com/
spaCy, https://spacy.io/
Spark Beyond, http://www.sparkbeyond.com/
SparkCognition, http://sparkcognition.com/
Splunk, https://www.splunk.com/
Springrole, https://springrole.com/
Sudo, https://www.sudo.ai/
Tala (a InVenture), http://tala.co/
Talkiq, http://talkiq.com/
Talla, talla.com
Tamr Inc., http://www.tamr.com/
TensorFlow, https://www.tensorflow.org/
TerraVion, http://www.terravion.com/
Tesla, www.tesla.com

Textio, https://textio.com/
Theano, https://github.com/Theano/Theano
Thingworx, https://www.thingworx.com/
Torch7, http://torch.ch/
Trace Genomics, https://www.tracegenomics.com/
Tracxn, https://tracxn.com/
Trifacta, https://www.trifacta.com/
Trimble, https://agriculture.trimble.com/software/
Tule, https://www.tuletechnologies.com/
Twilio, https://www.twilio.com/
twoXAR, http://www.twoxar.com/
Uber, https://developer.uber.com/
Ubtech, http://www.ubtrobot.com/
Udio, http://udio.ai/
Unitive, http://www.unitive.works/
Uptake, https://uptake.com/
Verdigris, http://verdigris.co/
Verily, https://verily.com/
Vicarious, http://www.vicarious.com/
Volley, http://www.volley.com/
Voyager Labs, http://voyagerlabs.co/
Wade and Wendy, http://wadeandwendy.ai/
Wealthfront, https://www.wealthfront.com/
Weka, http://www.cs.waikato.ac.nz/ml/weka/
Wise.io, Wise.io
WorkFusion, https://www.workfusion.com/
X AI, x.ai
Yhat, https://www.yhat.com/
Yseop, https://yseop.com/
Zebra Medical Vision, https://www.zebra-med.com/
Zendesk, Zendesk.com
Zephyr Health, https://zephyrhealth.com/
ZestFinance, https://www.zestfinance.com/
Zimperium, www.zimperium.com
Zoom AI, zoom.ai
Zymergen, https://www.zymergen.com/, https://www.zymergen.com

References

Abramowicz, W., Kalczyński, P., & Węcel, K. (2002). Knowledge Representation Standards. In *Filtering the Web to Feed Data Warehouses* (pp. 41–74). London: Springer. https://doi.org/10.1007/978-1-4471-0137-6_3.

Adner, R., & Zemsky, P. B. (2004). A Demand Based View of Sustainable Competitive Advantage. *SSRN Electronic Journal* https://doi.org/10.2139/ssrn.651184.

Agrawal, A. K., Gans, J. S., & Tetlock, P. E. (2017). What to Expect From Artificial Intelligence. *MIT Sloan Management Review*, Spring.

Bednarz, J. (2011). Klasyczne a nowe teorie przewagi konkurencyjnej przedsiębiorstw. *Prace I Materiały Instytutu Handlu Zagranicznego Uniwersytetu Gdańskiego*, (nr 30), 112–122.

Bitran, G. R., Gurumurthi, S., & Sam, S. L. (2007). The Need for Third-Party Coordination in Supply Chain Governance. *MIT Sloan Management Review, 48*, 30–37.

Bostrom, N. (2014). *Superintelligence*. Oxford: Oxford University Press.

Bounfour, A., & Edvinsson, L. (2012). *Intellectual Capital for Communities*. London and New York: Routledge.

Bovet, D., & Martha, J. (2000). Value Nets: Reinventing the Rusty Supply Chain for Competitive Advantage. *Strategy & Leadership, 28*(4), 21–26. https://doi.org/10.1108/10878570010378654.

A. Wodecki, *Artificial Intelligence in Value Creation*,
https://doi.org/10.1007/978-3-319-91596-8

Bowman, C., & Ambrosini, V. (2000). Value Creation Versus Value Capture: Towards a Coherent Definition of Value in Strategy. *British Journal of Management, 11*(1), 1–15. https://doi.org/10.1111/1467-8551.00147.

Brockman, G., Cheung, V., Pettersson, L., Schneider, J., Schulman, J., Tang, J., & Zaremba, W. (2016, June 5). OpenAI Gym. arXiv:1606.01540

Bughin, J., Hazan, E., Ramaswamy, S., Chui, M., Allas, T., Dahlstrom, P., et al. (2017). *Artificial Intelligence.* McKinsey Global Institute. Retrieved from https://www.mckinsey.com/~/media/McKinsey/Industries/Advanced%20Electronics/Our%20Insights/How%20artificial%20intelligence%20can%20deliver%20real%20value%20to%20companies/MGI-Artificial-Intelligence-Discussion-paper.ashx

Chapman, P., Clinton, J., Kerber, R., Khabaza, T., Reinartz, T., Shearer, C., & Wirth, R. (2004). *CRISP-DM 1.0* (pp. 1–76). SPSS. Retrieved from https://www.the-modeling-agency.com/crisp-dm.pdf

Chen, J. (2017, April 24). The New Moats – Greylock Perspectives. Retrieved January 2, 2018, from https://news.greylock.com/the-new-moats-53f61aeac2d9

Cognitive Computing Defined. (n.d.). *Cognitive Computing Defined.* Retrieved January 31, 2018, from https://cognitivecomputingconsortium.com/resources/cognitive-computing-defined/

Cuesta, J. C., Luokkanen-Rabetino, K., & Stanoevska-Slabeva, K. (2010). Grid Value Chains – What Is a Grid Solution? In *Grid and Cloud Computing* (pp. 83–96). Berlin/Heidelberg: Springer. https://doi.org/10.1007/978-3-642-05193-7_6.

Davenport, T. H., & Prusak, L. (2000, August). Working Knowledge – How Organizations Manage What They Know. *Ubiquity, 2000,* 2-es. https://doi.org/10.1145/347634.348775.

Dennett, D. C. (2014). *Intuition Pumps and Other Tools for Thinking.* New York: W.W. Norton & Company.

Digitalization of Energy Systems. (2017). *Digitalization of Energy Systems* (pp. 1–61). New York: Bloomberg Finance LP. Retrieved from https://www.siemens.com/global/en/home/company/topic-areas/sustainable-energy/digitalization-of-energy-systems.html

Dyer, J. H., & Singh, H. (1998). The Relational View: Cooperative Strategy and Sources of Interorganizational Competitive Advantage. *Academy of Management Review, 23*(4), 660. https://doi.org/10.2307/259056.

Eaton, B. D., Elaluf-Calderwood, S. M., & Sørensen, C. (2010). *The Role of Control Points in Determining Business Models for Future Mobile Generative Systems* (pp. 459–463). Presented at the 2010 Ninth International Conference on Mobile Business and 2010 Ninth Global Mobility Roundtable (ICMB-GMR), IEEE. https://doi.org/10.1109/ICMB-GMR.2010.39.

Edvinsson, L., & Malone, M. S. (1997). *Intellectual Capital: Realizing Your Company's True Value by Finding It's Hidden Roots*. New York: Harper Business.

Ermine, J.-L. (2013). A Knowledge Value Chain for Knowledge Management. *Journal of Knowledge & Communication Management, 3*(2), 85–101. https://doi.org/10.5958/j.2277-7946.3.2.008.

Evans, P. B., & Wurster, T. S. (1997). Strategy and the New Economics of Information. *Harvard Business Review, Sept–Oct*, 70–82. Harvard University.

Five Management Strategies for Getting the Most from AI. (2017, September 19). *MIT Sloan Management Review*, pp. 1–6. Retrieved from https://sloanreview.mit.edu/article/five-management-strategies-for-getting-the-most-from-ai/

Foray, D. (2004). *Economics of Knowledge*. Cambridge: MIT Press.

For Robots to Work with People, They Must Understand People. (2017, August). For Robots to Work with People, They Must Understand People. *The Economist*. Retrieved from https://www.economist.com/science-andtechnology/2017/08/17/for-robots-to-work-with-people-they-must-understand-people

Frické, M. (2008). The Knowledge Pyramid: A Critique of the DIKW Hierarchy. *Journal of Information Science, 35*(2), 131–142. https://doi.org/10.1177/0165551508094050.

Friedrich, R., Iglezakis, I., Klein, W., & Pregizer, S. (2002). Experience-Based Decision Support for Project Management with Case-Based Reasoning. *German Workshop on Experience Management*.

Gabbatt, A. (2011, February 17). *IBM Computer Watson Wins Jeopardy Clash*. Retrieved January 31, 2018, from http://www.theguardian.com/technology/2011/feb/17/ibm-computer-watson-wins-jeopardy

Gazzaniga, M., & Ivry, R. B. (2013). *Cognitive Neuroscience: The Biology of the Mind*. New York: W.W. Norton.

Gebhart, M., Giessler, P., & Abeck, S. (2016). Flexible and Maintainable Service-Oriented Architectures with Resource-Oriented Web Services. *Emerging Trends in the Evolution of Service-Oriented and Enterprise Architectures, 111*(1&2), 23–39. https://doi.org/10.1007/978-3-319-40564-3_3.

Gleick, J. (2011). *The Information: A History, a Theory, a Flood*. New York: Pantheon Books.

Godlewska-Majkowska, H., Łyciuk-Bzdyra, M., Wodecki, A., Zarębski, P., & Zarębski, K. (2010). Atrakcyjność inwestycyjna polskich regionów w 2007 roku. *Studia I Analizy Instytutu Przedsiębiorstwa, Innowacyjność jako czynnik wzrostu atrakcyjności inwestycyjnej polskich regionów w latach 2002–2007*, 55–234.

Goertzel, B. (2017, September 5). *What Counts as a Conscious Thinking Machine?* Retrieved December 26, 2017, from https://www.newscientist.com/article/mg21528813.600-what-counts-as-a-conscious-thinking-machine/

Grudzewski, W. M., Hejduk, I. K., Sankowska, A., & Wańtuchowicz, M. (2008). Cultural Determinants of Creating Modern Organisations – The Role of Trust. In *Pervasive Collaborative Networks* (Vol. 283, pp. 323–332). Boston: Springer. https://doi.org/10.1007/978-0-387-84837-2_33.

Gunasekaran, A., & Ngai, E. W. T. (2004). Information Systems in Supply Chain Integration and Management. *European Journal of Operational Research, 159*(2), 269–295. https://doi.org/10.1016/j.ejor.2003.08.016.

Gunning, D. (2017). Explainable Artificial Intelligence (XAI). Retrieved June 13, 2018, from https://www.darpa.mil/program/explainable-artificial-intelligence

Hall, R. (1993). A Framework Linking Intangible Resources and Capabilities to Sustainable Competitive Advantage. *Strategic Management Journal, 14*(8), 607–618. https://doi.org/10.1002/smj.4250140804.

Hartford, J. S., Wright, J. R., & Leyton-Brown, K. (2016). *Deep Learning for Predicting Human Strategic Behavior* (pp. 2424–2432).

Hassabis, D., Kumaran, D., Summerfield, C., & Botvinick, M. (2017). Neuroscience-Inspired Artificial Intelligence. *Neuron, 95*(2), 245–258. https://doi.org/10.1016/j.neuron.2017.06.011.

Hern, A. (2017, April 18). Netflix's Biggest Competitor? *Sleep*. Retrieved January 31, 2018, from http://www.theguardian.com/technology/2017/apr/18/netflix-competitor-sleep-uber-facebook

Hoyt, J., & Huq, F. (2000). From Arms-Length to Collaborative Relationships in the Supply Chain. *International Journal of Physical Distribution & Logistics Management, 30*(9), 750–764. https://doi.org/10.1108/09600030010351453.

Hurwitz, J., Kaufman, M., & Bowles, A. (2015). *Cognitive Computing and Big Data Analytics*. Indianapolis: Wiley.

Iafrate, F. (2015). *From Big Data to Smart Data*. Hoboken: Wiley https://doi.org/10.1002/9781119116189.

Iansiti, M., & Levien, R. (2004). *The Keystone Advantage*. Boston: Harvard Business Press.

Kahneman, D. (2011). *Thinking, Fast and Slow*. New York: Farrar, Straus and Giroux.

Karras, T., Aila, T., Laine, S., & Lehtinen, J. (n.d.). *Progressive Growing of GANs for Improved Quality, Stability, and Variation*. Retrieved December 28, 2017, from http://research.nvidia.com/publication/2017-10_Progressive-Growing-of

Kelly, J. E. (2015). *Computing, Cognition and the Future of Knowing*. Retrieved January 31, 2018, from https://www.research.ibm.com/software/IBMResearch/multimedia/Computing_Cognition_WhitePaper.pdf

Kemelmacher-Shlizerman, I., Seitz, S. M., Miller, D., & Brossard, E. (2015). The MegaFace Benchmark – 1 Million Faces for Recognition at Scale. *2016 IEEE Conference on Computer Vision and Pattern Recognition (CVPR)*.

Retrieved from http://arxiv.org/pdf/1512.00596. For more details: https://www.researchgate.net/publication/311609513_The_MegaFace_Benchmark_1_Million_Faces_for_Recognition_at_Scale
Kimball, R., & Caserta, J. (2004). *The Data Warehouse ETL Toolkit*. Indianapolis: Wiley.
Kimball, R., Ross, M., Thornthwaite, W., Mundy, J., & Becker, B. (2008). *The Data Warehouse Lifecycle Toolkit* (2nd ed.). Indianapolis: Wiley.
Koelblin, S. (2017, April 3). *Robots Take Over – The Apparel Production*. Retrieved January 31, 2018, from https://www.linkedin.com/pulse/robots-take-over-apparel-production-susanna-koelblin
Kolodner, J. L. (1992). An Introduction to Case-Based Reasoning. *Artificial Intelligence Review, 6*(1), 3–34. https://doi.org/10.1007/BF00155578.
Le Blanc, B., & Ermine, J.-L. (2011). A Shannon's Theory of Knowledge. In *Creating Collaborative Advantage Through Knowledge and Innovation* (Vol. 5, pp. 51–67). World Scientific. https://doi.org/10.1142/9789812707482_0004.
Leibo, J. Z., Zambaldi, V., Lanctot, M., Marecki, J., & Graepel, T. (2017, February 10). *Multi-agent Reinforcement Learning in Sequential Social Dilemmas*. https://arxiv.org/abs/1702.03037
Levine, P. (2016, December 16). *The End of Cloud Computing*. Retrieved January 30, 2018, from https://a16z.com/2016/12/16/the-end-of-cloud-computing/
Li, Y., Roy, U., Shin, S.-J., & Lee, Y. T. (2015). *A "Smart Component" Data Model in PLM* (pp. 1388–1397). Presented at the 2015 IEEE International Conference on Big Data (Big Data), IEEE. https://doi.org/10.1109/BigData.2015.7363899.
Lin, Y., & Xiao, W. (2017). *Implementing a Smart Data Platform*. Beijing: O'Reilly. Retrieved from https://www.oreilly.com/data/free/implementing-a-smart-data-platform.csp
Lippman, S. A., & Rumelt, R. P. (2003). A Bargaining Perspective on Resource Advantage. *Strategic Management Journal, 24*(11), 1069–1086. https://doi.org/10.1002/smj.345.
Lohr, S. (2014, August 17). For Big-Data Scientists, "Janitor Work" Is Key Hurdle to Insights. Retrieved December 31, 2017, from https://www.nytimes.com/2014/08/18/technology/for-big-data-scientists-hurdleto-insights-is-janitor-work.html
Lusch, R. F., Vargo, S. L., & Malter, A. J. (2006). Marketing as Service-Exchange: Taking a Leadership Role in Global Marketing Management. *Organizational Dynamics, 35*, 264–278.
Lusch, R. F., Vargo, S. L., & O'Brien, M. (2007). Competing Through Service: Insights from Service-Dominant Logic. *Journal of Retailing, 83*(1), 5–18. https://doi.org/10.1016/j.jretai.2006.10.002.

Lusch, R. F., Vargo, S. L., & Tanniru, M. (2009). Service, Value Networks and Learning. *Journal of the Academy of Marketing Science, 38*(1), 19–31. https://doi.org/10.1007/s11747-008-0131-z.

MacDonald, G., & Ryall, M. D. (2004). How Do Value Creation and Competition Determine Whether a Firm Appropriates Value? *Management Science, 50*(10), 1319–1333. https://doi.org/10.1287/mnsc.1030.0152.

Mazur, M. (1970). *Jakościowa teoria informacji.* Warsaw: Wydawnictwa Naukowo-Techniczne.

Mercier-Laurent, E., Owoc, M. L., & Boulanger, D. (2016). In E. Mercier-Laurent, M. L. Owoc, & D. Boulanger (Eds.), *Artificial Intelligence for Knowledge Management* (Vol. 469). Cham: Springer. https://doi.org/10.1007/978-3-319-28868-0.

Messaging Apps Are Now Bigger Than Social Networks. (2016). *Business Insider.* http://www.businessinsider.com/the-messaging-app-report-2015-11

Min, S., Mentzer, J. T., & Ladd, R. T. (2007). A Market Orientation in Supply Chain Management. *Journal of the Academy of Marketing Science, 35*(4), 507–522. https://doi.org/10.1007/s11747-007-0020-x.

Montani, S. (2010). In S. Montani & L. C. Jain (Eds.), *Successful Case-Based Reasoning Applications* (Vol. 305). Berlin/Heidelberg: Springer Science & Business Media. https://doi.org/10.1007/978-3-642-14078-5.

Moravčík, M., Schmid, M., Burch, N., Lisý, V., Morrill, D., Bard, N., et al. (2017). DeepStack: Expert-Level Artificial Intelligence in Heads-Up No-Limit Poker. *Science, 356*(6337), 508–513. https://doi.org/10.1126/science.aam6960.

Nelson, P. (2016, December 7). *One Autonomous Car Will Use 4,000 GB of Data Per Day.* Retrieved January 20, 2018, from https://www.networkworld.com/article/3147892/internet/one-autonomous-car-will-use-4000-gb-of-dataday.html

Ng, A. Y., & Russell, S. (2017, August 17). *Algorithms for Inverse Reinforcement Learning.* Retrieved December 27, 2017, from http://bair.berkeley.edu/blog/2017/08/17/cooperatively-learning-human-values/

Nilsson, N. J. (2005). Human-Level Artificial Intelligence? Be Serious! *AI Magazine,* Winter, *26*(4), 68–75. https://doi.org/10.1609/aimag.v26i4.1850.

Nisbett, R. E. (2015). *Mindware.* New York: Farrar, Straus and Giroux.

Nonaka, I. (1994). A Dynamic Theory of Organizational Knowledge Creation. *Organization Science, 5*(1), 14–37. https://doi.org/10.1287/orsc.5.1.14.

Normann, R., & Ramirez, R. (1993). From Value Chain to Value Constellation: Designing Interactive Strategy. *Harvard Business Review, 71*(4), 65–77.

Normann, R. (2001). *Reframing Business.* Chichester: Wiley.

Norvig, P., & Russell, S. (2016). *Artificial Intelligence: Modern Approach* (3rd ed.). Upper Saddle River: Prentice Hall.

On Orbitz, Mac Users Steered to Pricier Hotels. (2012, August 23). On Orbitz, Mac Users Steered to Pricier Hotels. Retrieved December 29, 2017, from https://www.wsj.com/articles/SB1000142405270230445860457748822667325882

Osuszek, L., & Stanek, S. (2015). Case Based Reasoning as an Improvement of Decision Making and Case Processing in Adaptive Case Management Systems. *FedCSIS Position Papers, 6*, 217–223.

Pagani, M. (2013). Digital Business Strategy and Value Creation: Framing the Dynamic Cycle of Control Points. *MIS Quarterly, 37*, 617–632.

Pil, F. K., & Holweg, M. (2006). Evolving from Value Chain to Value Grid. *MIT Sloan Management Review, 47*, 72–80.

Porter, M. E. (2008). *Competitive Advantage*. New York: Simon and Schuster.

Porter, M. E., & Heppelmann, J. E. (2014). How Smart, Connected Products Are Transforming Competition. *Harvard Business Review, 92*, 64–88.

Porter, M. E., & Heppelmann, J. E. (2015). How Smart, Connected Products Are Transforming Companies. *Harvard Business Review, 93*(10), 96–114.

Porter, M. E., & Heppelmann, J. E. (2017). A Manager's Guide to Augmented Reality. *Harvard Business Review*, 11–12.

Porter, M. E., & Millar, V. A. (1985). How Information Gives You Competitive Advantage. *Harvard Business Review, 63*(4), 149–160.

Prahalad, C. K., & Hamel, G. (1990). The Core Competence of the Corporation. *Harvard Business Review, 68*(3), 79–91.

Quinn, J. B. (1992). *Intelligent Enterprise*. New York: Simon and Schuster.

Ransbotham, S. (2017a). AI and the Need for Speed. *MIT Sloan Management Review*, 1–4. Retrieved from https://sloanreview.mit.edu/article/ai-and-the-need-for-speed/

Ransbotham, S. (2017b, January 26). *Managing with Immature AI*. Retrieved December 18, 2017, from https://sloanreview.mit.edu/article/managing-with-immature-ai/

Ransbotham, S., Kiron, D., Gerbert, P., & Reeves, M. (2017). Reshaping Business with Artificial Intelligence. *MIT Sloan Management Review*. Retrieved from http://sloanreview.mit.edu/projects/reshaping-business-with-artificial-intelligence/

Raschka, S. (2015). *Python Machine Learning*. Birmingham: Packt Publishing Ltd.

Ross, J. (2017). The Fundamental Flaw in AI Implementation. *MITSloan Review,* Winter 2017, 1–5. Retrieved from https://sloanreview.mit.edu/article/the-fundamental-flaw-in-ai-implementation/

Rószkiewicz, M., Węziak, D., & Wodecki, A. (2007). Kapitał intelektualny Lubelszczyzny – Propozycja operacjonalizacji i pomiaru. *Studia Regionalne I Lokalne*, *2*(28), 59–88.

Rowley, J. (2007). The Wisdom Hierarchy – Representations of the DIKW Hierarchy. *Journal of Information Science, 33*(2), 163–180. https://doi.org/10.1177/0165551506070706.

Sambamurthy, V., Bharadwaj, A. S., & Grover, V. (2003). Shaping Agility Through Digital Options – Reconceptualizing the Role of Information Technology in Contemporary Firms. *Management Information Systems Quarterly* https://doi.org/10.2307/30036530.

Shannon, C. E., & Weaver, W. (1949). *The Mathematical Theory of Information.* https://doi.org/10.1234/12345678.

Shoham, Y., Perrault, R., Brynjolfsson, E., Clark, J., & LeGassick, C. (2017). *Artificial Intelligence Index* (pp. 1–101). Retrieved from https://aiindex.org/#report

Simon, H. A. (1977). *The New Science of Management Decision* (Rev. ed.). Englewood Cliffs: Prentice Hall.

Stabell, C. B., & Fjeldstad, Ø. D. (1998). Configuring Value for Competitive Advantage: On Chains, Shops, and Networks. *Strategic Management Journal, 19*(5), 413–437. http://doi.org/10.1002/(SICI)1097-0266(199805)19:5<413::AID-SMJ946>3.3.CO;2-3.

Stanoevska-Slabeva, K., & Talamanca, C. (2007). Development of a Generic Value Chain for the Grid Industry. *Grid Economics and Business Models: 4th International Workshop, GECON 2007, Rennes, France, August 28, 2007, Proceedings* (pp. 44–57).

Suwajanakorn, S., Seitz, S. M., & Kemelmacher-Shlizerman, I. (n.d.). Synthesizing Obama: Learning Lip Sync from Audio. Retrieved December 28, 2017, from http://grail.cs.washington.edu/projects/AudioToObama/siggraph17_obama.pdf

The Effect of Acceleration Techniques on Product Development Time J. Zirger and Janet L. Hartley, IEEE Transactions on Engineering Management (May 1996). pp. 143–152. (1996). *Journal of Product Innovation Management, 13*(6), 555–556. https://doi.org/10.1016/S0737-6782(96)89830-4.

The Four V's of Big Data. Retrieved May 18, 2018, from http://www.ibmbigdatahub.com/infographic/four-vs-big-data

The Future Lies in Automation. (2017 April 8). *The Economist.* Retrieved from https://www.economist.com/special-report/2017/04/08/the-future-lies-in-automation

The HFT Algo-Computers Crash FX Markets - Bert Dohmen. (2016, December 30). *The HFT Algo-Computers Crash FX Markets – Bert Dohmen.* Retrieved January 23, 2018, from http://bertdohmen.com/hft-algo-computers-crash-fx-markets/

Thompson, J. D. (1967). *Organizations in Action.* New York: McGraw Hill.

Trossen, D., & Fine, C. (2005). Value Chain Dynamics in the Communication Industry. MIT Communications Future Programme, MIT.

Turing, A. M. (1950). Computing Machinery and Intelligence. *Mind, LIX*(236), 433–460. https://doi.org/10.1093/mind/LIX.236.433.

Vargo, S. L., & Lusch, R. F. (2004). Evolving to a New Dominant Logic for Marketing. *Journal of Marketing, 68*(1), 1–17. https://doi.org/10.1509/jmkg.68.1.1.24036.

Vargo, S. L., & Lusch, R. F. (2008). Service-Dominant Logic: Continuing the Evolution. *Journal of the Academy of Marketing Science, 36*(1), 1–10. https://doi.org/10.1007/s11747-007-0069-6.

Vondrick, C., Pirsiavash, H., & Torralba, A. (2016). *Generating Videos with Scene Dynamics.* Neural Information Processing Systems Foundation, Inc. Presented at the 30th Neural Information Processing Systems (NIPS) 2016, Barcelona.

von Tunzelmann, N. (2005). J. Mokyr, The Gifts of Athena – Historical Origins of the Knowledge Economy, Princeton University Press, Princeton and Oxford (2002). *Information Economics and Policy, 17*(2), 271–273. https://doi.org/10.1016/j.infoecopol.2004.10.001.

Wang, C. L., & Ahmed, P. K. (2013). The Knowledge Value Chain: A Pragmatic Knowledge Implementation Network. *Handbook of Business Strategy, 6*(1), 321–326. https://doi.org/10.1108/08944310510558115.

Wang, Y., Skerry-Ryan, R. J., Stanton, D., Wu, Y., Weiss, R. J., Jaitly, N., et al. (2017, March 29). *Tacotron: Towards End-to-End Speech Synthesis.* https://arxiv.org/abs/1703.10135

Wernerfelt, B. (1984). A Resource-Based View of the Firm. *Strategic Management Journal, 5*(2), 171–180. https://doi.org/10.1002/smj.4250050207.

What Main Methodology Are You Using for Your Analytics, Data Mining, or Data Science Projects? Poll. (n.d.). Retrieved January 10, 2018, from https://www.kdnuggets.com/polls/2014/analytics-data-mining-data-science-methodology.html

Wilson, H. J., Daugherty, P. R., & Morini-Bianzino, N. (2017). The Jobs That Artificial Intelligence Will Create. *MIT Sloan Management Review*, Summer.

Woodward, J. (1970). *Industrial Organization Behavior and Control.* Oxford: Oxford University Press.

Wozniak, S. (n.d.). Wozniak: Could a Computer Make a Cup of Coffee? Retrieved December 26, 2017, from https://www.fastcompany.com/1568187/wozniak-could-computer-make-cup-coffee

Zawiła-Niedźwiecki, J. (2015a). Structuring Knowledge Management – Classical Theory, Strategic Initiation and Operational Knowledge Management (Part I). *Foundations of Management, 7*(1). https://doi.org/10.1515/fman-2015-0041.

Zawiła-Niedźwiecki, J. (2015b). Structuring Knowledge Management – Levels, Resources and Efficiency Areas of Knowledge Management (Part II). *Foundations of Management, 7*(1). https://doi.org/10.1515/fman-2015-0042.

Zawiła-Niedźwiecki, J., & Byczkowski, M. (2009). Information Security Aspect of Operational Risk Management. *Foundations of Management, 1*(2), 162. https://doi.org/10.2478/v10238-012-0010-2.

Zhao, J. L., Tanniru, M., & Zhang, L.-J. (2007). Services Computing as the Foundation of Enterprise Agility: Overview of Recent Advances and Introduction to the Special Issue. *Information Systems Frontiers, 9*(1), 1–8. https://doi.org/10.1007/s10796-007-9023-x.

Zhu, J.-Y., Park, T., Isola, P., & Efros, A. A. (n.d.). *Unpaired Image-to-Image Translation Using Cycle-Consistent Adversarial Networks*. Retrieved December 27, 2017, from https://arxiv.org/pdf/1703.10593.pdf

Zilis, S., & Cham, J. (2016, November). The Competitive Landscape for Machine Intelligence. *Harvard Business Review*. Retrieved from https://hbr.org/2016/11/the-competitive-landscape-for-machine-intelligence

Index

A. Wodecki, *Artificial Intelligence in Value Creation*,
https://doi.org/10.1007/978-3-319-91596-8

The manufacturer's authorised representative in the EU is Springer Nature Customer Service Centre GmbH, Europaplatz 3, 69115 Heidelberg, Germany. If you have any concerns regarding our products, please contact ProductSafety@springernature.com

Printed and bound by CPI Group (UK) Ltd, Croydon, CR0 4YY
22/09/2026
02220950-0007